TABLE OF CONTENTS

Top 15 Test Taking Tips

1. Know the test directions, duration, topics, question types, how many questions
2. Setup a flexible study schedule at least 3-4 weeks before test day
3. Study during the time of day you are most alert, relaxed, and stress free
4. Maximize your learning style; visual learner use visual study aids, auditory learner use auditory study aids
5. Focus on your weakest knowledge base
6. Find a study partner to review with and help clarify questions
7. Practice, practice, practice
8. Get a good night's sleep; don't try to cram the night before the test
9. Eat a well balanced meal
10. Wear comfortable, loose fitting, layered clothing; prepare for it to be either cold or hot during the test
11. Eliminate the obviously wrong answer choices, then guess the first remaining choice
12. Pace yourself; don't rush, but keep working and move on if you get stuck
13. Maintain a positive attitude even if the test is going poorly
14. Keep your first answer unless you are positive it is wrong
15. Check your work, don't make a careless mistake

Chapter 1 - Whole Numbers

In this chapter you will learn about large whole numbers. It is important to understand these concepts because you will need them throughout the rest of the book.

Here are the things you will learn about:

- Place Value
- Rounding
- Estimating
- Addition
- Subtraction

Lesson 1

Place Value 1-10,000,000

The place value of a digit is determined by where it is in a number.

Ten Millions	Millions	Hundred Thousands	Ten Thousands	Thousands	Hundreds	Tens	Ones
1	2	3	4	5	6	7	8

12,345,678

Twelve million, three hundred forty-five thousand, six hundred seventy-eight

Match the numbers below to the correct place value boxes.

1. 15,632,782 =

1	5	6	3	2	7	8	2
Ten Millions	Millions	Hundred Thousands	Ten Thousands	Thousands	Hundreds	Tens	Ones

2. 24,879,360 =

Ten Millions	Millions	Hundred Thousands	Ten Thousands	Thousands	Hundreds	Tens	Ones

3. 62,158,524 =

Ten Millions	Millions	Hundred Thousands	Ten Thousands	Thousands	Hundreds	Tens	Ones

4. 30,671,234 =

Ten Millions	Millions	Hundred Thousands	Ten Thousands	Thousands	Hundreds	Tens	Ones

5. 52,197,305 =

Ten Millions	Millions	Hundred Thousands	Ten Thousands	Thousands	Hundreds	Tens	Ones

6. 83,498,147 =

Ten Millions	Millions	Hundred Thousands	Ten Thousands	Thousands	Hundreds	Tens	Ones

Place Value 1-100,000,000

The place value of a digit is determined by where it is in a number.

Hundred Millions	Ten Millions	Millions	Hundred Thousands	Ten Thousands	Thousands	Hundreds	Tens	Ones
1	2	3	4	5	6	7	8	9

123,456,789

One hundred twenty-three million, four hundred fifty-six thousand, seven hundred eighty-nine

Match the numbers below to the correct place value boxes.

1. 748,422,719 =

Hundred Millions	Ten Millions	Millions	Hundred Thousands	Ten Thousands	Thousands	Hundreds	Tens	Ones

2. 329,608,114 =

Hundred Millions	Ten Millions	Millions	Hundred Thousands	Ten Thousands	Thousands	Hundreds	Tens	Ones

3. 124,375,277 =

Hundred Millions	Ten Millions	Millions	Hundred Thousands	Ten Thousands	Thousands	Hundreds	Tens	Ones

4. 741,588,379 =

Hundred Millions	Ten Millions	Millions	Hundred Thousands	Ten Thousands	Thousands	Hundreds	Tens	Ones

5. 504,267,332 =

Hundred Millions	Ten Millions	Millions	Hundred Thousands	Ten Thousands	Thousands	Hundreds	Tens	Ones

6. 972,114,089 =

Hundred Millions	Ten Millions	Millions	Hundred Thousands	Ten Thousands	Thousands	Hundreds	Tens	Ones

Lesson 2

Rounding up to 100,000

Round the following numbers to the nearest thousand.

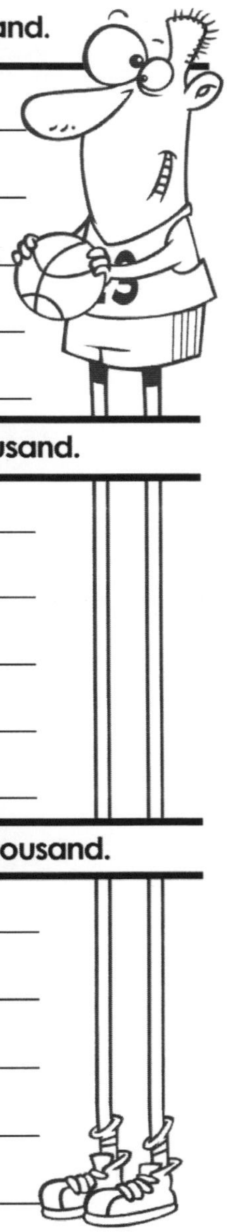

1. 2,563 ___3,000___

2. 9,198 ____________

3. 1,423 ____________

4. 7,712 ____________

5. 3,300 ____________

6. 4,219 ____________

7. 5,756 ____________

8. 8,154 ____________

9. 6,069 ____________

10 1,995 ____________

Round the following numbers to the nearest ten-thousand.

11. 39,092 ____________

12. 19,917 ____________

13. 93,254 ____________

14. 56,055 ____________

15. 70,856 ____________

16. 77,150 ____________

17. 33,809 ____________

18. 35,451 ____________

19. 20,901 ____________

20. 48,599 ____________

Round the following numbers to the nearest hundred-thousand.

21. 274,333 ____________

22. 596,559 ____________

23. 221,324 ____________

24. 530,708 ____________

25. 189,365 ____________

26. 317,110 ____________

27. 882,658 ____________

28. 610,567 ____________

29. 789,381 ____________

30. 109,277 ____________

Lesson 3

Building Numbers

Use what you learned about place value to sort and solve the problems below.

1. 3 + 400 + 4,000 + 20,000 + 50 = 24,453

2. 50,000 + 700 + 10 + 5,000 + 8 = __________

3. 500 + 50 + 10,000 + 9,000 + 4 = __________

4. 8,000 + 100 + 30 + 2 + 20,000 = __________

5. 10,000 + 900 + 60 + 2,000 + 6 = __________

6. 90,000 + 300 + 50 + 9 + 3,000 = __________

7. 1 + 500 + 6,000 + 90,000 + 90 = __________

8. 700 + 70 + 50,000 + 6,000 + 2 = __________

9. 3,000 + 200 + 90 + 7 + 80,000 = __________

10. 5 + 900 + 7,000 + 20,000 + 10 = __________

11. 5,000 + 200 + 10 + 2 + 30,000 = __________

12. 600 + 80 + 60,000 + 2,000 + 9 = __________

13. 40,000 + 200 + 10 + 9,000 + 2 = __________

14. 9,000 + 300 + 50 + 9 + 70,000 = __________

15. 6 + 700 + 3,000 + 90,000 + 50 = __________

16. 8 + 300 + 1,000 + 40,000 + 20 = __________

17. 3,000 + 7 + 50 + 900 + 40,000 = __________

18. 100 + 60 + 10,000 + 4,000 + 1 = __________

19. 500 + 60 + 90,000 + 3,000 + 4 = __________

20. 7 + 800 + 9,000 + 30,000 + 10 = __________

Lesson 4

Estimating 1

To estimate a sum or difference, round each number.
Then add or subtract the rounded numbers.

Addition:

688 →	700
+ 231 →	+ 200
	900

Subtraction:

4,491 →	4,500
- 789 →	- 800
	3,700

Estimate and solve the problems below.

1. 858 → 900
+ 391 → + 400
1,300

2. 461 →
+ 545 →

3. 129 →
+ 607 →

4. 399 →
+ 731 →

5. 943 →
- 499 →

6. 768 →
- 207 →

7. 630 →
- 452 →

8. 356 →
- 175 →

Estimating 2

To estimate a sum or difference, round each number.
Then add or subtract the rounded numbers.

Estimate and solve the problems below.

1. 6,281 → + 3,552 →	**2.** 4,782 → + 1,321 →	**3.** 9,423 → + 6,599 →
4. 5,192 → + 4,807 →	**5.** 2,991 → + 5,841 →	**6.** 7,510 → + 7,291 →
7. 1,690 → + 4,501 →	**8.** 3,908 → + 4,687 →	**9.** 9,499 → + 532 →
10. 3,641 → - 2,487 →	**11.** 8,961 → - 4,540 →	**12.** 7,299 → - 5,607 →
13. 4,701 → - 3,112 →	**14.** 9,475 → - 7,500 →	**15.** 3,559 → - 1,890 →
16. 4,115 → - 805 →	**17.** 5,602 → - 2,199 →	**18.** 7,999 → - 5,999 →

Lesson 5

Addition with Regrouping

To add multiple-digit numbers together, start in the ones place and then use basic addition rules. When a number equals ten or more the first digit carries over to the next spot. This is called **regrouping**.

Step 1:
Add the digits in the one's column and carry over the 1 to the ten's column.

	1000's	100's	10's	1's
			1	
		7	5	9
+		5	6	4
				[3]

Step 2:
Next add the digits in the ten's column and carry over the 1 to the hundred's column.

	1000's	100's	10's	1's
		1	1	
		7	5	9
+		5	6	4
			[2]	3

Step 3:
Next add the digits in the hundred's column.

	1000's	100's	10's	1's
		1	1	
		7	5	9
+		5	6	4
		[3]	2	3

Step 4:
Finally, carry over the 1 from the hundred's column to the thousand's column.

	1000's	100's	10's	1's
		1	1	
		7	5	9
+		5	6	4
	[1]	3	2	3

Solve the problems below. Use regrouping when needed.

1. 944 + 281 = 1,225

2. 603 + 421

3. 946 + 634

4. 407 + 335

5. 289 + 972

6. 572 + 539

7. 491 + 862

8. 945 + 687

9. 999 + 237

10. 755 + 675

Lesson 6

4-Digit Addition 1

Solve the problems below using regrouping.

1. 1,091 2,157 + 3,267	**2.** 9,815 803 + 2,216	**3.** 3,891 1,259 + 7,520	**4.** 2,552 8,406 + 271
5. 5,330 1,211 + 9,801	**6.** 4,881 2,009 + 1,987	**7.** 3,072 1,650 + 578	**8.** 1,985 8,105 + 1,776
9. 9,841 2,750 + 1,349	**10.** 5,400 501 + 3,814	**11.** 7,072 6,152 + 1,785	**12.** 707 1,804 + 2,950
13. 2,400 962 + 815	**14.** 6,074 1,255 + 8,079	**15.** 8,180 2,755 + 2,577	**16.** 9,064 9,607 + 6,074
17. 4,911 2,757 + 3,025	**18.** 5,787 6,962 + 1,570	**19.** 7,705 5,321 + 1,766	**20.** 3,033 1,447 + 9,632

4-Digit Addition 2

Solve the problems below using regrouping.

1. 4,982 6,350 9,811 + 2,652	**2.** 5,578 1,669 8,902 + 191	**3.** 2,121 9,279 3,364 + 2,127	**4.** 4,880 6,524 9,967 + 2,115	**5.** 6,159 1,250 1,975 + 9,364
6. 3,160 9,497 5,222 + 4,596	**7.** 6,890 1,457 9,058 + 3,126	**8.** 2,459 9,087 1,134 + 705	**9.** 6,110 993 1,678 + 5,157	**10.** 3,692 1,157 7,239 + 7,058
11. 4,457 9,280 1,170 + 2,357	**12.** 6,898 6,157 3,309 + 675	**13.** 3,070 1,007 4,911 + 7,963	**14.** 5,158 4,058 3,982 + 1,360	**15.** 4,869 6,048 9,263 + 2,009
16. 1,222 1,378 3,157 + 9,009	**17.** 3,089 6,164 7,665 + 5,035	**18.** 2,172 4,339 6,057 + 1,197	**19.** 3,887 3,105 1,007 + 332	**20.** 7,982 3,350 2,811 + 4,652

Lesson 7

5-Digit Addition

Solve the problems below using regrouping.

1. 54,691 10,847 + 39,116	**2.** 90,861 77,392 + 20,691	**3.** 44,388 35,512 + 64,172	**4.** 50,233 46,397 + 92,846
5. 58,732 33,020 + 12,571	**6.** 19,570 27,694 + 56,630	**7.** 90,691 51,072 + 14,321	**8.** 35,450 82,300 + 23,124
9. 60,805 84,997 + 39,111	**10.** 66,349 70,244 + 11,188	**11.** 15,000 39,289 + 2,723	**12.** 99,785 35,562 + 48,078
13. 38,058 36,298 + 57,613	**14.** 66,951 23,207 + 10,881	**15.** 47,381 61,273 + 75,507	**16.** 94,080 11,636 + 9,860
17. 39,005 29,678 + 14,567	**18.** 48,399 15,467 + 5,005	**19.** 18,222 90,309 + 66,009	**20.** 99,863 99,067 + 65,331

Lesson 8

6-Digit Addition

Solve the problems below using regrouping.

1. 102,220 366,357 + 127,475	**2.** 557,365 166,204 + 254,129	**3.** 325,299 770,351 + 64,658	**4.** 129,195 632,744 + 335,163
5. 641,001 237,925 + 210,137	**6.** 752,112 209,482 + 322,165	**7.** 480,129 638,635 + 218,001	**8.** 500,051 217,521 + 127,937
9. 637,817 289,364 + 123,994	**10.** 491,065 278,605 + 316,221	**11.** 841,316 958,375 + 175,363	**12.** 150,633 534,110 + 156,925
13. 655,119 230,754 + 524,239	**14.** 163,159 952,364 + 402,846	**15.** 752,005 647,119 + 841,715	**16.** 363,175 119,376 + 237,860
17. 445,123 967,525 + 364,129	**18.** 638,117 500,682 + 438,385	**19.** 781,975 237,105 + 285,367	**20.** 908,129 117,765 + 637,032

Lesson 9

7-Digit Addition

Solve the problems below using regrouping.

1. 3,541,277 6,129,245 + 2,382,107	**2.** 2,711,015 3,844,362 + 1,332,745	**3.** 5,008,694 3,992,406 + 8,264,367	**4.** 8,267,200 7,164,245 + 6,277,594
5. 5,466,999 3,050,638 + 6,105,347	**6.** 7,548,007 2,215,635 + 1,365,815	**7.** 9,147,129 6,308,905 + 4,315,707	**8.** 5,113,799 5,564,002 + 6,465,355
9. 1,648,912 3,154,099 + 5,367,474	**10.** 6,905,011 4,322,966 + 3,375,378	**11.** 6,475,619 9,504,242 + 7,289,071	**12.** 1,299,151 3,637,889 + 8,652,234
13. 3,552,910 7,313,577 + 4,429,964	**14.** 6,008,799 5,027,346 + 6,244,310	**15.** 1,224,799 1,496,843 + 9,841,000	**16.** 4,208,577 5,995,685 + 5,372,129
17. 6,141,654 1,764,889 + 7,633,924	**18.** 5,639,047 6,129,885 + 3,445,369	**19.** 9,665,007 8,682,420 + 4,341,204	**20.** 5,245,895 6,636,635 + 8,547,118

Lesson 10

Subtraction with Borrowing

To subtract and borrow, start with the ones column. If the bottom number is of a greater value, you have to borrow from the next column.

Step 1:	**Step 2:**	**Step 3:**	**Step 4:**
Any time the bottom number in a column is of greater value than the top number, you need to borrow.	Borrow 10 from the next column. This reduces the 6 to 5 and increases the number in the first column from 3 to 13.	Now we need to borrow 10 from the hundreds column. This reduces the 7 to 6 and increases the numbers in the tens column from 5 to 15.	Now you are ready for the final step. Finish by subtracting the numbers in all the columns.
100's | 10's | 1's 7 6 3 - 4 8 5	100's | 10's | 1's 5 7 ~~6~~ 13 - 4 8 5	100's | 10's | 1's 6 15 ~~7~~ ~~6~~ 13 - 4 8 5	100's | 10's | 1's 6 15 ~~7~~ ~~6~~ 13 - 4 8 5 2 7 8

Use borrowing to solve the problems below.

1. 682 - 239 443	**2.** 909 - 457	**3.** 342 - 199	**4.** 511 - 227	**5.** 704 - 165
6. 467 - 349	**7.** 919 - 58	**8.** 609 - 158	**9.** 711 - 459	**10.** 197 - 68
11. 679 - 388	**12.** 537 - 87	**13.** 892 - 604	**14.** 906 - 449	**15.** 637 - 205

Lesson 11

4-Digit Subtraction

Use what you learned about borrowing to solve the problems below.

1. 6,432 − 5,320	**2.** 2,675 − 1,564	**3.** 4,233 − 452	**4.** 5,428 − 2,649
5. 1,995 − 239	**6.** 7,321 − 834	**7.** 9,211 − 1,700	**8.** 3,946 − 1,682
9. 2,463 − 1,939	**10.** 8,959 − 3,274	**11.** 1,295 − 968	**12.** 9,942 − 7,895
13. 7,542 − 2,907	**14.** 3,649 − 1,590	**15.** 9,864 − 4,389	**16.** 3,888 − 999
17. 5,001 − 3,547	**18.** 1,775 − 859	**19.** 3,880 − 1,125	**20.** 9,567 − 6,820

Lesson 12

5-Digit Subtraction

Use what you learned about borrowing to solve the problems below.

1. 25,911 - 23,125	**2.** 40,127 - 15,089	**3.** 68,956 - 47,580	**4.** 42,207 - 5,699
5. 30,113 - 9,357	**6.** 92,253 - 75,449	**7.** 57,115 - 36,608	**8.** 21,659 - 17,102
9. 81,678 - 44,169	**10.** 47,827 - 9,018	**11.** 35,157 - 16,658	**12.** 50,011 - 23,956
13. 29,368 - 13,504	**14.** 48,638 - 5,174	**15.** 59,239 - 14,107	**16.** 66,250 - 20,078
17. 36,754 - 18,265	**18.** 54,587 - 33,058	**19.** 63,017 - 5,582	**20.** 92,236 - 15,297

Lesson 13

6-Digit Subtraction

Use what you learned about borrowing to solve the problems below.

1. 627,343 - 495,861	**2.** 854,115 - 346,264	**3.** 506,925 - 229,167	**4.** 129,239 - 95,226
5. 958,062 - 179,687	**6.** 297,343 - 105,907	**7.** 961,343 - 550,097	**8.** 639,447 - 287,334
9. 339,081 - 117,118	**10.** 520,142 - 287,963	**11.** 728,253 - 681,175	**12.** 550,008 - 368,764
13. 785,780 - 358,999	**14.** 902,144 - 751,100	**15.** 811,654 - 436,907	**16.** 495,861 - 399,000
17. 447,675 - 258,007	**18.** 781,115 - 369,098	**19.** 265,017 - 65,336	**20.** 965,305 - 345,999

Lesson 14

7-Digit Subtraction

Use what you learned about borrowing to solve the problems below.

1. 2,135,209 - 1,542,921	**2.** 4,275,394 - 2,866,100	**3.** 6,429,925 - 699,295	**4.** 5,985,324 - 3,547,935
5. 7,122,956 - 5,009,122	**6.** 5,588,133 - 367,794	**7.** 9,002,357 - 1,688,188	**8.** 8,652,116 - 5,775,209
9. 6,339,100 - 3,203,548	**10.** 9,000,142 - 3,872,482	**11.** 7,125,951 - 5,324,007	**12.** 5,689,008 - 1,005,956
13. 9,958,111 - 6,832,504	**14.** 7,194,926 - 2,607,299	**15.** 4,305,842 - 635,184	**16.** 8,965,122 - 5,594,009
17. 6,487,070 - 8,199	**18.** 9,488,267 - 7,129,098	**19.** 6,125,199 - 2.658,037	**20.** 5,600,204 - 3,317,869

Lesson 15

8-Digit Subtraction

Use what you learned about borrowing to solve the problems below.

1. 32,445,311 - 19,306,805
2. 54,009,812 - 23,329,605
3. 72,511,420 - 49,964,122
4. 43,652,019 - 7,994,364
5. 17,457,333 - 9,864,127
6. 85,674,152 - 39,200,997
7. 55,925,321 - 365,544
8. 90,899,425 - 1,621,678
9. 69,129,364 - 34,330,657
10. 84,994,657 - 65,732,566
11. 88,299,882 - 2,164,295
12. 39,599,635 - 10,124,988
13. 67,290,975 - 2,364,963
14. 50,400,991 - 6,536,027
15. 42,633,635 - 12,396,864
16. 95,155,964 - 57,377,337
17. 82,112,650 - 820,941
18. 75,644,340 - 38,637,652
19. 59,965,122 - 3,637,569
20. 93,050,002 - 54,864,632
21. 66,965,362 - 167,064
22. 92,338,674 - 17,211,995
23. 44,294,632 - 29,009,367
24. 84,962,366 - 52,507,999

Chapter 2 - Multiplication and Exponents

Chapter 2 - Multiplication and Exponents

In this chapter you will learn about multiplication and exponents.

Here is what you will learn:

- Multiplication tables
- Multiplying 2-digit numbers
- Multiplying 3-digit numbers
- Multiplying 4-digit numbers
- Multiplying 5-digit numbers
- Understanding Exponents
- Comparing exponents
- Writing exponents

Multiplication Table

x	1	2	3	4	5	6	7	8	9	10
1	1	2	3	4	5	6	7	8	9	10
2	2	4	6	8	10	12	14	16	18	20
3	3	6	9	12	15	18	21	24	27	30
4	4	8	12	16	20	24	28	32	36	40
5	5	10	15	20	25	30	35	40	45	50
6	6	12	18	24	30	36	42	48	54	60
7	7	14	21	28	35	42	49	56	63	70
8	8	16	24	32	40	48	56	64	72	80
9	9	18	27	36	45	54	63	72	81	90
10	10	20	30	40	50	60	70	80	90	100

Lesson 1

Blank Multiplication Table

This is a multiplication table. Multiply the numbers in the top row by the numbers in the side row to get the product.

x	1	2	3	4	5	6	7	8	9	10
1										
2										
3										
4										
5										
6										
7										
8										
9										
10										

Multiplication Table Mix-up

X	1	2	3
1	1	2	3
2	2	4	6

This is a multiplication table. Multiply the numbers in the top row by the numbers in the side row to get the product.

1.

X	4	5	6
6			
5			
4			
3			
2			

2.

X	0	6	8	4	9
5					
4					
3					

3.

X	2	3	4	5	6
10					
11					
12					

4.

X	5	4	3
6			
5			
4			
3			
2			

Lesson 2

Multiplication

To multiply a one-digit number by a two-digit number with regrouping, start in the ones place and then use basic multiplication rules. When the number equals ten or more the first digit carries over to the next spot. This is called **regrouping**.

Step 1: Multiply the numbers in the ones column and carry the first digit over to the tens column.

	Hundreds	Tens	Ones
		2	
		4	7
x			3
			1

3 x 7 = 21

Step 2: Multiply the digit in at the bottom of the ones column by the digit in the tens column and add the regrouped number.

	Hundreds	Tens	Ones
		2 +	
		4	7
x			3
		4	1

4 x 3 = 12 Then 12 + 2 = 14

Step 3: The one then carries over to the hundreds place.

	Hundreds	Tens	Ones
		2	
		4	7
x			3
	1	4	1

Answer = 141

Solve the problems below.

1. 65 x 4 = 260
2. 49 x 3
3. 12 x 9
4. 92 x 6
5. 57 x 8
6. 49 x 8
7. 29 x 4
8. 32 x 5
9. 68 x 7
10. 83 x 9

Lesson 3

Multiplication by 2-Digit Numbers

To multiply a two-digit number by a two-digit number, start in the ones place and then use basic multiplication and addition rules. Don't forget to use what you've learned about regrouping.

1. Multiply by the **ones** multiplier.

Hundreds	Tens	Ones
	2	
	+	
	4	6
x	2	4
1	8	4

4 is the first multiplier
4 x 46 = 184

2. Multiply by the **tens** multiplier.

Hundreds	Tens	Ones
	1	
	+	
	4	6
x	2	4
1	8	4
+ 9	2	0

20 is the second multiplier
20 x 46 = 104

3. Add the products.

Hundreds	Tens	Ones
	4	6
x	2	4
1	8	4
+ 9	2	0
1 1	0	4

Add the two products
184 + 920 = 1,104

Solve the problems below.

1. 82 x 24
328
+1640
1,968

2. 99 x 32

3. 27 x 16

4. 54 x 36

5. 72 x 29

6. 37 x 28

7. 55 x 17

8. 62 x 33

9. 92 x 18

10. 24 x 12

Lesson 4

Multiplying 2-Digit Numbers by 2-Digit Numbers

To multiply a two-digit number by a two-digit number, start in the ones place and then use basic multiplication and addition rules. Dont forget to use what you've learned about regrouping.

Solve the problems below.

1. 49 x 15	**2.** 64 x 24	**3.** 54 x 36	**4.** 67 x 48	**5.** 85 x 65
6. 74 x 46	**7.** 86 x 39	**8.** 35 x 29	**9.** 68 x 47	**10.** 72 x 25
11. 54 x 54	**12.** 87 x 64	**13.** 62 x 43	**14.** 95 x 92	**15.** 42 x 39
16. 96 x 75	**17.** 84 x 15	**18.** 98 x 67	**19.** 76 x 28	**20.** 65 x 57

Lesson 5

Multiplication Word Problems

Use multiplication to solve the problems below.

1. If Tommy plays 7 soccer games, and he blocks 6 shots in each game, how many shots will he block?

2. Larry loves photography and takes a lot of pictures. If he takes 32 pictures a day for 20 days, how many pictures will he take?

3. James is a great painter. He can paint 3 paintings a day. If he paints for 19 days how many paintings will he have?

4. Brian eats pizza every day. If he eats 8 slices a day for 9 days how many slices of pizza will he eat?

Lesson 6

Multiplying 3-Digit Numbers by 2-Digit Numbers 1

To multiply a three-digit number by a two-digit number, start in the ones place and then use basic multiplication and addition rules. Dont forget to use what you've learned about regrouping.

Solve the problems below.

1. 321 x 23 = 963 + 6420 = 7,383

2. 259 x 19

3. 512 x 43

4. 459 x 36

5. 608 x 25

6. 641 x 39

7. 539 x 62

8. 235 x 24

9. 684 x 31

10. 843 x 64

11. 892 x 83

12. 399 x 95

13. 705 x 34

14. 633 x 79

15. 514 x 92

16. 455 x 99

17. 950 x 64

18. 696 x 82

19. 789 x 34

20. 865 x 96

Multiplying 3-Digit Numbers by 2-Digit Numbers 2

To multiply a three-digit number by a two-digit number, start in the ones place and then use basic multiplication and addition rules. Dont forget to use what you've learned about regrouping.

Solve the problems below.

1. 491 x 52	**2.** 903 x 32	**3.** 384 x 94	**4.** 689 x 17	**5.** 732 x 57
6. 559 x 73	**7.** 197 x 44	**8.** 294 x 54	**9.** 316 x 29	**10.** 917 x 34
11. 827 x 12	**12.** 494 x 37	**13.** 659 x 96	**14.** 749 x 61	**15.** 527 x 72
16. 399 x 57	**17.** 899 x 75	**18.** 421 x 34	**19.** 625 x 84	**20.** 964 x 66

Lesson 7

Multiplication Word Problems 2

Use multiplication to solve the problems below.

1. George has lots of pigs. He keeps 147 pigs in each pen. He has 23 pens. How many pigs does he have in all?

2. Penny is cooking muffins. She can cook 4 muffins per pan. She has 239 pans. How many muffins can she cook?

3. Mickey is going trick or treating. If he goes to 128 houses and collects 12 pieces of candy at each house, how much candy will Mickey have?

4. Nathan is a talented basketball player. If he scores 19 points in each of his next 32 games, how many points will he score?

Lesson 8

Multiplying 4-Digit Numbers by 2-Digit Numbers 1

To multiply a four-digit number by a two-digit number, start in the ones place and then use basic multiplication and addition rules. Don't forget to use what you've learned about regrouping.

Solve the problems below.

1. 1,491 × 52
2982
+ 74550
77,532

2. 6,861 × 15

3. 4,532 × 37

4. 2,725 × 93

5. 3,116 × 29

6. 7,683 × 49

7. 4,492 × 66

8. 2,374 × 97

9. 5,051 × 31

10. 8,790 × 29

11. 2,778 × 86

12. 6,627 × 61

13. 3,055 × 57

14. 6,812 × 89

15. 4,558 × 64

16. 5,109 × 51

17. 9,582 × 75

18. 7,716 × 68

19. 3,337 × 35

20. 8,274 × 59

Multiplying 4-Digit Numbers by 2-Digit Numbers 2

To multiply a four-digit number by a two-digit number, start in the ones place and then use basic multiplication and addition rules. Don't forget to use what you've learned about regrouping.

Solve the problems below.

1. 2,631 × 12	**2.** 3,437 × 20	**3.** 6,115 × 25	**4.** 1,037 × 31	**5.** 4,624 × 29
6. 5,297 × 33	**7.** 1,608 × 37	**8.** 4,809 × 47	**9.** 5,194 × 10	**10.** 3,578 × 36
11. 8,167 × 57	**12.** 5,802 × 66	**13.** 4,950 × 42	**14.** 9,568 × 67	**15.** 7,827 × 74
16. 9,972 × 27	**17.** 5,302 × 37	**18.** 8,185 × 97	**19.** 6,375 × 88	**20.** 9,219 × 96

Lesson 9

Multiplying 3-Digit Numbers by 3-Digit Numbers 1

To multiply a three-digit number by a three-digit number, start in the ones place and then use basic multiplication and addition rules. Don't forget to use what you've learned about regrouping.

Solve the problems below.

1.
$$\begin{array}{r} 432 \\ \times\ 365 \\ \hline 2{,}160 \\ 25{,}920 \\ +\ 129{,}600 \\ \hline 157{,}680 \end{array}$$

2. $\begin{array}{r} 359 \\ \times\ 619 \\ \hline \end{array}$

3. $\begin{array}{r} 482 \\ \times\ 165 \\ \hline \end{array}$

4. $\begin{array}{r} 742 \\ \times\ 363 \\ \hline \end{array}$

5. $\begin{array}{r} 476 \\ \times\ 134 \\ \hline \end{array}$

6. $\begin{array}{r} 895 \\ \times\ 135 \\ \hline \end{array}$

7. $\begin{array}{r} 922 \\ \times\ 617 \\ \hline \end{array}$

8. $\begin{array}{r} 384 \\ \times\ 475 \\ \hline \end{array}$

9. $\begin{array}{r} 524 \\ \times\ 277 \\ \hline \end{array}$

10. $\begin{array}{r} 915 \\ \times\ 674 \\ \hline \end{array}$

11. $\begin{array}{r} 595 \\ \times\ 186 \\ \hline \end{array}$

12. $\begin{array}{r} 807 \\ \times\ 132 \\ \hline \end{array}$

13. $\begin{array}{r} 915 \\ \times\ 337 \\ \hline \end{array}$

14. $\begin{array}{r} 935 \\ \times\ 476 \\ \hline \end{array}$

15. $\begin{array}{r} 482 \\ \times\ 982 \\ \hline \end{array}$

Multiplying 3-Digit Numbers by 3-Digit Numbers 2

To multiply a three-digit number by a three-digit number, start in the ones place and then use basic multiplication and addition rules. Don't forget to use what you've learned about regrouping.

Solve the problems below.

1. 367 x 182	**2.** 227 x 307	**3.** 521 x 497	**4.** 139 x 927	**5.** 865 x 267
6. 556 x 234	**7.** 682 x 264	**8.** 905 x 114	**9.** 946 x 371	**10.** 568 x 436
11. 637 x 220	**12.** 274 x 369	**13.** 857 x 237	**14.** 475 x 602	**15.** 552 x 189
16. 648 x 422	**17.** 592 x 305	**18.** 200 x 967	**19.** 637 x 137	**20.** 659 x 884

Lesson 10

Multiplying 4-Digit Numbers by 3-Digit Numbers 1

To multiply a four-digit number by a three-digit number, start in the ones place and then use basic multiplication and addition rules. Don't forget to use what you've learned about regrouping.

Solve the problems below.

1.
```
  1,291
  x 324
   5164
  25820
+387300
418,284
```

2. 2,177 x 115

3. 4,264 x 137

4. 3,387 x 244

5. 5,189 x 320

6. 3,654 x 439

7. 5,307 x 148

8. 2,273 x 259

9. 4,892 x 341

10. 5,952 x 326

11. 6,489 x 566

12. 2,701 x 424

13. 3,119 x 178

14. 5,297 x 626

15. 9,436 x 339

16. 3,624 x 749

17. 7,117 x 572

18. 5,930 x 897

19. 8,175 x 688

20. 6,408 x 960

Multiplying 4-Digit Numbers by 3-Digit Numbers 2

To multiply a four-digit number by a three-digit number, start in the ones place and then use basic multiplication and addition rules. Don't forget to use what you've learned about regrouping.

Solve the problems below.

1. 6,584 x 324	**2.** 3,291 x 105	**3.** 8,347 x 137	**4.** 4,551 x 244	**5.** 9,067 x 320
6. 6,561 x 439	**7.** 7,812 x 140	**8.** 3,302 x 259	**9.** 5,191 x 341	**10.** 4,073 x 326
11. 8,651 x 560	**12.** 3,291 x 424	**13.** 5,067 x 682	**14.** 5,297 x 119	**15.** 9,436 x 207
16. 3,624 x 329	**17.** 7,117 x 708	**18.** 5,930 x 132	**19.** 8,175 x 985	**20.** 6,408 x 560

Lesson 11

Exponents 1

An **exponent** is a number that tells how many times the base is used as a factor. It is written as a smaller number placed above and to the right of the base number.

Example:	Example:
$5^3 = 125$ $(5 \times 5 \times 5) = 125$ 5 is the base number and 3 is the exponent	$3^4 = 81$ $(3 \times 3 \times 3 \times 3) = 81$ 3 is the base number and 4 is the exponent

Write the exponents for each set of numbers.

1. $6 \times 6 \times 6 \times 6 = \underline{6^4}$
2. $3 \times 3 \times 3 =$ _____
3. $5 \times 5 \times 5 =$ _____
4. $7 \times 7 \times 7 \times 7 =$ _____
5. $9 \times 9 \times 9 \times 9 \times 9 =$ _____
6. $8 \times 8 \times 8 \times 8 \times 8 \times 8 =$ _____
7. $2 \times 2 \times 2 \times 2 \times 2 \times 2 =$ _____
8. $4 \times 4 \times 4 \times 4 =$ _____
9. $5 \times 5 \times 5 =$ _____
10. $6 \times 6 \times 6 \times 6 \times 6 =$ _____
11. $7 \times 7 \times 7 \times 7 \times 7 \times 7 \times 7 =$ _____
12. $2 \times 2 \times 2 =$ _____
13. $3 \times 3 \times 3 \times 3 =$ _____
14. $9 \times 9 \times 9 \times 9 \times 9 \times 9 =$ _____

Lesson 12

Exponents 2

Write out the exponents below and solve. Use the boxes to work out the problems,

1. 9^3 = 9 x 9 x 9 = 729

2. 5^5 = ________________ = ____

3. 8^4 = ________________ = ____

4. 2^9 = ________________ = ____

5. 6^4 = ________________ = ____

6. 4^5 = ________________ = ____

Lesson 13

Exponents 3

Write out the exponents below and solve. Use the boxes to work out the problems,

1. 8^2 = ________________ = ____

2. 6^5 = ________________ = ____

3. 7^4 = ________________ = ____

4. 3^8 = ________________ = ____

5. 4^3 = ________________ = ____

6. 5^5 = ________________ = ____

Comparing Exponents

An **exponent** is a number that tells how many times the base is used as a factor. It is written as a smaller number placed above and to the right of the base number.

Fill in the blanks to answer if each set is greater than, less than or equal.

1. 3^2 [<] 2^4

2. 4^3 [ ] 3^2

3. 2^4 [ ] 5^2

4. 6^5 [ ] 4^3

5. 3^3 [ ] 5^2

6. 5^3 [ ] 7^2

7. 8^4 [ ] 5^3

8. 6^3 [ ] 9^3

9. 4^4 [ ] 8^4

10. 5^2 [ ] 9^2

11. 7^3 [ ] 2^2

12. 4^4 [ ] 3^2

13. 8^3 [ ] 4^2

14. 3^4 [ ] 9^3

15. 6^2 [ ] 7^2

Chapter 3 - Division

In this chapter you will learn about division of large numbers.

Here are the things you will learn:

- Understanding Division
- Division with Remainders
- Division of 2-digit numbers
- Division of 3-digit numbers
- Division of 4-digit numbers
- Division of 5-digit numbers

Division

- Division is a way to find out how many times one number is counted in another number.
- The $\div$ sign means " divided by".
- Use this symbol $\overline{)}$ to set up a division problem.
- The dividend is the larger number that is divided by the smaller number, the divisor.
- The answer of a division problem is called the quotient.

$\div$ is the symbol for division

$$6 \div 2 = 3$$

dividend **divisor** **quotient**

- $6 \div 2 = 3$ is read "6 divided by 2 is equal to 3".
- In $6 \div 2 = 3$, the divisor is 2, the dividend is 6 and the quotient is 3.

$\overline{)}$ is used to divide

$$\begin{array}{r} 5 \\ 2\overline{)10} \end{array}$$

divisor **dividend** **quotient**

- $\begin{array}{r} 5 \\ 2\overline{)10} \end{array}$ is read "10 divided by 2 is equal to 5".
- In $\begin{array}{r} 5 \\ 2\overline{)10} \end{array}$, the divisor is 2, the dividend is 10 and the quotient is 5.

Lesson 1

Division with a 2-Digit Dividend 1

When dividing a **two-digit number** by a **one-digit number**, the quotient can have one or two digits. That is why it is easier to start by breaking the problem down into steps.

Estimate	**Divide the tens**	**Bring down the ones and repeat the steps.**	The answer is: **28 r 1**
2 3)85	2 3)85 - 6 2	28 3)85 - 6↓ 25 - 24 1	Remember these steps: **1.** Divide **2.** Multiply **3.** Subtract **4.** Bring down
Take a look at the first digit. Estimate how many times 3 will go into 8 without going over the number.	3 can go into 8 twice. Multiply 3 x 2 and get 6. Subtract the 6 from 8 leaving 2.	Bring down the 5 from the one's column and repeat the steps. **The remainder is 1**	Repeat these steps until there are no more digits to bring down.

Solve these problems. Some may not have remainders.

1. 6)97 = 16 r 1
- 6
37
- 36
1

2. 5)38

3. 7)89

4. 2)91

4. 4)99

6. 3)44

7. 5)58

8. 2)67

Lesson 2

Division with a 2-Digit Dividend 2

Solve these problems. Some may not have remainders.

1. $5\overline{)67}$ **2.** $8\overline{)99}$ **3.** $3\overline{)53}$ **4.** $9\overline{)92}$

5. $2\overline{)78}$ **6.** $7\overline{)80}$ **7.** $5\overline{)73}$ **8.** $3\overline{)64}$

9. $4\overline{)61}$ **10.** $2\overline{)83}$ **11.** $9\overline{)97}$ **12.** $6\overline{)77}$

Lesson 3

Division Word Problems

Use division to solve the problems below.

1. Jerry has 24 boxes to move. He can only carry 3 boxes at a time. How many trips will he have to make to move all the boxes?

2. Sandy has 15 chores to do around the house this week. If she does 3 chores a day, how many days will it take her to do all her chores?

3. Mitchell has 42 apples. He wants to divide them into 6 groups. How many apples will be in each group?

4. Andy has 63 cookies in his jar that he wants to share with his friends. If he has 7 friends, how many cookies will each friend get?

Lesson 4

Dividing 3-Digit Dividends by a 1-Digit Divisor 1

When dividing a larger number by a one-digit number, it is easier to start by breaking the problem down into steps.

Always remember these steps

1. Estimate
2. Divide
3. Multiply
4. Subtract
5. Compare
6. Bring down

Repeat the steps as needed

Here is an example:

Estimate	**Divide the hundreds**	**Bring down the tens and repeat the steps.**	**Bring down the ones and repeat the steps.**
2 4)975	2 4)975 - 8 1	24 4)975 - 8↓ 17 - 16 1	243r3 4)975 - 8 17 - 16↓ 15 - 12 3
Take a look at the first digit. Estimate how many times 4 will go into 9 without going over the number.	4 can go into 9 twice. Multiply 4 x 2 and get 8. Subtract the 8 from 9 leaving 1.	4 can go into 17 four times. Multiply 4 x 4 and get 16. Subtract 16 from 17 leaving 1.	The remainder is **3**

Solve these problems. Some may not have remainders.

1. 2)735

367 r 1
- 6
13
-12
15
- 14
1

2. 3)892

3. 7)938

Lesson 5

Dividing 3-Digit Dividends by a 1-Digit Divisor 2

Solve these problems. Some may not have remainders.

1. $\begin{array}{r} 153\text{r}2 \\ 3\overline{)461} \\ -3 \\ \hline 16 \\ -15 \\ \hline 11 \\ -9 \\ \hline 2 \end{array}$

2. $4\overline{)128}$

3. $2\overline{)392}$

4. $7\overline{)975}$

5. $9\overline{)815}$

6. $6\overline{)892}$

7. $3\overline{)564}$

8. $2\overline{)297}$

9. $3\overline{)622}$

10. $4\overline{)930}$

11. $5\overline{)556}$

12. $7\overline{)986}$

13. $2\overline{)846}$

14. $3\overline{)134}$

15. $2\overline{)408}$

16. $2\overline{)276}$

17. $3\overline{)578}$

18. $8\overline{)556}$

19. $9\overline{)681}$

20. $4\overline{)599}$

Dividing 3-Digit Dividends by a 1-Digit Divisor 3

Solve these problems. Some may not have remainders.

1. $9\overline{)592}$	2. $5\overline{)344}$	3. $7\overline{)907}$	4. $2\overline{)677}$	5. $6\overline{)128}$
6. $3\overline{)750}$	7. $4\overline{)417}$	8. $8\overline{)982}$	9. $9\overline{)337}$	10. $3\overline{)827}$
11. $6\overline{)679}$	12. $2\overline{)736}$	13. $5\overline{)422}$	14. $7\overline{)175}$	15. $8\overline{)697}$
16. $9\overline{)858}$	17. $2\overline{)907}$	18. $4\overline{)335}$	19. $9\overline{)875}$	20. $5\overline{)785}$

Lesson 6

Dividing 4-Digit Dividends by a 1-Digit Divisor

Solve these problems. Some may not have remainders.

1. $5\overline{)6,207}$
2. $8\overline{)4,557}$
3. $2\overline{)3,045}$
4. $9\overline{)5,671}$
5. $7\overline{)9,278}$
6. $4\overline{)8,715}$
7. $3\overline{)1,896}$
8. $6\overline{)5,809}$
9. $5\overline{)2,254}$
10. $2\overline{)3,735}$
11. $6\overline{)6,854}$
12. $9\overline{)8,994}$

Lesson 7

Dividing 5-Digit Dividends by a 1-Digit Divisor 1

Solve these problems. Some may not have remainders.

1. $4\overline{)33,791}$ = 8,447 r3

```
   8,447r3
4)33,791
 -32
   17
  -16
    19
   -16
     31
    -28
      3
```

2. $3\overline{)64,872}$

3. $6\overline{)43,951}$

4. $2\overline{)89,305}$

5. $7\overline{)51,372}$

6. $5\overline{)90,139}$

7. $9\overline{)81,225}$

8. $3\overline{)54,981}$

9. $4\overline{)78,241}$

10. $7\overline{)28,356}$

11. $6\overline{)99,807}$

12. $9\overline{)70,207}$

Dividing 5-Digit Dividends by 1-Digit Divisor 2

Solve these problems. Some may not have remainders.

1. $9\overline{)40{,}863}$
2. $6\overline{)92{,}025}$
3. $8\overline{)17{,}283}$
4. $7\overline{)59{,}518}$
5. $2\overline{)64{,}761}$
6. $5\overline{)51{,}909}$
7. $3\overline{)73{,}871}$
8. $8\overline{)81{,}095}$
9. $6\overline{)79{,}812}$
10. $4\overline{)33{,}299}$
11. $9\overline{)30{,}956}$
12. $7\overline{)99{,}068}$

Lesson 8

Division Word Problems 2

Use division to solve the problems below.

1. Reggie has 312 letters to deliver. If he delivers 6 letters an hour, how many hours will it take him to deliver all the letters?

2. Suzy is running a marathon. She needs to run 286 miles to finish. She can run 22 miles a day. How many days will it take her to finish the marathon?

3. Ray has 714 square feet of snow to shovel from his yard. He can shovel 14 square feet an hour. How many hours will it take him to shovel all the snow?

4. Dad is building a fence. He has 595 boards. It takes 5 boards to build each section of the fence. How many sections of fence can he make with the boards he has?

Lesson 9

Division with 2-Digit Divisors

When dividing a larger number by a two-digit number, it is easier to start by breaking the problem down into steps.

Here is an example:

Always remember these steps

1. Estimate
2. Divide
3. Multiply
4. Subtract
5. Compare
6. Bring down

Repeat the steps as needed

Estimate	Divide the first set.	Bring down the ones and repeat the steps.	Bring the remainder back up top.
3 24)865	3 24)865 - 72 14	36 24)865 - 72↓ 145 - 144 1	36r1 24)865 - 72↓ 145 - 144 1
Take a look at the first digits. Estimate how many times 24 will go into 86 without going over the number.	24 can go into 86 three times equaling 72. Subtract 72 from 86 leaving 14.	24 can go into 145 six times giving us 144. Subtract 144 from 145 leaving 1.	The remainder is 1

Solve these problems. Some may not have remainders.

1. 31)659 → 21r8
-62
39
- 31
8
2. 46)884
3. 21)429
4. 19)708
5. 38)594
6. 75)999
7. 53)864
8. 60)729
9. 91)963
10. 43)836

Lesson 10

Dividing 3-Digit Dividends by a 2-Digit Divisor

Solve these problems. Some may not have remainders.

1. 12)269 = 22r5
```
   22r5
12)269
  -24
    29
   -24
     5
```

2. 30)738 **3.** 22)449 **4.** 41)209

5. 20)861 **6.** 12)271 **7.** 45)994 **8.** 33)735

9. 35)755 **10.** 11)195 **11.** 29)312 **12.** 63)656

13. 24)681 **14.** 15)575 **15.** 20)468 **16.** 41)630

17. 43)129 **18.** 39)705 **19.** 51)362 **20.** 67)197

Lesson 11

Dividing 4-Digit Dividends by a 2-Digit Divisor

Solve these problems. Some may not have remainders.

1. $13\overline{)2{,}691}$

2. $24\overline{)3{,}558}$

3. $65\overline{)8{,}945}$

4. $54\overline{)6{,}021}$

5. $41\overline{)9{,}278}$

6. $23\overline{)5{,}968}$

7. $36\overline{)7{,}682}$

8. $17\overline{)4{,}950}$

9. $44\overline{)8{,}962}$

10. $16\overline{)1{,}891}$

11. $21\overline{)3{,}398}$

12. $32\overline{)6{,}570}$

Lesson 12

Dividing 5-Digit Dividends by a 2-Digit Divisor 1

Solve these problems. Some may not have remainders.

1.

```
     3,229r8
12)38,756
  -36
    27
   -24
     35
    -24
     116
    -108
       8
```

2. 34)85,097

3. 57)96,134

4. 29)64,893

5. 45)95,507

6. 61)35,692

7. 32)96,599

8. 43)77,039

9. 59)32,072

10. 86)90,965

11. 71)80,099

12. 27)43,992

Dividing 5-Digit Dividends by a 2-Digit Divisor 2

Solve these problems. Some may not have remainders.

1. 29)66,126 **2.** 18)40,834 **3.** 43)54,957 **4.** 36)37,993

5. 56)76,013 **6.** 84)99,957 **7.** 70)32,142 **8.** 33)33,962

9. 44)59,195 **10.** 91)85,809 **11.** 62)65,135 **12.** 89)99,066

Chapter 4 - Fractions

Chapter 4 - Fractions

Lesson 1

Adding Fractions with Common Denominators

To add fractions with common denominators, just add the numerators. The denominators will remain the same.

Numerators →	$\frac{2}{9} + \frac{3}{9} = \frac{2+3}{9} = \frac{5}{9}$
Common Denominators →	

Add the fractions below.

1. $\frac{6}{15} + \frac{5}{15} + \frac{2}{15} = \underline{\frac{13}{15}}$

2. $\frac{12}{37} + \frac{7}{37} + \frac{4}{37} =$ ____

3. $\frac{13}{80} + \frac{9}{80} + \frac{27}{80} =$ ____

4. $\frac{8}{109} + \frac{77}{109} + \frac{15}{109} =$ ____

5. $\frac{17}{64} + \frac{3}{64} + \frac{10}{64} =$ ____

6. $\frac{3}{21} + \frac{7}{21} + \frac{4}{21} =$ ____

7. $\frac{205}{865} + \frac{111}{865} + \frac{67}{865} =$ ____

8. $\frac{14}{55} + \frac{8}{55} + \frac{11}{55} =$ ____

9. $\frac{2}{13} + \frac{7}{13} + \frac{1}{13} =$ ____

10. $\frac{2}{74} + \frac{12}{74} + \frac{31}{74} =$ ____

11. $\frac{9}{250} + \frac{140}{250} + \frac{89}{250} =$ ____

12. $\frac{3}{94} + \frac{3}{94} + \frac{1}{94} =$ ____

Lesson 2

Subtracting Fractions with Common Denominators

To subtract fractions with common denominators, just subtract the numerators. The denominators will remain the same.

Numerators →	$\dfrac{10}{12} - \dfrac{8}{12} = \dfrac{10-8}{12} = \dfrac{2}{12}$
Common Denominators →	

Subtract the fractions below.

1. $\dfrac{32}{73} - \dfrac{11}{73} = \dfrac{21}{73}$
2. $\dfrac{12}{28} - \dfrac{5}{28} =$ ____
3. $\dfrac{78}{89} - \dfrac{56}{89} =$ ____
4. $\dfrac{112}{146} - \dfrac{92}{146} =$ ____
5. $\dfrac{233}{634} - \dfrac{119}{634} =$ ____
6. $\dfrac{8}{12} - \dfrac{4}{12} =$ ____
7. $\dfrac{608}{759} - \dfrac{325}{759} =$ ____
8. $\dfrac{45}{56} - \dfrac{19}{56} =$ ____
9. $\dfrac{178}{207} - \dfrac{99}{207} =$ ____
10. $\dfrac{30}{49} - \dfrac{17}{49} =$ ____
11. $\dfrac{246}{277} - \dfrac{79}{277} =$ ____
12. $\dfrac{439}{534} - \dfrac{201}{534} =$ ____
13. $\dfrac{77}{88} - \dfrac{11}{88} =$ ____
14. $\dfrac{68}{129} - \dfrac{29}{129} =$ ____
15. $\dfrac{894}{952} - \dfrac{705}{952} =$ ____

Lesson 3

Fraction Word Problems

Write the correct fractions for each question below.

1. Daryl is working on his garden. He has planted 28 plants so far. He has 13 tomato plants, 6 eggplants and 9 potato plants. Write the fraction that represents each type of plant.

Tomatoes: $\frac{13}{28}$ **Eggplants:** $\frac{6}{28}$ **Potatoes:** $\frac{9}{28}$

2. Mom's favorite hobby is bird watching. Today she saw 15 different birds. She saw 3 blue jays, 9 sparrows, 6 ducks and 1 eagle. Write the fraction that represents each set of birds.

Blue Jays: ______ **Sparrows:** ______ **Ducks:** ______ **Eagles:** ______

3. Johnny went fishing today and caught 17 fish. He caught 2 bass, 6 trout, 5 guppies and 4 goldfish. Write the fraction that represents each type of fish.

Bass: ______ **Trout:** ______ **Guppies:** ______ **Goldfish:** ______

4. Dad is barbequing for the party this afternoon. He has 76 items to cook. He is going to cook 15 hamburgers, 22 chicken wings and 39 sausages.

Hamburgers: ______ **Chicken Wings:** ______ **Sausages:** ______

Lesson 4

Equivalent Fractions

Equivalent Fractions are fractions that have the same value. Even though each shape is divided into a different amount of parts, the shaded parts are equal.

$\frac{2}{4}$ of the circle is shaded in.

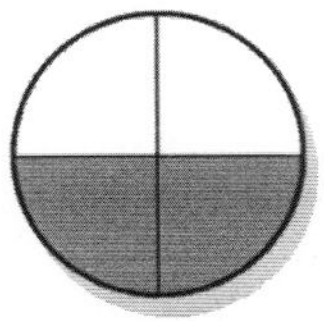

$\frac{4}{8}$ of the circle is shaded in.

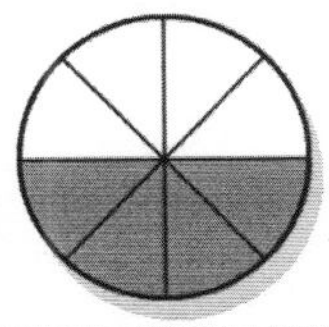

$\frac{2}{4}$ and $\frac{4}{8}$ are equivalent fractions. $\frac{2}{4} = \frac{4}{8}$

Shade in the equivalent fractions on the right to equal the fractions on the left.

$\frac{1}{4}$ 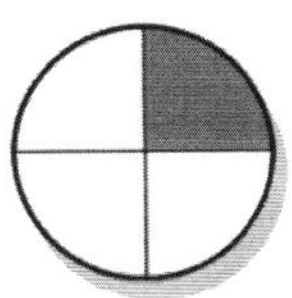 $=$ $\frac{2}{8}$ 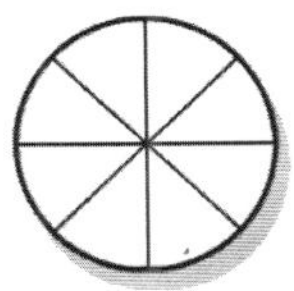

$\frac{2}{4}$ 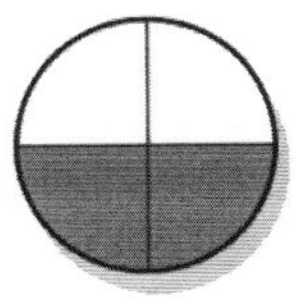 $=$ $\frac{4}{8}$ 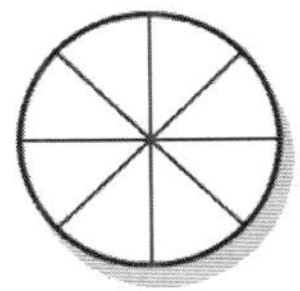

$\frac{3}{8}$ 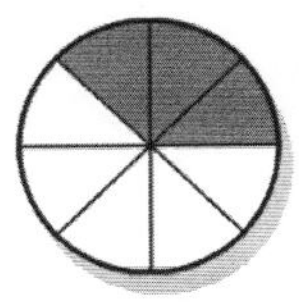 $=$ $\frac{6}{16}$ 

$\frac{5}{8}$ 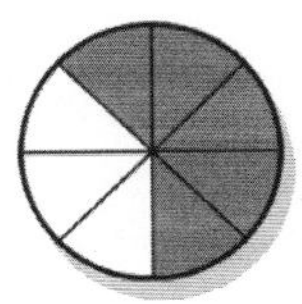 $=$ $\frac{10}{16}$ 

Lesson 5

Reducing to Equivalent Fractions

- Reducing (or simplifying) fractions means reducing a fraction to an equivalent fraction that has the smallest possible numbers.
- To do this, find the largest number that both the numerator and denominator are divisible by. Then divide both by that number.

Example 1:	Example 2:
$\frac{15}{21} \div \left[\frac{3}{3}\right] = \frac{5}{7}$	$\frac{12}{20} \div \left[\frac{4}{4}\right] = \frac{3}{5}$
$\frac{15}{21} = \frac{5}{7}$	$\frac{12}{20} = \frac{3}{5}$

Reduce the fractions to lowest terms.

1. $\frac{18}{27} \div \frac{9}{9} = \frac{2}{3}$

2. $\frac{4}{12} \div$ ____ = ____

3. $\frac{20}{35} \div$ ____ = ____

4. $\frac{9}{24} \div$ ____ = ____

5. $\frac{15}{21} \div$ ____ = ____

6. $\frac{16}{40} \div$ ____ = ____

7. $\frac{10}{25} \div$ ____ = ____

8. $\frac{16}{36} \div$ ____ = ____

9. $\frac{12}{30} \div$ ____ = ____

10. $\frac{9}{27} \div$ ____ = ____

11. $\frac{8}{14} \div$ ____ = ____

12. $\frac{16}{32} \div$ ____ = ____

Lesson 6

Reducing to Equivalent Fractions with Common Denominators

Before we can add or subtract fractions, we must make sure they have common denominators. There are two ways to do this–using multiplication or division. Let's look at division first.

$$\frac{9}{12} - \frac{1}{4}$$

In order to subtract these fractions, we must change one to an equivalent fraction with a common denominator (in this case, 4).
To change a fraction to an equivalent fraction, divide the numerator and the denominator by the same number (in this case, 3).

Numerator ⟶ / **Denominator** ⟶ $\frac{9}{12} = \frac{9 \div 3}{12 \div 3} = \frac{3}{4}$

$\frac{1}{4}$ and $\frac{3}{4}$ now have common denominators.

Example:

Before we can find the difference, we must find an equivalent fraction with a common denominator.

Change this: $\frac{9}{12} - \frac{1}{4} =$

To this & subtract: $\frac{3}{4} - \frac{1}{4} = \frac{2}{4}$

1. $\frac{6}{10} + \frac{1}{5} = \frac{3}{5} + \frac{1}{5} = \frac{4}{5}$
2. $\frac{8}{12} + \frac{1}{6} = \underline{\quad} + \frac{1}{6} = \underline{\quad}$
3. $\frac{9}{21} + \frac{2}{7} = \underline{\quad} + \frac{2}{7} = \underline{\quad}$
4. $\frac{12}{32} + \frac{3}{8} = \underline{\quad} + \frac{3}{8} = \underline{\quad}$
5. $\frac{15}{25} - \frac{1}{5} = \underline{\quad} - \frac{1}{5} = \underline{\quad}$
6. $\frac{15}{20} - \frac{1}{4} = \underline{\quad} - \frac{1}{4} = \underline{\quad}$
7. $\frac{25}{35} - \frac{3}{7} = \underline{\quad} - \frac{3}{7} = \underline{\quad}$
8. $\frac{32}{36} - \frac{4}{9} = \underline{\quad} - \frac{4}{9} = \underline{\quad}$

Lesson 7

Adding Fractions with Different Denominators - Using Division

To add fractions with different denominators, first find a common denominator. Then add the numerators.

Solve each problem. Find each common denominator and sum.

1. $\frac{15}{21} = \frac{5}{7}$; $+\frac{2}{7} = +\frac{2}{7}$; sum: $\frac{7}{7}$

2. $\frac{1}{5} = \_\_$; $+\frac{8}{20} = +\_\_$; sum: $\_\_$

3. $\frac{21}{30} = \_\_$; $+\frac{2}{10} = +\_\_$; sum: $\_\_$

4. $\frac{10}{12} = \_\_$; $+\frac{6}{36} = +\_\_$; sum: $\_\_$

5. $\frac{2}{9} = \_\_$; $+\frac{18}{54} = +\_\_$; sum: $\_\_$

6. $\frac{25}{35} = \_\_$; $+\frac{2}{7} = +\_\_$; sum: $\_\_$

7. $\frac{54}{81} = \_\_$; $+\frac{1}{9} = +\_\_$; sum: $\_\_$

8. $\frac{27}{36} = \_\_$; $+\frac{2}{12} = +\_\_$; sum: $\_\_$

9. $\frac{6}{7} = \_\_$; $+\frac{28}{49} = +\_\_$; sum: $\_\_$

10. $\frac{56}{64} = \_\_$; $+\frac{1}{8} = +\_\_$; sum: $\_\_$

11. $\frac{3}{9} = \_\_$; $+\frac{20}{36} = +\_\_$; sum: $\_\_$

12. $\frac{81}{90} = \_\_$; $+\frac{7}{10} = +\_\_$; sum: $\_\_$

Lesson 8

Subtracting Fractions with Different Denominators - Using Division

To add fractions with different denominators, first find a common denominator. Then add the numerators.

Solve each problem. Find each common denominator and sum.

1. $\frac{12}{18} = \frac{12}{18}$

$- \frac{2}{9} = \frac{4}{18}$

$\frac{8}{18}$

2. $\frac{4}{7} =$ ___

$- \frac{3}{21} =$ ___

___

3. $\frac{7}{9} =$ ___

$- \frac{20}{45} =$ ___

___

4. $\frac{28}{35} =$ ___

$- \frac{3}{5} =$ ___

___

5. $\frac{3}{7} =$ ___

$- \frac{18}{63} =$ ___

___

6. $\frac{36}{42} =$ ___

$- \frac{5}{7} =$ ___

___

7. $\frac{81}{81} =$ ___

$- \frac{6}{9} =$ ___

___

8. $\frac{8}{9} =$ ___

$- \frac{12}{36} =$ ___

___

9. $\frac{6}{7} =$ ___

$- \frac{21}{49} =$ ___

___

10. $\frac{8}{9} =$ ___

$- \frac{12}{54} =$ ___

___

11. $\frac{5}{6} =$ ___

$- \frac{16}{48} =$ ___

___

12. $\frac{32}{36} =$ ___

$- \frac{5}{9} =$ ___

___

Lesson 9

Finding Common Denominators using Multiplication 1

Before we can add or subtract fractions, we must make sure they have common denominators. There are two ways to do this–using multiplication or division. Let's look at multiplication .

To change a fraction to an equivalent fraction, multiply the numerator and the denominator by the same number.

Example: Before we can add these fractions we must find a common denominator.

Change this: $\frac{2}{6} + \frac{2}{12}$ = **To this & add:** $\frac{4}{12} + \frac{2}{12} = \frac{6}{12}$

Numerator / Denominator → $\frac{2}{6} = \frac{2 \times 2}{6 \times 2} = \frac{4}{12}$

$\frac{2}{12}$ and $\frac{4}{12}$ now have a common denominator.

Fill in the blanks to complete the equivalent fractions.

1. $\frac{2}{6} \times \frac{2}{2} = \frac{4}{12}$
2. $\frac{3}{5} \times \frac{\quad}{\quad} = \frac{9}{15}$
3. $\frac{6}{8} \times \frac{\quad}{\quad} = \frac{24}{32}$
4. $\frac{5}{7} \times \frac{\quad}{\quad} = \frac{15}{21}$
5. $\frac{2}{3} \times \frac{\quad}{\quad} = \frac{16}{24}$
6. $\frac{3}{4} \times \frac{\quad}{\quad} = \frac{15}{20}$
7. $\frac{3}{7} \times \frac{\quad}{\quad} = \frac{9}{21}$
8. $\frac{2}{6} \times \frac{\quad}{\quad} = \frac{22}{66}$
9. $\frac{2}{6} \times \frac{\quad}{\quad} = \frac{18}{54}$

Lesson 10

Finding Common Denominators Using Multiplication 2

- We just learned that one way to find **equivalent fractions** is to multiply both the numerator and denominator by the same number.
- So this means $\frac{2}{6} = \frac{4}{12}$

$$\frac{2}{6} = \frac{2 \times 2}{6 \times 2} = \frac{4}{12}$$

← **Numerator**

← **Denominator**

$\frac{2}{6}$ and $\frac{4}{12}$ are now **equivalent fractions.**

Fill in the blanks to make the fractions below equivalent fractions.

1. $\frac{3}{5} = \frac{\quad}{20}$	**2.** $\frac{2}{4} = \frac{6}{\quad}$	**3.** $\frac{1}{2} = \frac{\quad}{20}$	**4.** $\frac{6}{8} = \frac{30}{\quad}$
5. $\frac{1}{7} = \frac{\quad}{35}$	**6.** $\frac{2}{6} = \frac{30}{\quad}$	**7.** $\frac{4}{5} = \frac{\quad}{100}$	**8.** $\frac{2}{4} = \frac{\quad}{32}$
9. $\frac{4}{12} = \frac{\quad}{84}$	**10.** $\frac{5}{10} = \frac{45}{\quad}$	**11.** $\frac{3}{7} = \frac{6}{\quad}$	**12.** $\frac{3}{5} = \frac{33}{\quad}$
13. $\frac{9}{16} = \frac{72}{\quad}$	**14.** $\frac{1}{3} = \frac{\quad}{45}$	**15.** $\frac{15}{25} = \frac{30}{\quad}$	**16.** $\frac{16}{18} = \frac{\quad}{90}$
17. $\frac{3}{16} = \frac{\quad}{64}$	**18.** $\frac{3}{5} = \frac{\quad}{25}$	**19.** $\frac{4}{6} = \frac{4}{\quad}$	**20.** $\frac{2}{8} = \frac{4}{\quad}$

Lesson 11

Adding Fractions with Different Denominators - Using Multiplication

To change a fraction to an equivalent fraction, multiply the numerator and the denominator by the same number.

Fill in the blanks to find equivalent fractions, then add the fractions.

1. $\frac{2}{4} = \frac{4}{8}$; $+\frac{1}{8} = +\frac{1}{8}$; $= \frac{5}{8}$

2. $\frac{4}{12} = \frac{\quad}{12}$; $+\frac{3}{6} = +\frac{\quad}{12}$; $= \frac{\quad}{\quad}$

3. $\frac{2}{7} = \frac{\quad}{21}$; $+\frac{5}{21} = +\frac{\quad}{21}$; $= \frac{\quad}{\quad}$

4. $\frac{4}{28} = \frac{\quad}{28}$; $+\frac{3}{4} = +\frac{\quad}{28}$; $= \frac{\quad}{\quad}$

5. $\frac{3}{5} = \frac{\quad}{50}$; $+\frac{12}{50} = +\frac{\quad}{50}$; $= \frac{\quad}{\quad}$

6. $\frac{6}{24} = \frac{\quad}{24}$; $+\frac{5}{8} = +\frac{\quad}{24}$; $= \frac{\quad}{\quad}$

7. $\frac{21}{48} = \frac{\quad}{48}$; $+\frac{2}{6} = +\frac{\quad}{48}$; $= \frac{\quad}{\quad}$

8. $\frac{5}{9} = \frac{\quad}{81}$; $+\frac{12}{81} = +\frac{\quad}{81}$; $= \frac{\quad}{\quad}$

9. $\frac{9}{36} = \frac{\quad}{36}$; $+\frac{3}{6} = +\frac{\quad}{36}$; $= \frac{\quad}{\quad}$

10. $\frac{4}{9} = \frac{\quad}{63}$; $+\frac{5}{63} = +\frac{\quad}{63}$; $= \frac{\quad}{\quad}$

11. $\frac{39}{72} = \frac{\quad}{72}$; $+\frac{3}{9} = +\frac{\quad}{72}$; $= \frac{\quad}{\quad}$

12. $\frac{17}{56} = \frac{\quad}{56}$; $+\frac{5}{8} = +\frac{\quad}{56}$; $= \frac{\quad}{\quad}$

Lesson 12

Subtracting Fractions with Different Denominators - Using Multiplication

To change a fraction to an equivalent fraction, multiply the numerator and the denominator by the same number.

Fill in the blanks to find equivalent fractions, then subtract.

1. $\frac{2}{4} = \frac{10}{20}$; $-\frac{6}{20} = -\frac{6}{20}$; $\frac{4}{20}$

2. $\frac{14}{15} = \frac{\quad}{15}$; $-\frac{4}{5} = -\frac{\quad}{15}$; $\frac{\quad}{\quad}$

3. $\frac{13}{18} = \frac{\quad}{18}$; $-\frac{2}{6} = -\frac{\quad}{18}$; $\frac{\quad}{\quad}$

4. $\frac{35}{40} = \frac{\quad}{40}$; $-\frac{2}{4} = -\frac{\quad}{40}$; $\frac{\quad}{\quad}$

5. $\frac{5}{6} = \frac{\quad}{48}$; $-\frac{29}{48} = -\frac{\quad}{48}$; $\frac{\quad}{\quad}$

6. $\frac{16}{24} = \frac{\quad}{24}$; $-\frac{5}{8} = -\frac{\quad}{24}$; $\frac{\quad}{\quad}$

7. $\frac{36}{49} = \frac{\quad}{49}$; $-\frac{3}{7} = -\frac{\quad}{49}$; $\frac{\quad}{\quad}$

8. $\frac{5}{6} = \frac{\quad}{54}$; $-\frac{29}{54} = -\frac{\quad}{54}$; $\frac{\quad}{\quad}$

9. $\frac{63}{81} = \frac{\quad}{81}$; $+\frac{6}{9} = -\frac{\quad}{81}$; $\frac{\quad}{\quad}$

10. $\frac{54}{63} = \frac{\quad}{63}$; $-\frac{5}{9} = -\frac{\quad}{63}$; $\frac{\quad}{\quad}$

11. $\frac{27}{48} = \frac{\quad}{48}$; $-\frac{4}{8} = -\frac{\quad}{48}$; $\frac{\quad}{\quad}$

12. $\frac{35}{50} = \frac{\quad}{100}$; $-\frac{50}{100} = -\frac{\quad}{100}$; $\frac{\quad}{\quad}$

Lesson 13

Mixed Numbers with Common Denominators

When we add or subtract mixed numbers with common denominators, we need to first add or subtract the fractions. Next add or subtract the whole numbers.

Example 1: $2\frac{2}{8} + 6\frac{3}{8}$

Step 1: Add the fractions	**Step 2:** Add the whole numbers
$\begin{array}{r} 2\frac{2}{8} \\ +6\frac{3}{8} \\ \hline \frac{5}{8} \end{array}$	$\begin{array}{r} 2\frac{2}{8} \\ +6\frac{3}{8} \\ \hline 8\frac{5}{8} \end{array}$

Example 2: $5\frac{9}{12} - 3\frac{5}{12}$

Step 1: Subtract the fractions	**Step 2:** Subtract the whole numbers
$\begin{array}{r} 5\frac{9}{12} \\ -3\frac{5}{12} \\ \hline \frac{4}{12} \end{array}$	$\begin{array}{r} 5\frac{9}{12} \\ -3\frac{5}{12} \\ \hline 2\frac{4}{12} \end{array}$

Add or subtract the mixed numbers below.

1. $\begin{array}{r} 3\frac{6}{12} \\ +2\frac{4}{12} \\ \hline 5\frac{10}{12} \end{array}$

2. $\begin{array}{r} 5\frac{3}{9} \\ +1\frac{1}{9} \\ \hline \end{array}$

3. $\begin{array}{r} 4\frac{2}{5} \\ +3\frac{2}{5} \\ \hline \end{array}$

4. $\begin{array}{r} 1\frac{8}{23} \\ +1\frac{12}{23} \\ \hline \end{array}$

5. $\begin{array}{r} 9\frac{2}{8} \\ +4\frac{4}{8} \\ \hline \end{array}$

6. $\begin{array}{r} 6\frac{3}{15} \\ +7\frac{7}{15} \\ \hline \end{array}$

7. $\begin{array}{r} 8\frac{21}{39} \\ +5\frac{9}{39} \\ \hline \end{array}$

8. $\begin{array}{r} 3\frac{4}{10} \\ +9\frac{5}{10} \\ \hline \end{array}$

9. $\begin{array}{r} 6\frac{12}{19} \\ -2\frac{7}{19} \\ \hline \end{array}$

10. $\begin{array}{r} 8\frac{7}{8} \\ -5\frac{2}{8} \\ \hline \end{array}$

11. $\begin{array}{r} 10\frac{14}{16} \\ -7\frac{8}{16} \\ \hline \end{array}$

12. $\begin{array}{r} 14\frac{5}{6} \\ -9\frac{1}{6} \\ \hline \end{array}$

13. $\begin{array}{r} 24\frac{21}{25} \\ -19\frac{17}{25} \\ \hline \end{array}$

14. $\begin{array}{r} 36\frac{9}{10} \\ -25\frac{8}{10} \\ \hline \end{array}$

15. $\begin{array}{r} 46\frac{39}{44} \\ -38\frac{12}{44} \\ \hline \end{array}$

Lesson 14

Reducing Mixed Numbers with Common Denominators

- When we add or subtract mixed numbers with common denominators, first we need to add or subtract the fractions. Next add or subtract the whole numbers.
- When reducing, remember to divide by the largest number possible.

Add or subtract the mixed numbers below, then reduce to the simplest form.

1. $4\frac{3}{10} + 1\frac{2}{10}$ = $5\frac{5}{10} = 5\frac{1}{2}$

2. $4\frac{8}{12} + 5\frac{1}{12}$

3. $3\frac{2}{18} + 6\frac{4}{18}$

4. $3\frac{1}{8} + 5\frac{3}{8}$

5. $7\frac{7}{24} + 5\frac{5}{24}$

6. $9\frac{10}{36} + 6\frac{8}{36}$

7. $4\frac{5}{56} + 7\frac{16}{56}$

8. $8\frac{22}{81} + 6\frac{23}{81}$

9. $12\frac{10}{16} - 9\frac{2}{16}$

10. $17\frac{5}{12} - 5\frac{1}{12}$

11. $11\frac{21}{28} - 3\frac{7}{28}$

12. $29\frac{9}{9} - 17\frac{3}{9}$

13. $48\frac{37}{42} - 9\frac{9}{42}$

14. $72\frac{25}{63} - 54\frac{7}{63}$

15. $50\frac{18}{21} - 25\frac{6}{21}$

16. $36\frac{32}{50} - 25\frac{12}{50}$

Lesson 15

Converting Mixed Numbers

To add, subtract, multiply or divide mixed numbers by other fractions, we need to convert the mixed number to an improper fraction.

Step 1:	Step 2:	Step 3:
Multiply the whole number by the denominator. $2\frac{1}{4} = \frac{2\times4}{4}$	Add the numerator to the product. $2\frac{1}{4} = \frac{2\times4+1}{4} = \frac{9}{4}$	Keep the denominator the same. $2\frac{1}{4} = \frac{9}{4}$

Convert each mixed number to an improper fraction.

1. $3\frac{4}{3} = \frac{13}{3}$ **2.** $8\frac{6}{4} = \_\_$ **3.** $2\frac{9}{2} = \_\_$ **4.** $6\frac{2}{5} = \_\_$

5. $9\frac{5}{10} = \_\_$ **6.** $4\frac{1}{5} = \_\_$ **7.** $3\frac{4}{7} = \_\_$ **8.** $1\frac{11}{3} = \_\_$

9. $5\frac{1}{5} = \_\_$ **10.** $8\frac{6}{3} = \_\_$ **11.** $4\frac{7}{5} = \_\_$ **12.** $2\frac{2}{8} = \_\_$

13. $9\frac{7}{5} = \_\_$ **14.** $7\frac{6}{3} = \_\_$ **15.** $6\frac{3}{11} = \_\_$ **16.** $3\frac{7}{3} = \_\_$

17. $1\frac{15}{22} = \_\_$ **18.** $2\frac{6}{9} = \_\_$ **19.** $8\frac{2}{4} = \_\_$ **20.** $9\frac{5}{3} = \_\_$

Lesson 16

Improper Fractions

Improper fractions are fractions that have a numerator greater than or equal to the denominator.

Numerator → 8, 49, 10
Denominator → 8, 7, 5

$\frac{8}{8}, \frac{49}{7}, \frac{10}{5}$

To convert an **improper fraction** into a whole number or mixed number, divide the numerator by the denominator.

$\frac{8}{8} = 8\overline{)8}$ → 1 $\frac{49}{7} = 7\overline{)49}$ → 7

$\frac{10}{5} = 5\overline{)10}$ → 2

When converting improper fractions, sometimes you get remainders. This means you will get **mixed numbers.** Write the remainder as a fraction with the divisor as the bottom number.

$\frac{9}{5} = 5\overline{)9}$ → $2\frac{1}{5}$
-8
1

Convert the fractions below.

Convert these fractions to whole numbers:

1. $\frac{35}{5} = $ 7

2. $\frac{12}{3} = $ ____

3. $\frac{24}{8} = $ ____

4. $\frac{27}{3} = $ ____

5. $\frac{48}{6} = $ ____

6. $\frac{93}{3} = $ ____

7. $\frac{25}{5} = $ ____

8. $\frac{84}{2} = $ ____

Convert these fractions to mixed numbers:

9. $\frac{15}{6} = 2\frac{3}{6}$

10. $\frac{10}{4} = $ ____

11. $\frac{7}{2} = $ ____

12. $\frac{19}{8} = $ ____

13. $\frac{23}{4} = $ ____

14. $\frac{26}{3} = $ ____

15. $\frac{50}{9} = $ ____

16. $\frac{46}{8} = $ ____

Chapter 5 - Decimals

Lesson 1

Decimal Points Addition

Adding decimals is like most normal addition. You just have to remember to line up the decimals.

Hint: Decimal points always go at the end of a whole number (3 = 3.0 or 3.00)

Example: Add 6.33, 5 and 9.5

Step 1: Line up the numbers	**Step 2:** Add zeros	**Step 3:** Find the total
6.33 5. + 9.5	6.33 5.00 + 9.50	6.33 5.00 + 9.50 20.83

Line up the numbers and solve the problems below. Show your work in the boxes.

1: 5.84 + 1.7 + 3.29

5.84
1.70
+ 3.29
10.83

2: 8.09 + 2.97 + .49

3: 6.94 + 3.07 + 7

4: 24 + 11.09 + 39.74

5: 70.05 + .95 + .38

6: 9.99 + .83 + 60.4

Lesson 2

Arranging and Adding Decimals 1

Use what you learned about adding numbers with decimals to find the totals to the questions below. Show your work in the boxes.

1: 10.54 + 8.01 + .89

2: 6.32 + 9.51 + 1.99

3: .99 + 5.15 + 12.47

4: 4.21 + 3.57 + 15.05

5: 11.97 + 246.1 + 6.50

6: .23 + 13.31 + 72.08

7: 61.59 + 31.64 + .08

8: 84 + 16.99 + 14.89

9: 8.50 + 7.27 + 985

Arranging and Adding Decimals 2

Use what you learned about adding numbers with decimals to find the totals to the questions below. Show your work in the boxes.

1: .154 + 28.46 + 11.751

2: 9.81 + .011 + 6.907

3: 3.645 + 5.707 + 99

4: 6.59 + 1.194 + 5.99

5: 29.175 + 35.19 + 3.809

6: 1.567 + 88.09 + 41.78

7: 58.079 + 44.015 + 7.09

8: 1.955 + 44.19 + 70.091

9: 9.89 + .275 + 67.001

Arranging and Adding Decimals 3

Use what you learned about adding numbers with decimals to find the totals to the questions below. Show your work in the boxes.

1: 164.99 + 805.46 + .75

2: 150.92 + 321 + 50.24

3: 95.56 + 128.7 + 9.23

4: 389.04 + 84.99 + 6.15

5: 18.56 + 991.5 + 525.09

6: 61.91 + 571.17 + 223.09

7: 7.56 + 75.61 + 756.1

8: 395.1 + 395.11 + 39.51

9: 91.8 + 9.18 + 918.8

Lesson 3

Decimal Addition Word Problems

Solve the problems below.

1. Jeremy is a great basketball player. In season one he averaged 9.3 points with 6.2 rebounds per game. In season two he averaged 24.9 points and 3.6 rebounds per game. In season three he averaged 41.2 points with 6.4 rebounds per game. What was the total of his points and rebound averages for all three seasons?

2. Randy eats way too much ice cream. He ate 1.5 ounces on Monday, 2.3 ounces on Tuesday and 3.6 ounces on Wednesday. Thursday he ate 6.9 ounces . Then on Friday he ate 4.2 ounces of ice cream. How much ice cream did Randy eat in total this week?

3. Cynthia has a parrot named Hank. Hank gets his exercise everyday by flying. On Monday he flew 5.1 miles. On Tuesday he flew 6.85 miles. On Wednesday he flew 2.97 miles. Then on Thursday he flew 4.63 miles. How many miles has Hank flown this week?

4. Dad went fishing today. The first fish he caught weighed 12.39 pounds. The second fish he caught weighed 16.05 pounds. The third fish he caught weighed 2.76 pounds. Finally the last fish he caught weighed 9.14 pounds. What is the total weight of all the fish Dad caught today?

Lesson 4

Adding Decimals 1

Find the totals below.

1. 123.47 34.10 + 8.36	**2.** 106.05 23.21 + 1.36	**3.** 253.75 73.36 + 10.15	**4.** 387.12 49.70 + 6.65
5. 513.08 309.12 + 76.59	**6.** 480.21 759.96 + 88.07	**7.** 624.71 267.35 + 20.99	**8.** 945.37 651.83 + 79.41
9. 11.892 20.624 57.393 + 8.102	**10.** .937 13.419 23.757 + 9.144	**11.** 12.587 6.794 90.725 + 24.431	**12.** 67.599 11.180 9.413 + 21.924
13. 22.408 641.119 36.327 + 52.176	**14.** 18.649 97.321 531.655 + 944.299	**15.** 782.113 430.627 67.511 + 12.549	**16.** 72.399 194.912 381.134 + 26.709
17. 11.852 224.379 3.991 + 921.104	**18.** 127.537 363.224 40.916 + 598.644	**19.** 673.112 260.657 167.320 + 6.279	**20.** 587.611 76.435 539.907 + 322.621

Adding Decimals 2

Find the totals below.

1.
651.207
892.890
509.001
37.500
+ 201.605

2.
300.498
53.115
88.304
216.224
+ 366.367

3.
499.499
644.466
320.072
122.321
+ 783.009

4.
549.339
276.521
155.277
608.658
+ .151

5.
59.650
324.822
715.155
2.777
+ 500.000

6.
422.231
7.807
725.237
320.364
+ 967.957

7.
500.658
606.822
832.615
299.934
+ 1.307

8.
684.942
29.312
654.697
277.347
+ 306.754

9.
5.001
470.120
52.233
375.032
+ 960.197

10.
575.575
53.347
699.024
752.990
+ 247.367

11.
229.242
301.507
8.111
358.999
+ 295.031

12.
930.854
292.304
152.995
904.654
+ 35.002

13.
651.133
326.369
959.900
360.452
+ 995.521

14.
865.656
347.211
122.169
607.307
+ 744.654

15.
966.865
303.975
288.361
465.205
+ 217.000

16.
558.715
669.559
781.375
324.278
+ 587.662

Adding Decimals 3

Find the totals below.

1. 2,418.09 4,334.49 712.64 +1,482.11	**2.** 6,967.24 34.13 5,110.37 +2,326.22	**3.** 2,126.94 3,615.03 24.77 +4,331.62	**4.** 7,269.81 1,382.43 409.30 + 3.99
5. 604.88 7,291.39 3,036.13 +9,123.24	**6.** 4,168.68 5,055.33 4,333.07 + 659.37	**7.** 9,224.54 75.31 4.52 +3,012.10	**8.** 482.00 3,312.67 4,999.60 + 20.54
9. 6,287.90 961.24 823.36 +2,682.48	**10.** 329.58 3,677.41 9,003.36 + 51.27	**11.** 7,622.31 301.02 440.68 +2,539.88	**12.** 5,880.99 5,951.50 47.66 + 9.72
13. 4,408.12 8,399.99 254.17 2,765.55 +7,321.01	**14.** 88.78 9,100.59 65.34 3,036.66 + 7.92	**15.** 1,448.39 6,691.15 2,308.54 279.02 + 35.37	**16.** 5,651.14 9,842.59 2,000.77 2,621.22 +2,903.00

Lesson 5

Decimal Points Subtraction

Subtracting decimals is like normal subtraction.
You just have to remember to line up the decimals.

Hint: Decimal points always go at the end of a whole number (6 = 6.0 or 6.00)

Example: Subtract 20.99 from 44.5

Step 1: Line up the decimals.	**Step 2:** Add zeros and borrow when needed.	**Step 3:** Subtract all the numbers.
44.5 – 20.99	3 14 4 4. 5 10 (4 and 5 crossed out) – 20.99	3 14 4 4. 5 10 (4 and 5 crossed out) – 20.99 23.51

Line up the decimals and solve the problems below.
Show your work in the boxes.

1. 9.25 - 4.7

```
  9.25
- 4.70
------
  4.55
```

2. 30.5 - 17.05

3. 28.12 - .72

4. 605 - 45.07

5. 94.99 - 6.34

6. 339 - 40.09

Lesson 6

Arranging and Subtracting Decimals 1

Subtracting decimals is like normal subtraction.
You just have to remember to line up the decimals.

Hint: Decimal points always go at the end of a whole number (6 = 6.0 or 6.00)

Line up the decimals and solve the problems below.

1. 72.53 - 22.56

2. 99.58 - 71.90

3. 33.29 - 19.4

4. 40.06 - 24.1

5. 59.19 - 58.02

6. 82.33 - 51.73

7. 29.23 - 11.06

8. 95.19 - 48.44

9. 80 .46 - 62.9

Arranging and Subtracting Decimals 2

Subtracting decimals is like normal subtraction.
You just have to remember to line up the decimals.

Hint: Decimal points always go at the end of a whole number (6 = 6.0 or 6.00)

Line up the decimals and solve the problems below.

1. 695.53 - 103.08

2. 851.12 - 48.90

3. 305.94 - 12.44

4. 437.2 - 399.56

5. 229.16 - 116.95

6. 821.63 - 354.7

7. 537.21 - 37.59

8. 302.99 - 199.05

9. 900.56 - 621.07

Arranging and Subtracting Decimals 3

Subtracting decimals is like normal subtraction.
You just have to remember to line up the decimals.

Hint: Decimal points always go at the end of a whole number (6 = 6.0 or 6.00)

Line up the decimals and solve the problems below.

1. 81.953 - 2.641

2. 39.058 - 2.806

3. 66.491 - 11.08

4. 68.094 - 7.687

5. 22.916 - 11.695

6. 339.1 - .799

7. 53.210 - 37.059

8. 14 - 7.095

9. 579.802 - .07

Lesson 7

Subtracting Decimals 1

Subtract the amounts below.

1. 231.57 − 182.24	**2.** 432.66 − 106.27	**3.** 379.20 − 273.94	**4.** 628.12 − 504.39
5. 611.32 − 369.48	**6.** 461.30 − 119.82	**7.** 654.55 − 307.47	**8.** 859.00 − 689.38
9. 741.99 − 207.64	**10.** 584.37 − 119.01	**11.** 615.06 − 527.92	**12.** 363.19 − 329.75
13. 64.982 − 20.191	**14.** 32.100 − 12.086	**15.** 52.604 − 39.335	**16.** 11.325 − 5.425
17. 67.385 − 46.105	**18.** 90.488 − 53.914	**19.** 75.672 − 33.127	**20.** 36.854 − 11.367

Subtracting Decimals 2

Subtract the amounts below.

1. 1,334.62 − 451.39	**2.** 2,485.12 − 384.67	**3.** 4,645.14 − 185.33	**4.** 3,313.74 − 599.91
5. 5,482.49 − 420.24	**6.** 7,893.72 − 599.32	**7.** 6,820.47 − 875.97	**8.** 2,339.00 − 922.11
9. 5,894.27 −3,554.72	**10.** 8,775.54 −3,997.32	**11.** 7,654.41 −5,229.80	**12.** 9,501.64 −8,329.33
13. 628.399 − 175.508	**14.** 977.687 − 345.113	**15.** 710.910 − 84.456	**16.** 527.842 − 211.611
17. 139.209 − 44.364	**18.** 374.346 − 171.712	**19.** 452.833 − 299.425	**20.** 926.001 − 364.967

Subtracting Decimals 3

Subtract the amounts below.

1. 49.9262 − 32.6139	**2.** 69.8420 − 29.9609	**3.** 39.7124 − 18.2570	**4.** 84.4962 − 38.8691
5. 720.581 − 556.512	**6.** 521.003 − 352.109	**7.** 120.589 − 100.075	**8.** 264.892 − 155.684
9. 49,078.2 −38,865.1	**10.** 8,009.01 −6,420.57	**11.** 9,569.25 −3,365.72	**12.** 7.65940 − 2.29995
13. 3,965.21 −1,788.95	**14.** 548.722 − 345.871	**15.** 2.99265 − .95846	**16.** 90.0364 − 77.8205
17. 89,756.1 −15,672.7	**18.** 77,582.1 −56,963.8	**19.** 33,587.2 −19,985.7	**20.** 9,987.02 −8,908.25

Lesson 8

Decimal Subtraction Word Problems

Solve the problems below.

1. Mike needs to swim 6 miles a week to get strong enough to make the swim team. On Monday he swam 1.34 miles. On Tuesday he swam 2.49 miles. On Wednesday he swam .82 miles. How much further must he swim to reach his goal of 6 miles?

2. Jenny wants to lift 100 pounds of weight each day. First she lifted 10.57 pounds, then she lifted 29.96 pounds. Next she lifted 32.65 pounds. How much more weight does she need to lift to reach her goal ?

3. Newt needs a total of 300 points on his school projects to go on the field trip. On the first project he scored 86.57 points. On the second project he scored 95.36 points. On the next project he scored 64.11 points. How many more points must he score to go on the trip?

4. James was using so much water playing in the sprinkler that his mom set a limit of 15 gallons per week. On the first day he used 2.65 gallons. On the second day he used 3.21 gallons. On the third day James used 4.81 gallons. Then on the fourth day he used 1.92 gallons. How much water does James have left this week?

Lesson 9

Adding Money 1

The rules that we learned for adding decimals is also how we add money.

289.64 + 56.11 345.75	=	\$289.64 + \$56.11 \$345.75

Find the totals below.

1. \$103.32 + \$49.08 = \$152.40

2. \$315.15 + \$12.99

3. \$91.64 + \$296.12

4. \$144.75 + \$82.32

5. \$257.95 + \$189.05

6. \$642.44 + \$791.17

7. \$309.37 + \$276.24

8. \$914.70 + \$367.05

9. \$454.12, \$59.99 + \$375.36

10. \$708.51, \$623.78 + \$11.63

11. \$34.33, \$551.40 + \$186.17

12. \$691.11, \$320.95 + \$64.32

13. \$111.88, \$965.42 + \$375.30

14. \$399.23, \$499.67 + \$233.99

15. \$607.14, \$324.24 + \$178.17

16. \$119.67, \$394.66 + \$367.92

Adding Money 2

Find the totals below.

1. $108.22
$399.08
+ $12.28

2. $56.44
$275.17
+ $2.36

3. $480.55
$59.63
+ $237.11

4. $365.99
$264.56
+ $12.00

5. $564.23
$257.67
+ $106.63

6. $216.21
$347.96
+ $964.07

7. $754.55
$191.19
+ $267.67

8. $908.09
$124.64
+ $573.11

9. $245.77
$331.06
$24.33
+ $100.97

10. $210.11
$772.72
$186.80
+ $67.29

11. $662.95
$97.84
$205.04
+ $177.00

12. $302.34
$475.62
$65.24
+ $134.89

13. $905.15
$465.55
$992.61
+ $133.21

14. $488.88
$706.11
$300.37
+ $511.77

15. $625.33
$233.31
$914.45
+ $928.17

16. $723.99
$949.12
$811.34
+ $267.09

17. $635.01
$199.11
$208.28
+ $322.37

18. $500.49
$1.11
$600.59
+ $37.64

19. $368.84
$675.64
$99.30
+ $261.71

20. $299.02
$103.65
$690.31
+ $782.57

Lesson 10

Subtracting Money 1

Now that you know how to subtract decimals, use what you've learned to answer these money problems.

15.63		$15.63
- 2.12	=	- $ 2.12
13.51		$13.51

Subtract the amounts below.

1. $6.22 - $3.84 $2.38	**2.** $4.70 - $1.35	**3.** $3.84 - $1.99	**4.** $7.79 - $5.32
5. $8.84 - $3.53	**6.** $6.85 - $5.06	**7.** $9.98 - $6.16	**8.** $9.27 - $4.64
9. $8.99 - $6.13	**10.** $3.08 - $.94	**11.** $7.12 - $5.37	**12.** $6.39 - $2.17
13. $135.07 - $75.98	**14.** $209.47 - $105.12	**15.** $466.17 - $389.55	**16.** $349.68 - $127.35
17. $859.07 - $407.98	**18.** $654.00 - $332.37	**19.** $567.25 - $125.74	**20.** $804.91 - $722.05

Subtracting Money 2

Subtract the amounts below.

1. $275.29 - $107.72	**2.** $535.11 - $299.39	**3.** $332.88 - $111.49	**4.** $630.00 - $424.84
5. $643.17 - $307.51	**6.** $800.99 - $115.35	**7.** $772.63 - $631.51	**8.** $704.90 - $639.17
9. $551.12 - $337.94	**10.** $675.99 - $167.91	**11.** $240.11 - $177.54	**12.** $999.00 - $327.29
13. $490.17 - $215.05	**14.** $807.00 - $318.37	**15.** $420.34 - $385.94	**16.** $788.40 - $264.19
17. $711.72 - $499.07	**18.** $470.97 - $295.48	**19.** $849.84 - $601.31	**20.** $511.31 - $294.52

Lesson 11

Decimal Points Multiplication

To multiply decimals, start by multiplying the numbers just as if they were whole numbers.

Example: Multiply 4.22 by 3.5

Step 1:
Line up the numbers on the right - **do not align the decimal points.**

```
  4.22
x  3.5
```

Step 2:
Starting on the right, multiply each digit in the top number by each digit in the bottom number, just as with whole numbers. Then add the products.

```
   4.22
 x  3.5
   2110
+ 12660
  14770
```

Step 3:
Place the decimal point in the answer by starting at the right and moving the number of places equal to the sum of the decimal places in both numbers multiplied.

```
   4.22  ← 2 decimal places
            +
 x  3.5  ← 1 decimal place
   2110
+ 12660
  14.770 ← 3 decimal places
```

Multiply the problems below and correctly align the decimals.

1. 8.3 x 6.4

```
   8.3
 x 6.4
   3 3 2
+4 9 8 0
 5 3.1 2
```

2. 3.3 x 2.9

3. 6.7 x 4.4

4. 5.9 x 3.6

5. 4.5 x 2.9

6. 8.5 x 6.7

7. 4.9 x 2.7

8. 9.8 x 6.2

9. 7.7 x 5.8

10. 9.5 x 8.2

11. 8.8 x 7.4

12. 5.9 x 5.7

13. 6.2 x 4.9

14. 4.3 x 2.5

15. 8.7 x 3.9

Lesson 12

Multiplying Decimals 1

Multiply the problems below and correctly align the decimals.

1. 4.29 x 5.3 22.737	**2.** 6.85 x .86	**3.** 3.42 x 1.3	**4.** 5.37 x 6.4	**5.** 7.32 x 2.6
6. 85.5 x .32	**7.** 63.1 x .56	**8.** 29.4 x 49	**9.** 9.99 x .83	**10.** 67.2 x 2.9
11. .249 x .97	**12.** 43.3 x 23	**13.** 55.3 x .58	**14.** 68.2 x 4.3	**15.** .927 x 7.2
16. 77.3 x 2.4	**17.** 2.45 x .84	**18.** 82.7 x 2.7	**19.** 56.6 x 99	**20.** 6.08 x .67
21. 8.52 x 3.7	**22.** 59.9 x 6.6	**23.** 2.87 x 9.4	**24.** 36.2 x .55	**25.** 9.04 x 49

Multiplying Decimals 2

Multiply the problems below and correctly align the decimals.

1. 18.32 x 6.8	**2.** 44.09 x .33	**3.** 22.39 x 74	**4.** 57.82 x 2.9	**5.** 77.32 x .55
6. 3.447 x 4.1	**7.** 5.772 x 59	**8.** 33.47 x 3.3	**9.** 662.5 x 1.4	**10.** 4.262 x 5.7
11. 8299 x .88	**12.** 429.8 x 4.1	**13.** 5.723 x 63	**14.** 864.1 x .59	**15.** 93.22 x 2.9
16. 7.085 x 37	**17.** 367.5 x 4.5	**18.** 94.47 x .83	**19.** 7.245 x 7.6	**20.** 32.64 x 5.9
21. 995.3 x 8.4	**22.** 8127 x .99	**23.** 5.333 x 6.6	**24.** 81.24 x .34	**25.** 96.77 x 7.7

Multiplying Decimals 3

Multiply the problems below and correctly align the decimals.

1. 239.4 x 3.92	**2.** 7.863 x 45.5	**3.** 53.22 x 8.45	**4.** 4.977 x .368	**5.** 369.9 x 15.4
6. 23.18 x 53.6	**7.** 946.2 x .337	**8.** 4.556 x 66.8	**9.** 327.4 x 4.19	**10.** 5.585 x 72.5
11. .7269 x 342	**12.** 465.7 x 59.9	**13.** 3.697 x 23.5	**14.** 22.42 x 8.29	**15.** 6.823 x 37.7
16. 593.7 x 92.5	**17.** 7.557 x 82.7	**18.** 952.9 x 6.34	**19.** 3.669 x 29.2	**20.** 5247 x 7.94

Chapter 6 - Geometry

In this chapter you will learn about shapes and geometry. **Here is what you will learn:**

- Identifying Flat Shapes
- Polygons
- Finding Area of Shapes
- Finding Perimeter
- Identifying Solid Shapes
- Understanding Circles

  (Radius, Diameter, Circumference)
- Understanding Points, Lines and Rays
- Understanding Angles
- Understanding Volume

Flat Shapes

Shapes can come in any size and can have many sides. Here are the flat shapes you will learn about in this chapter.
Circle (1 side)
Triangle (3 sides)
Rectangle (4 sides)
Square (4 sides)
Rhombus (4 sides)
Parallelogram (4 sides)
Trapezoid (4 sides)
Pentagon (5 sides)
Hexagon (6 sides)
Heptagon (7 sides)
Octagon (8 sides)
Nonagon (9 sides)
Decagon (10 sides)

Lesson 1

Understanding Polygons

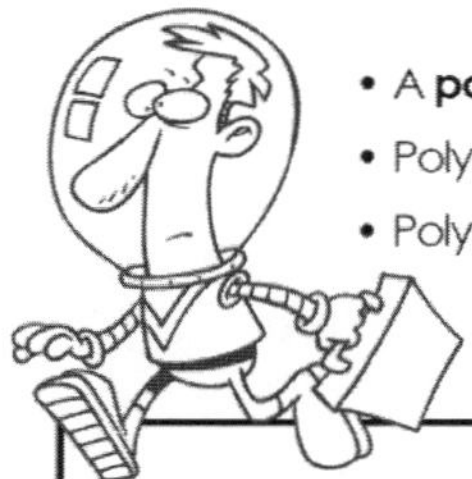

- A **polygon** is a closed plane figure made up of 3 or more line segments.
- Polygons that have all sides of equal length are called regular polygons.
- Polygons are named depending on the number of lines that form their boundaries.

Here are some examples of **polygons**:

Triangle:
A polygon with three sides

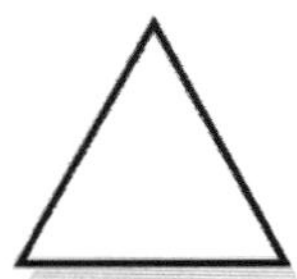

Quadrilateral
A polygon with four sides.

Pentagon
A polygon with five sides

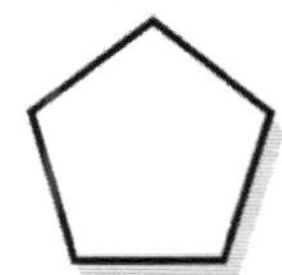

A **quadrilateral** is a four-sided polygon. Here are some types of **quadrilateral** shapes:

Rectangle: A parallelogram with four right angles.

Square: A parallelogram with four congruent sides and four right angles.

Trapezoid: A quadrilateral with only one pair of parallel sides.

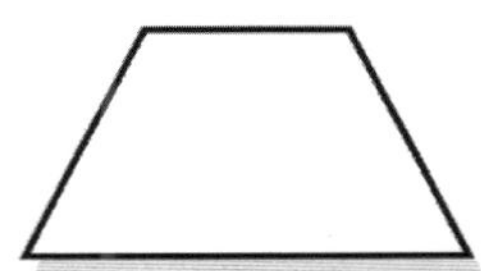

Parallelogram: A quadrilateral with two pairs of opposite sides parallel.

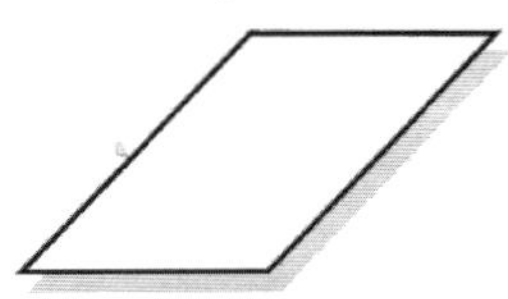

Rhombus: A parallelogram with four congruent sides.

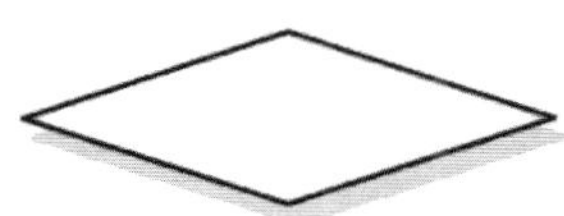

Lesson 2

Finding Area of Squares and Rectangles

Area is the measurement of a shape's surface area.
To find the **area** of a square, multiply the length by the width.

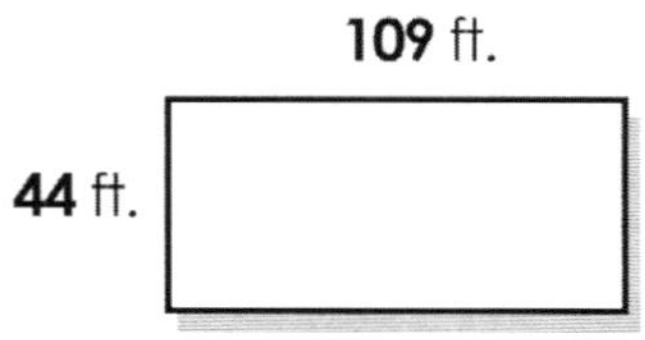

Area = 109 ft. x 44 ft. = 4,796 ft.^{2}

Area = 4,796 ft.^{2}

Find the area of each shape. Write the problem out.

1. 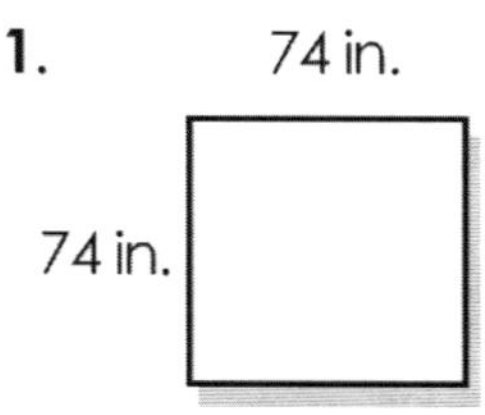

74in. x 74in. = 5,476 in.^{2}

2. 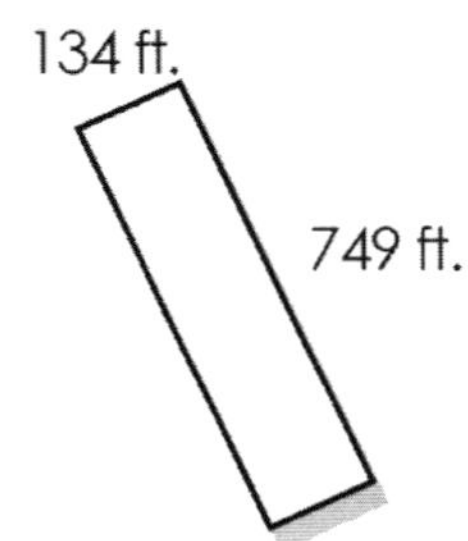

____

3. 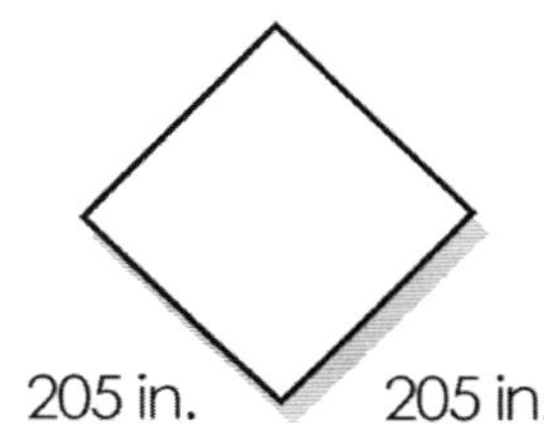

____

4. 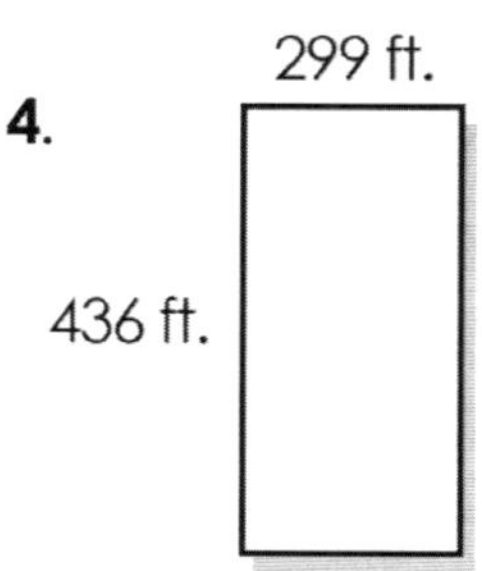

____

5. 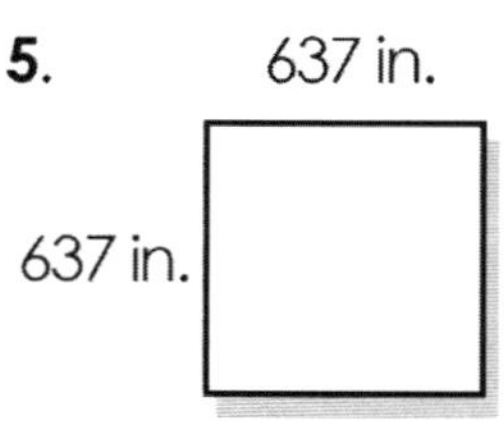

____

6. 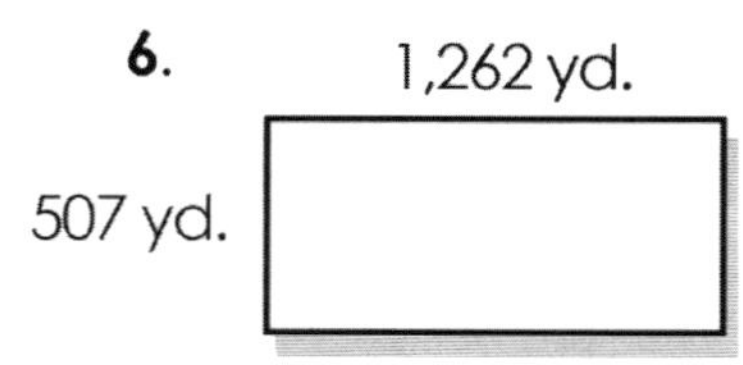

____

Lesson 3

Finding Area of Triangles

To find the **area** of a **triangle** use the formula below:

Area $= \frac{1}{2}$ of base x height

Area = 14in. x 8in. ÷ 2 = 56 in.^2

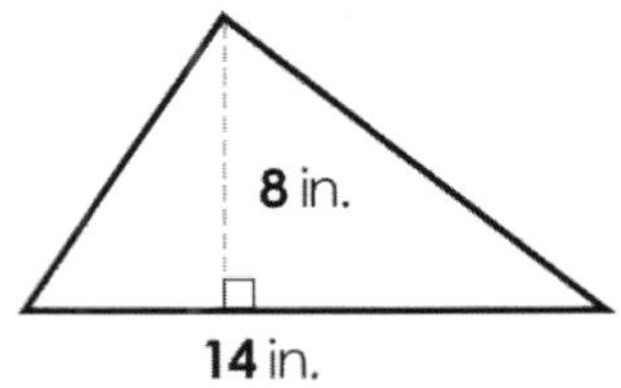

Find the area of each triangle. Write the problem out.

1.

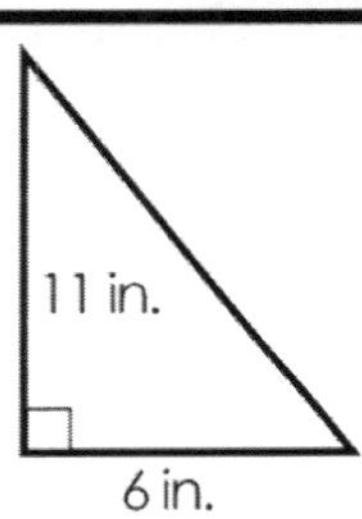

11in. x 6in. ÷ 2 = 33 in.^2

2.

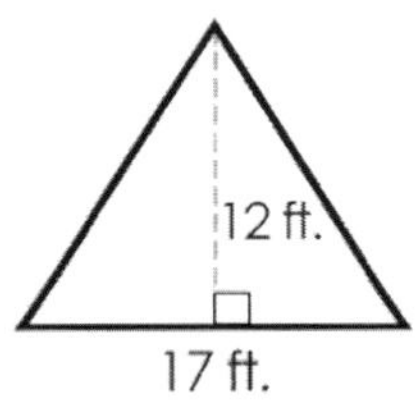

____

3.

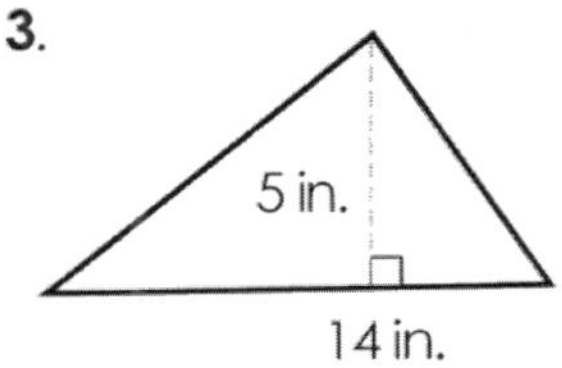

____

4.

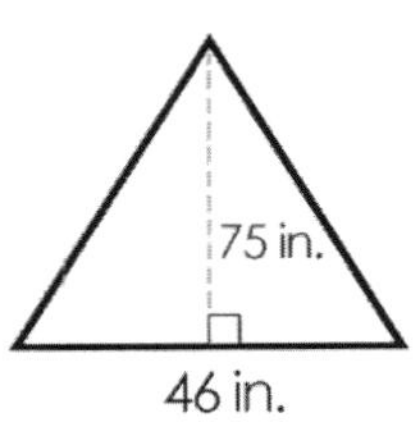

____

5.

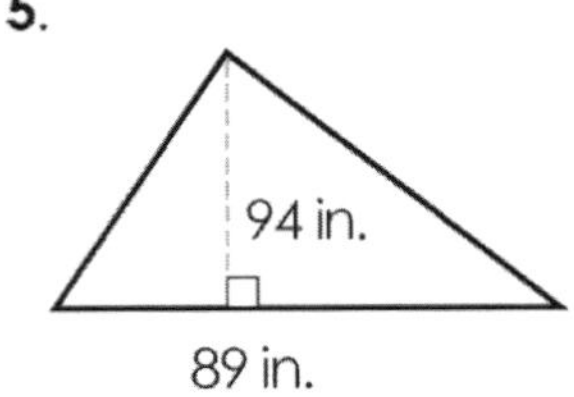

____

6.

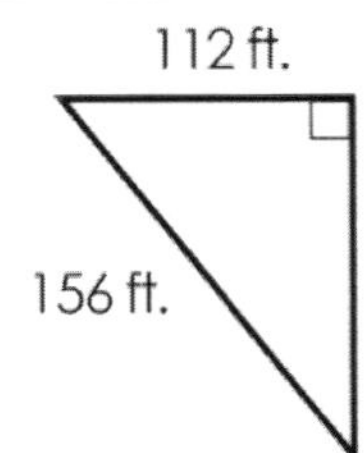

____

Lesson 4

Finding Area of Parallelograms

To find the area of a parallelogram use what we learned before and multiply height times width.

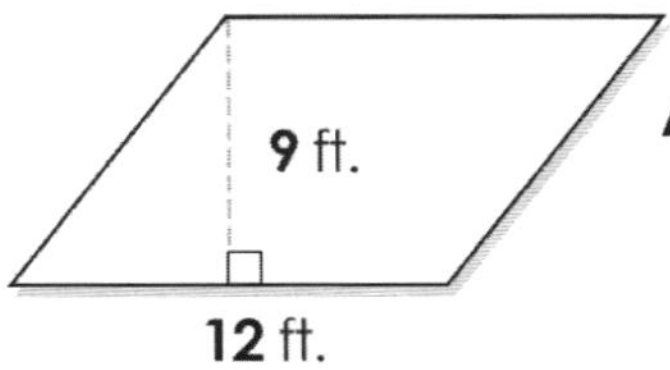

Area = 12 ft. x 9 ft. = 108 ft.^{2}

Area = 108 ft.^{2}

Find the area of each parallelogram. Write the problem out.

1.

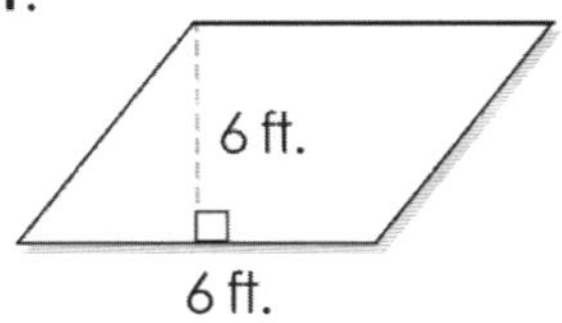

2.

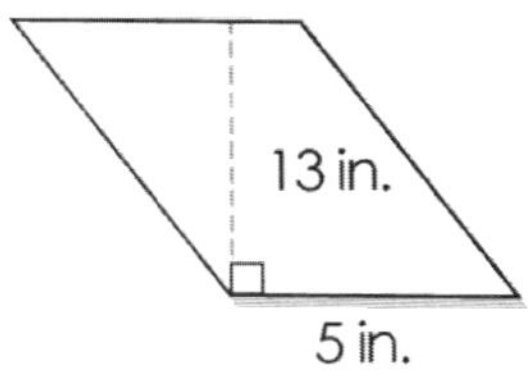

3.

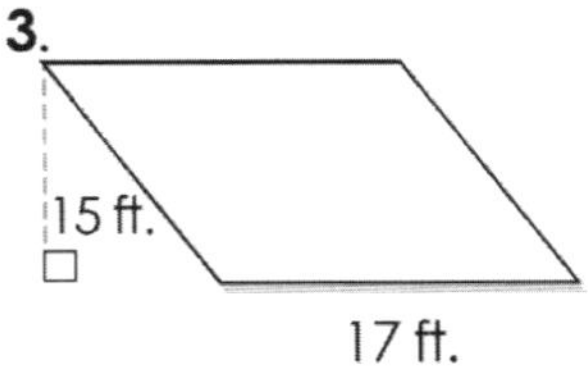

1. 6 ft. x 6 ft. = 36 ft.^{2}
2. ________________
3. ________________

4.

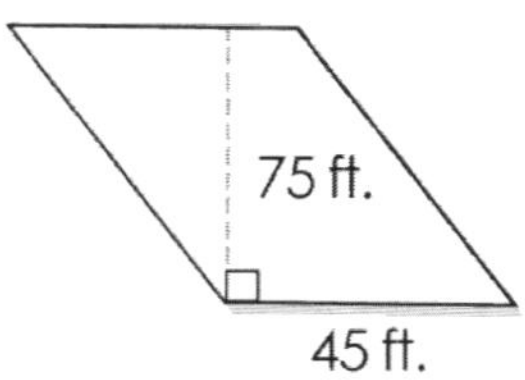

5.

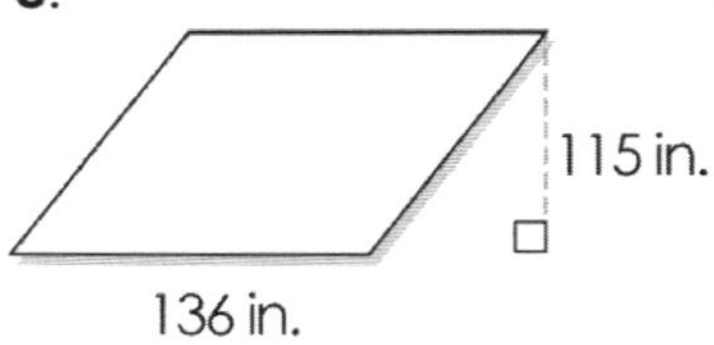

6.

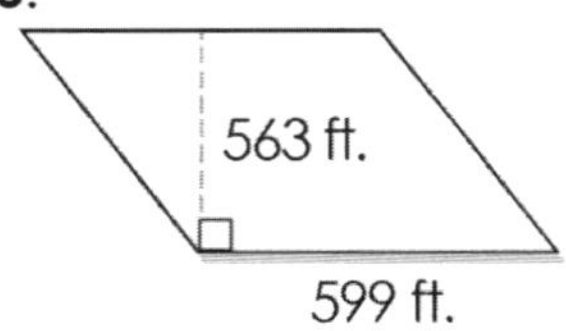

________________ ________________ ________________

Lesson 5

Finding Area of Trapezoids

To find the **area** of a **trapezoid** use this formula:

Area = $\frac{1}{2}$ of (base 1 + base 2 x height)

Step 1: Add the bases. 5 + 14 = 19	**Step 2:** Multiply base totals by height. 19 x 8 = 152	**Step 3:** Divide that total by 2. 152 ÷ 2 = 76
Area = 5 + 14 x 8 ÷ 2 = 76		

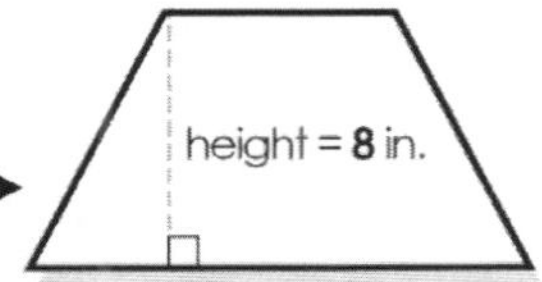

Area = 76 in.^{2}

Find the area of each trapezoid. Write the problem out.

1.

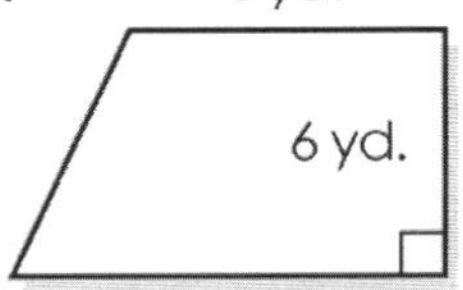

6 + 9 x 6 ÷ 2 = 45 yd.^{2}

2.

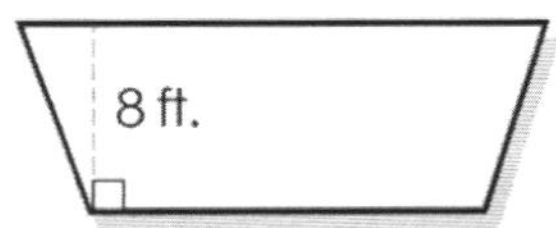

____

3.

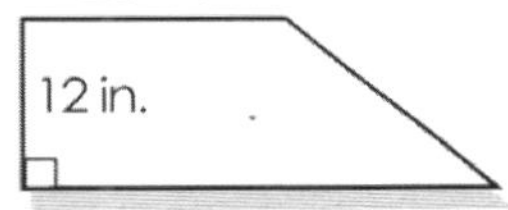

____

4.

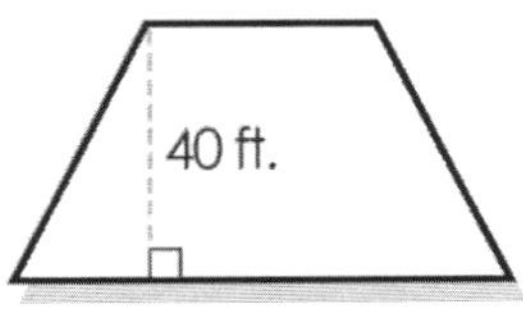

____

5.

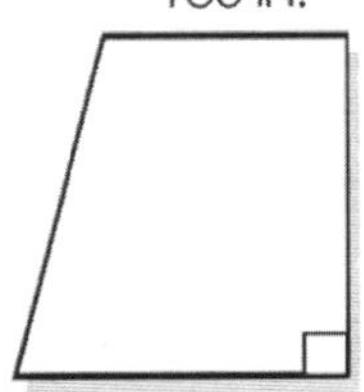

____

6.

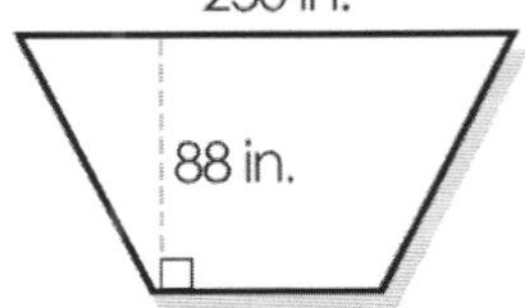

____

Lesson 6

Finding Perimeter 1

Perimeter is the distance around an object.
Find the perimeter of each object by adding all the sides.

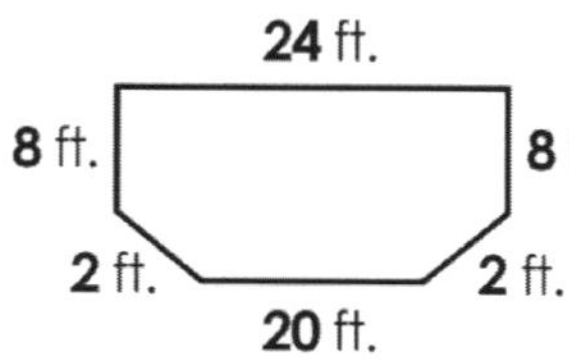

Perimeter = 24 ft. + 20 ft. + 8 ft. + 8 ft. + 2 ft. + 2 ft.

Perimeter = 64 ft.

Find the perimeter of each shape. Write the problem out.

1.

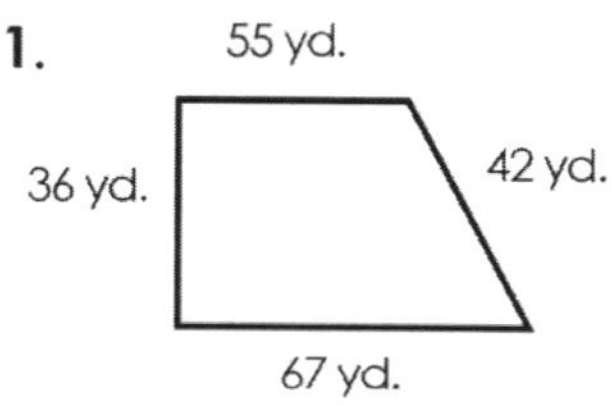

36 + 67 + 55 + 42 = 197 yd.

2.

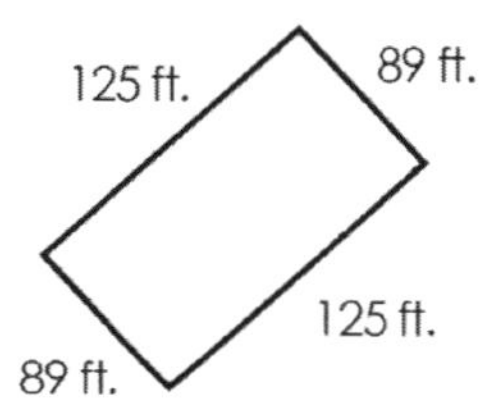

____

3.

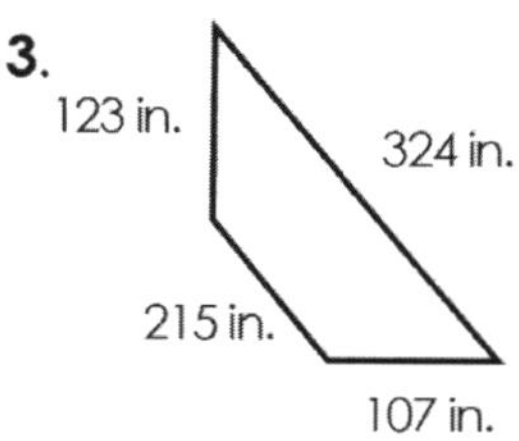

____

4.

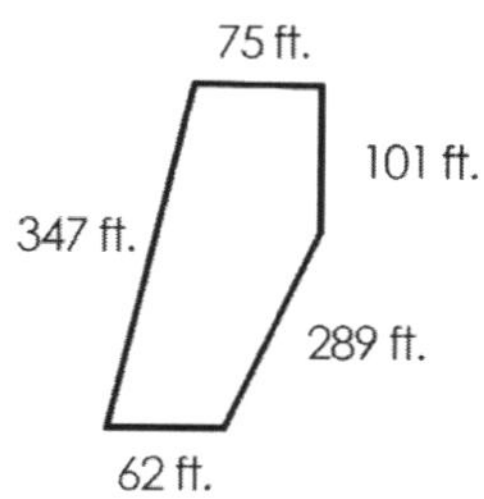

____

5.

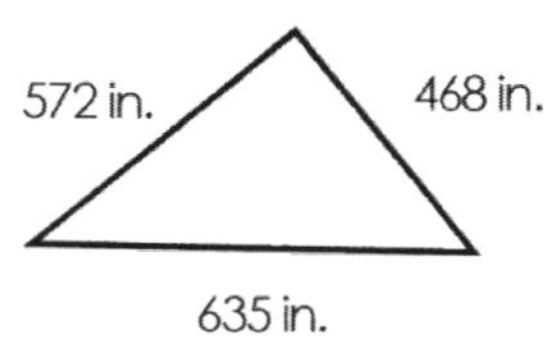

____

6.

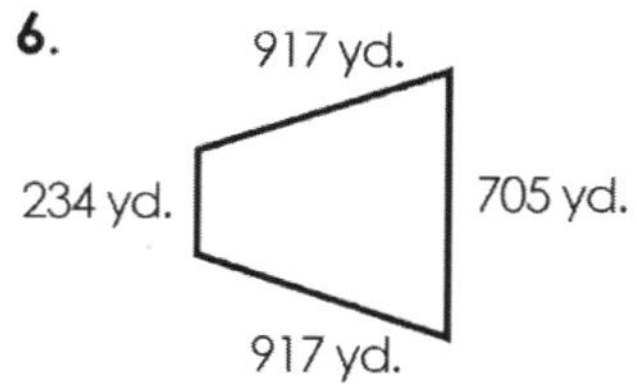

____

Finding Perimeter 2

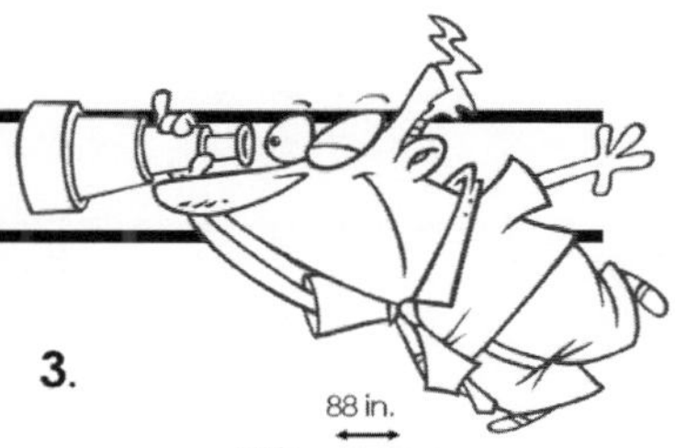

Find the perimeter of each shape. Write the problem out.

1. 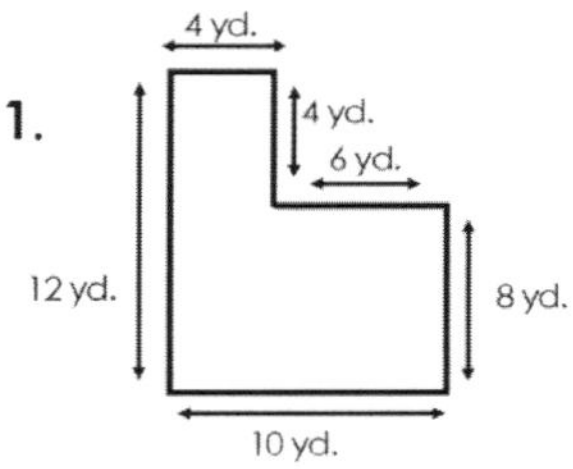

2. 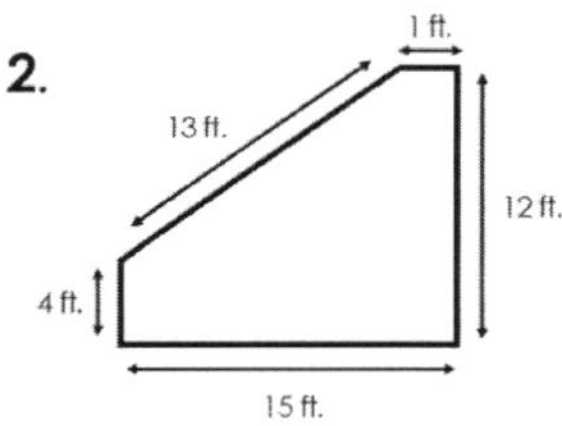

3. 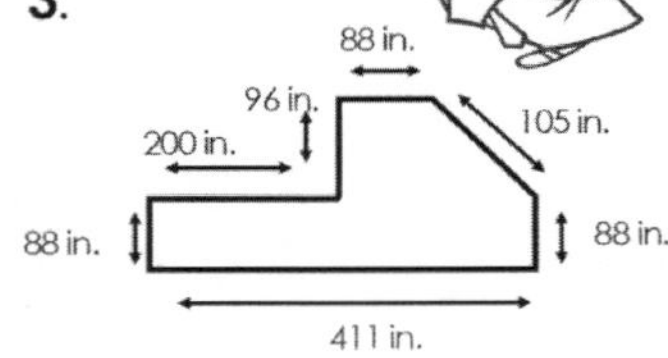

4. 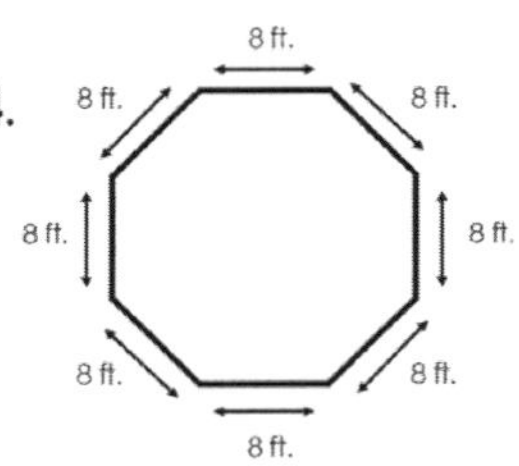

5. 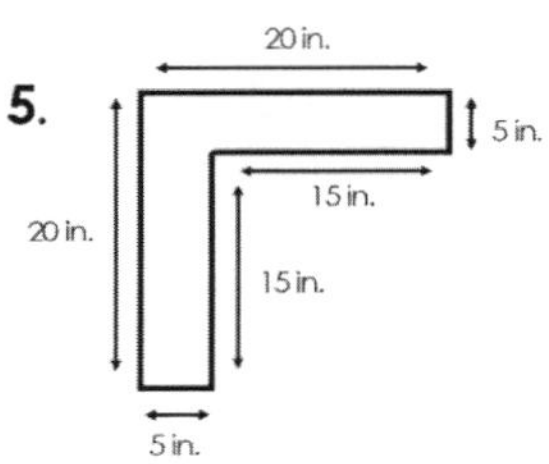

6. 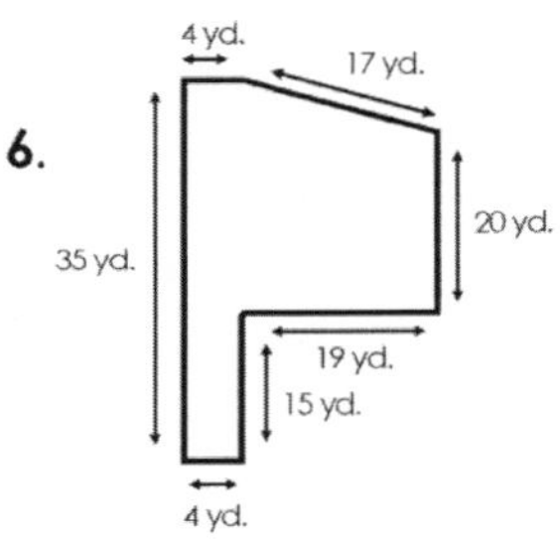

7. 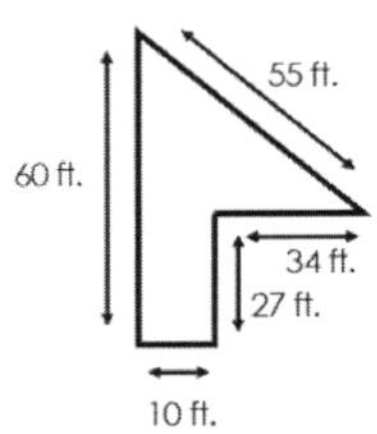

8. 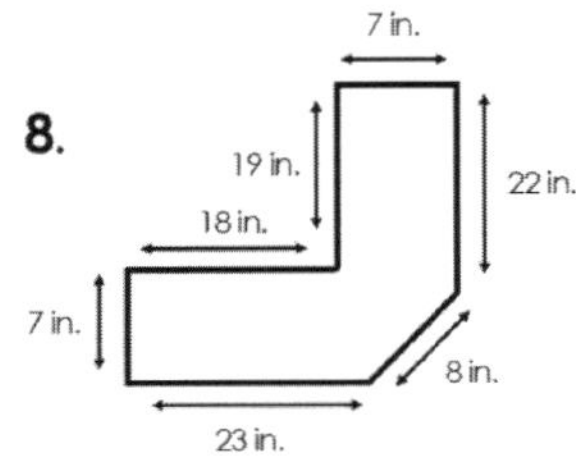

9. 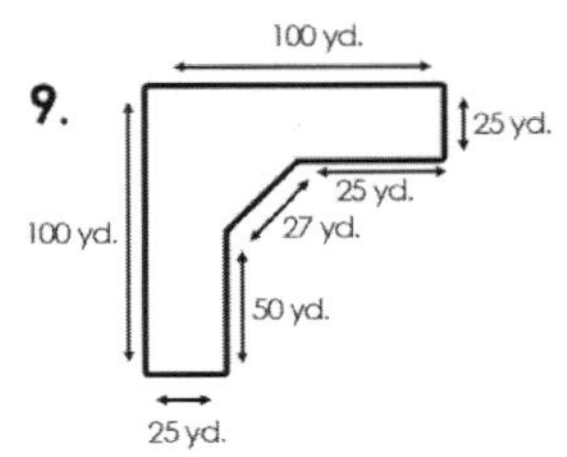

Lesson 7

Identifying Points, Lines and Rays

A **point** is an exact location in space.	A **line** is an endless straight path.	A **line segment** is a straight path between two points.	A **ray** is a part of a line; it has one endpoint and continues on in one direction.	A **vertex** is a point where two or more rays or line segments meet or cross.
•				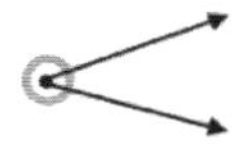

Identify and write how many of each set of figures below.

1\. 

vertex, 1

ray, 2

point, 2

2\. 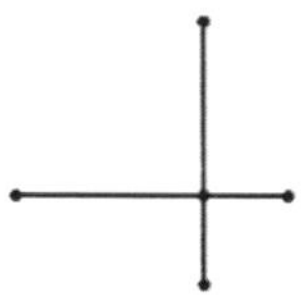

3\. 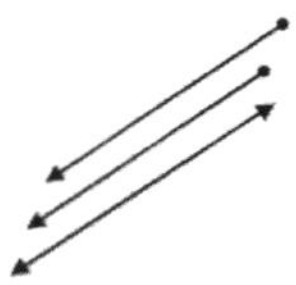

4\. 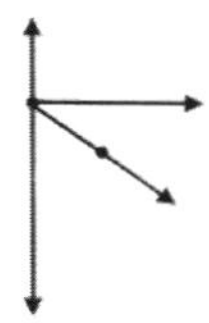

5\. 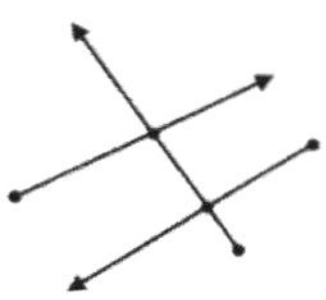

6\. 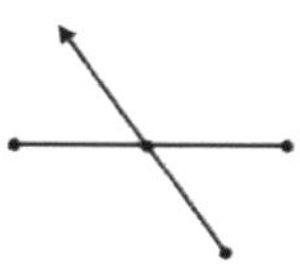

7\. 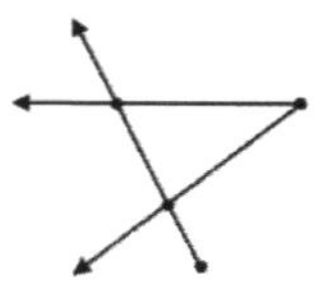

8\. 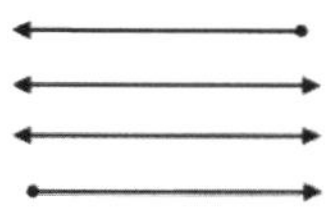

Lesson 8

Identifying Parts of an Angle

- Angles are determined by points and rays.
- This angle is named - ∠ABC.
- This angle is made up of rays AB and CB.
- The vertex of ∠ABC is the point B.

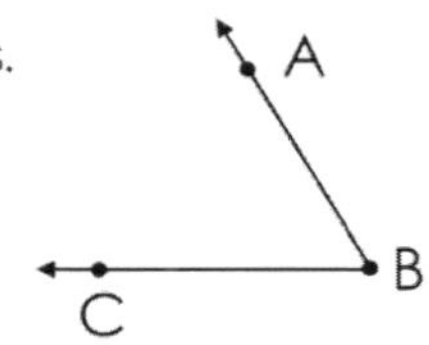

Identify the vertex, rays and names of each angle.

1.
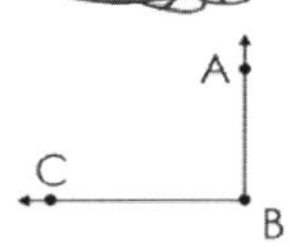

Angle: ABC
Vertex: B
Rays: AB, CB

2.
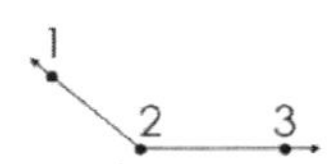

Angle: ______
Vertex: ______
Rays: ______

3.
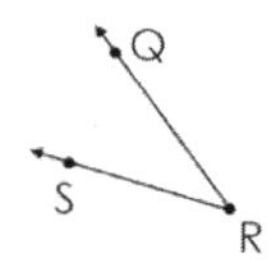

Angle: ______
Vertex: ______
Rays: ______

4.
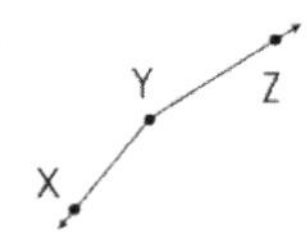

Angle: ______
Vertex: ______
Rays: ______

5.
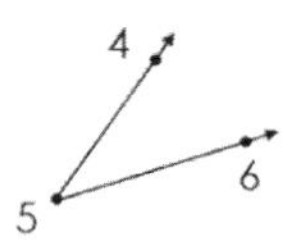

Angle: ______
Vertex: ______
Rays: ______

6.
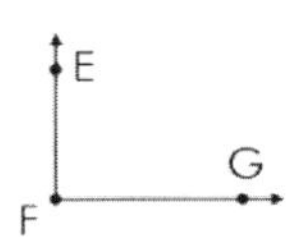

Angle: ______
Vertex: ______
Rays: ______

7.
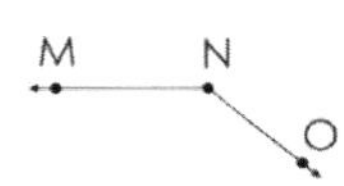

Angle: ______
Vertex: ______
Rays: ______

8.
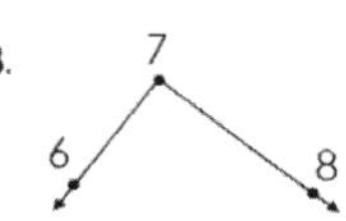

Angle: ______
Vertex: ______
Rays: ______

9.
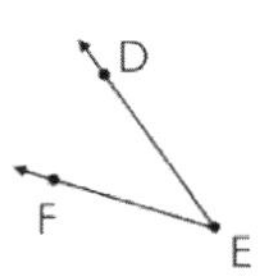

Angle: ______
Vertex: ______
Rays: ______

10.
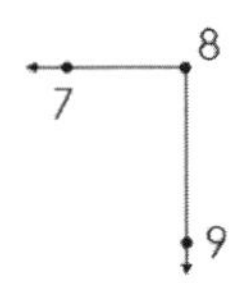

Angle: ______
Vertex: ______
Rays: ______

11.
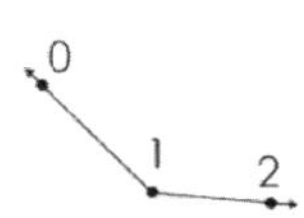

Angle: ______
Vertex: ______
Rays: ______

12.
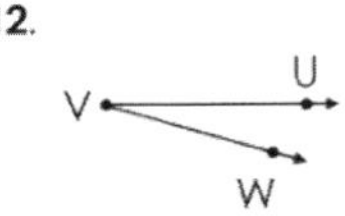

Angle: ______
Vertex: ______
Rays: ______

Solid Shapes

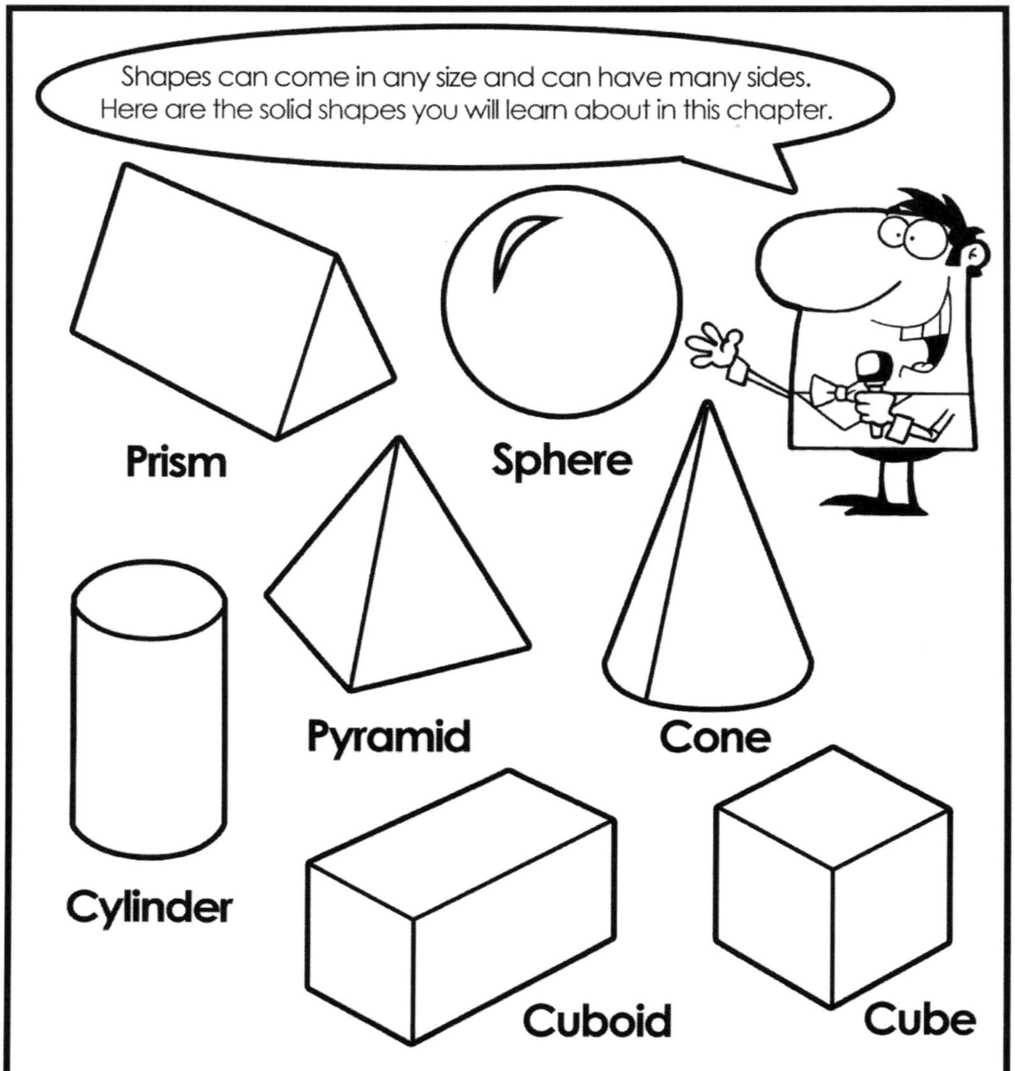

Lesson 9

Identifying Solid Shapes 1

Solid shapes are three-dimensional, non-flat figures. The names of the shapes are determined by the surfaces.

Solid shapes have surfaces, edges and vertices.

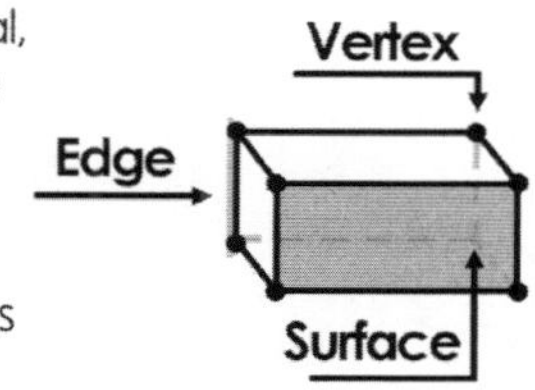

Write the name under each shape and answer the questions below.

1.

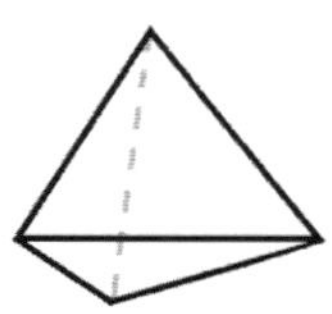

a. How many **vertices** does this shape have? ____________

b. How many **edges** does this shape have? ____________

c. How many **surfaces** does this shape have? ____________

____

2.

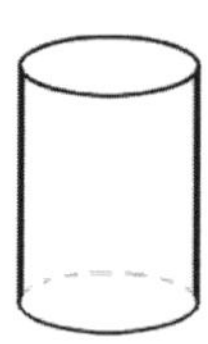

a. How many **vertices** does this shape have? ____________

b. How many **edges** does this shape have? ____________

c. How many **surfaces** does this shape have? ____________

____

3.

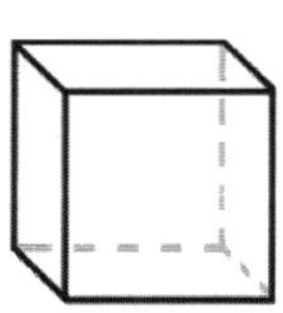

a. How many **vertices** does this shape have? ____________

b. How many **edges** does this shape have? ____________

c. How many **surfaces** does this shape have? ____________

____

Identifying Solid Shapes 2

Solid shapes are three-dimensional, non-flat figures. The names of the shapes are determined by the surfaces.

Solid shapes have surfaces, edges and vertices.

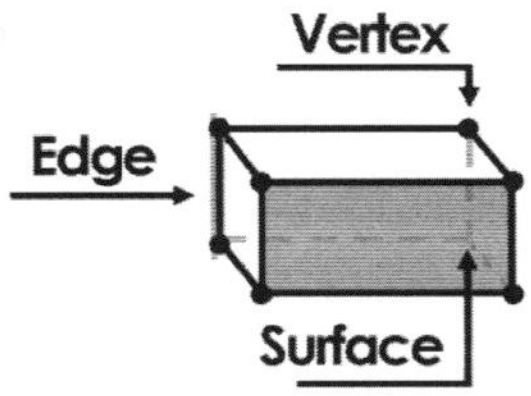

Write the name under each shape and answer the questions below.

1. 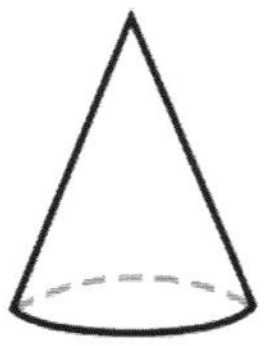

   a. How many **vertices** does this shape have? ______________

   b. How many **edges** does this shape have? ______________

   c. How many **surfaces** does this shape have? ______________

   ____

2. 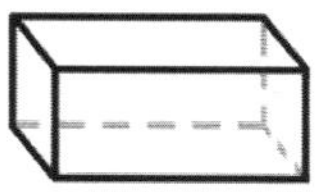

   a. How many **vertices** does this shape have? ______________

   b. How many **edges** does this shape have? ______________

   c. How many **surfaces** does this shape have? ______________

   ____

3. 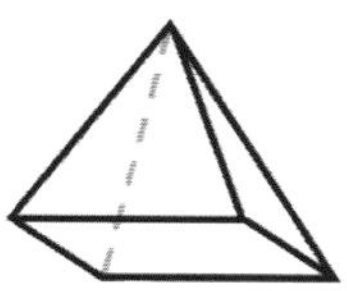

   a. How many **vertices** does this shape have? ______________

   b. How many **edges** does this shape have? ______________

   c. How many **surfaces** does this shape have? ______________

   ____

Lesson 10

Circles

Now we will learn about the components that make up a circle.
With a circle we have the **radius**, **diameter** and the **circumference**.
Knowing these components will help you to solve problems related to circles.

Radius

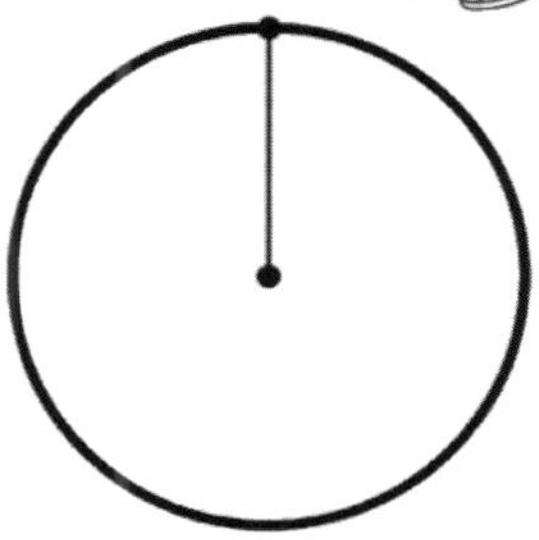

The **radius** of a circle is the distance from the circle's center point to any point on the circle. It can be used to determine a circle's diameter, circumference and area. Because of the circle's shape, the radius can be drawn in anywhere in the center of the circle.

Use this formula to find the radius of a circle:
Radius = Diameter ÷ 2

Diameter

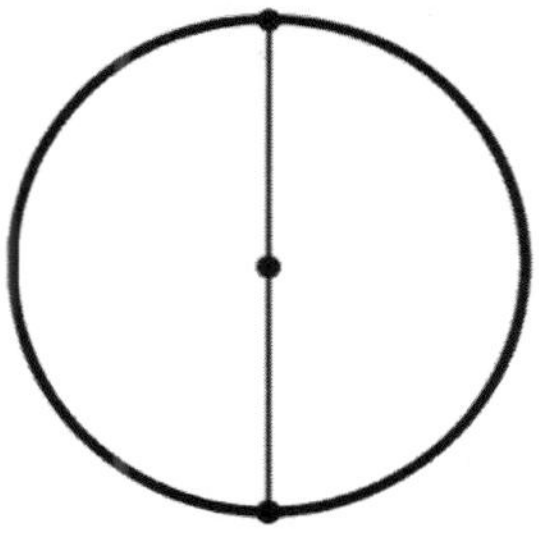

The **diameter** of a circle is the length of a straight line through the center of a circle and touching two points on its edge, the diameter is twice the measurement of the radius. It is the longest distance across the circle. If the diameter of a circle is known, dividing it by two will equal the radius.

Use this formula to find the diameter of a circle:
Diameter = Radius x 2

Circumference

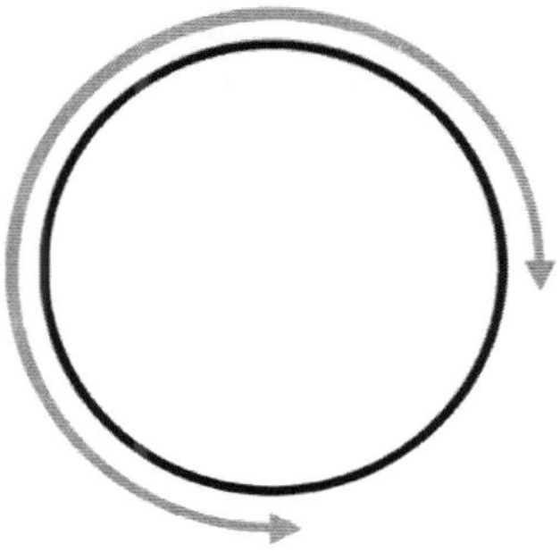

A circle's **circumference** is the distance around the circle. To determine the circumference of a circle, multiply the diameter by pi (π), or multiply the radius by 2 then multiply by pi (π). π is a Greek letter used in math to represent 3.14.

Use this formula to find the diameter of a circle:
Circumference = π x diameter or π x radius x 2

Lesson 11

Identifying Parts of a Circle

Identify the parts of the circles below.

1.

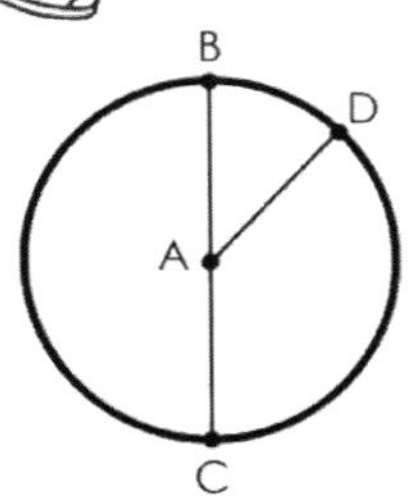

Circle: A

Radius: AB, AC, AD

Diameter: BC

2.

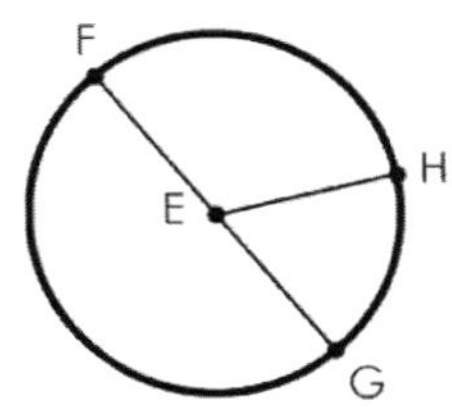

Circle: ______

Radius: ______

Diameter: ______

3.

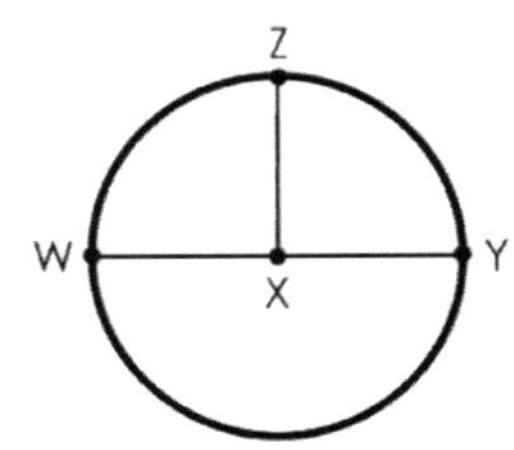

Circle: ______

Radius: ______

Diameter: ______

4.

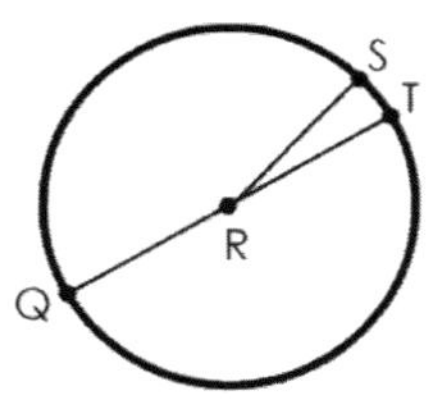

Circle: ______

Radius: ______

Diameter: ______

5.

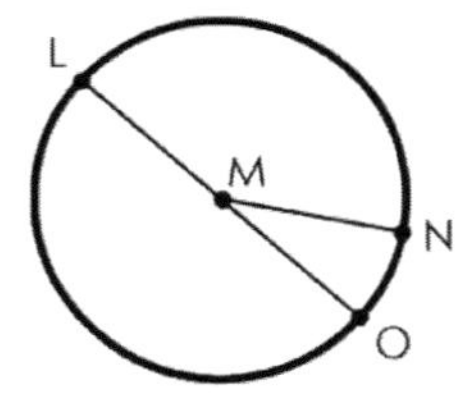

Circle: ______

Radius: ______

Diameter: ______

6.

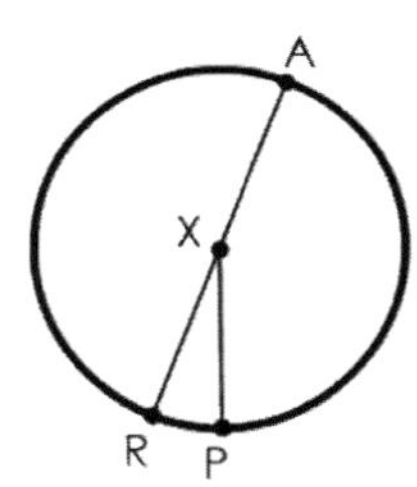

Circle: ______

Radius: ______

Diameter: ______

Lesson 12

Finding the Radius of a Circle

The **radius** of a circle is the distance from the circle's center point to any point on the circle. It can be used to determine a circle's diameter, circumference and area. To find the radius divide the diameter by 2.

Radius = Diameter ÷ 2

Diameter = 12 cm. **Radius** = 6 cm.

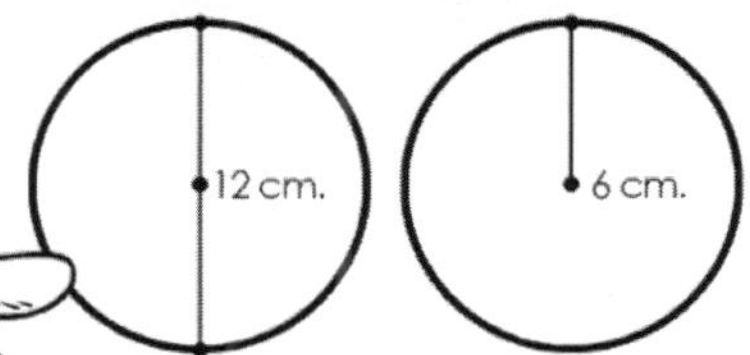

Radius = 12 ÷ 2 = 6 cm.

Using the diameter, determine the radius of each circle.

1. 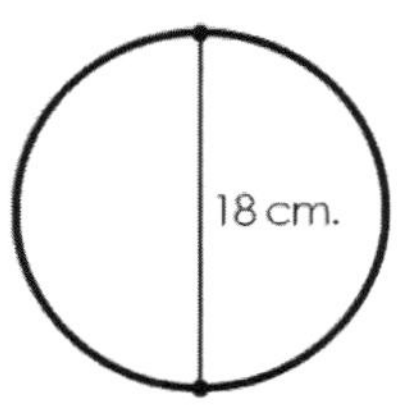

Radius: 18 ÷ 2 = 9 cm.

2. 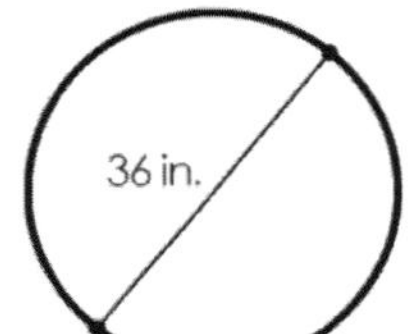

Radius: ________________

3. 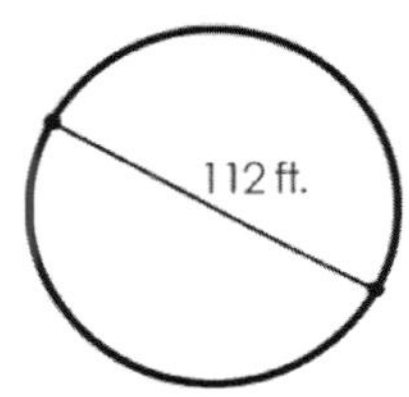

Radius: ________________

4. 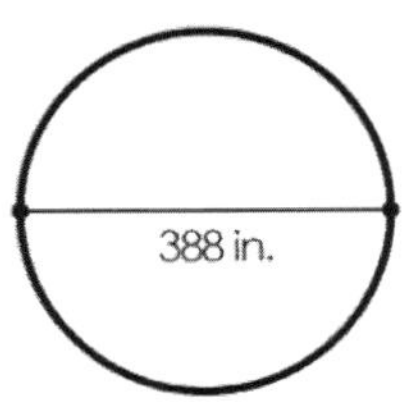

Radius: ________________

5. 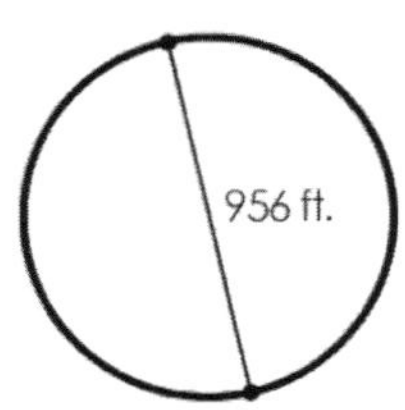

Radius: ________________

6. 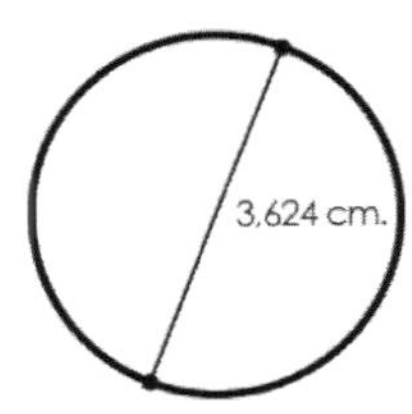

Radius: ________________

Lesson 12

Finding the Diameter of a Circle

The **diameter** of a circle is defined as the length of a straight line through the center of a circle and touching two points on its edge, the diameter is twice the measurement of the radius. It is the longest distance across the circle. If the radius of a circle is known, multiplying it by two will equal the diameter.

Diameter = Radius x 2

Radius = 8 cm.

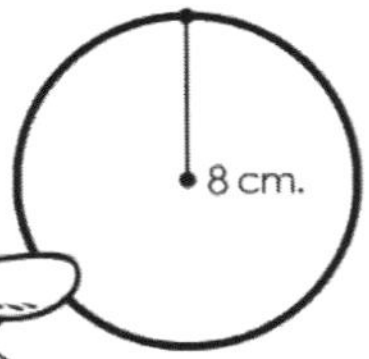

Diameter = 16 cm.

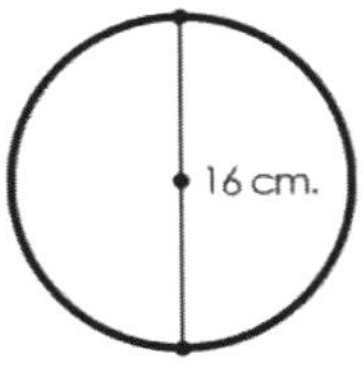

Diameter = 8 x 2 = 16cm.

Using the radius, determine the diameter of each circle.

1\.

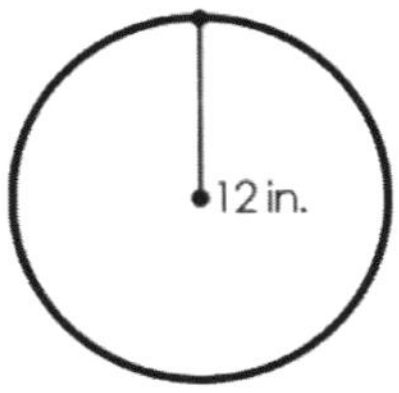

Radius: 12 x 2 = 24 in.

2\.

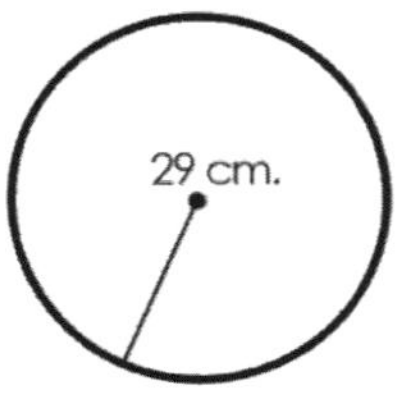

Radius: ______________

3\.

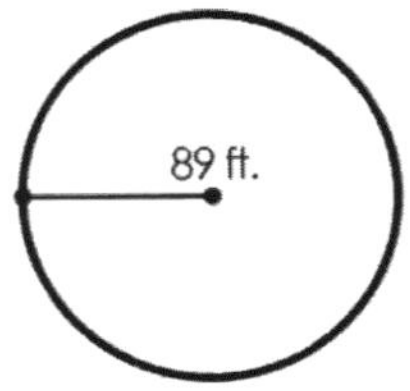

Radius: ______________

4\.

Radius: ______________

5\.

Radius: ______________

6\.

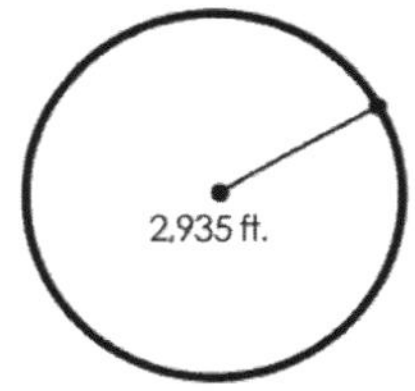

Radius: ______________

Lesson 13

Finding the Circumference of a Circle

A circle's **circumference** is the distance around the circle. To determine the circumference of a circle, multiply the diameter by pi (π), or multiply the radius by 2 then multiply by pi (π). π is a Greek letter used in mathematics to represent 3.14.

Radius = 4 cm. **Diameter** = 8 cm.

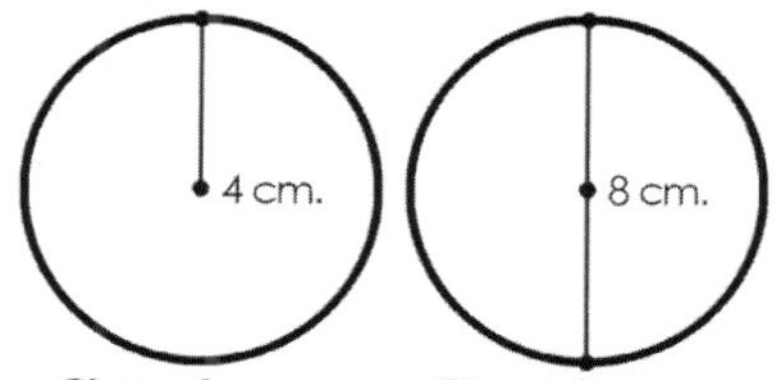

Circumference 4 x 3.14 x 2 = 25.12 **Circumference** 8 x 3.14 = 25.12

> Use these formulas to find the circumference of a circle:
> **Circumference** = (π x diameter) or (π x radius x 2)
> **Circumference** = (3.14 x diameter) or (3.14 x radius x 2)

Using the radius and diameter, determine the circumference of each circle below.

1.

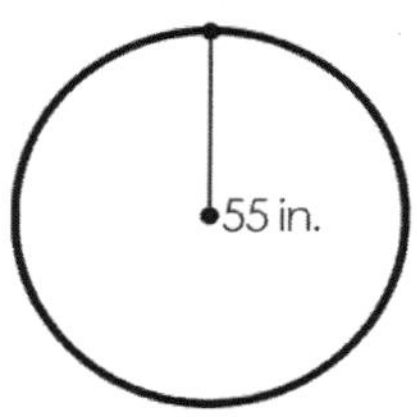

Circumference: 345.4 in.

2.

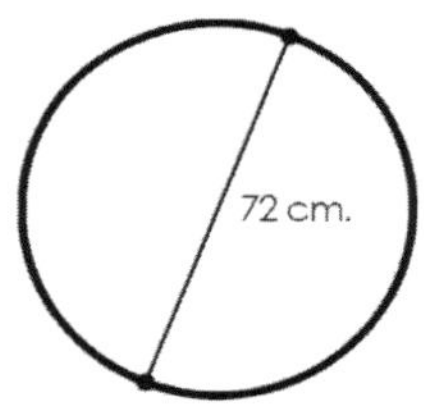

Circumference: ____________

3.

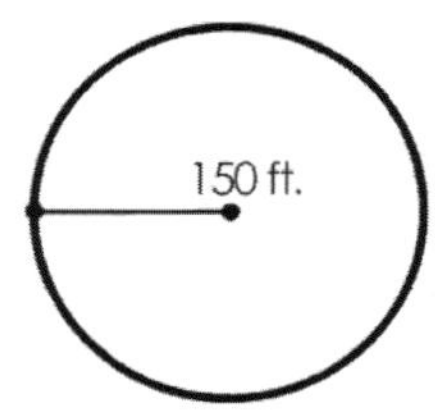

Circumference: ____________

4.

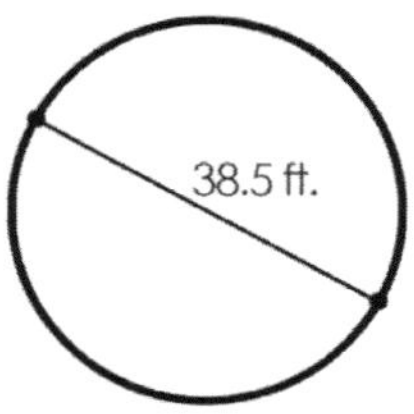

Circumference: ____________

5.

Circumference: ____________

6.

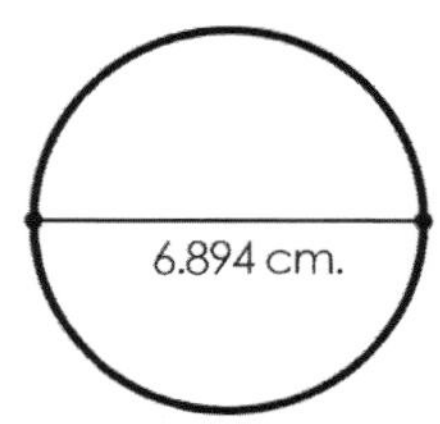

Circumference: ____________

Chapter 7 - Graphs

In this chapter you will learn about the different types of graphs.

You will learn to read and create these types of graphs:

- Bar Graphs
- Line Graphs
- Pie Graphs

Graphs

A graph or chart is a diagram used to display data or information visually. There are three types of graphs: **Bar Graphs**, **Line Graphs** and **Pie Graphs**.

In this chapter you will learn to read and create these types of graphs.

A **bar graph** is useful for comparing facts and comparing quantities in different categories.

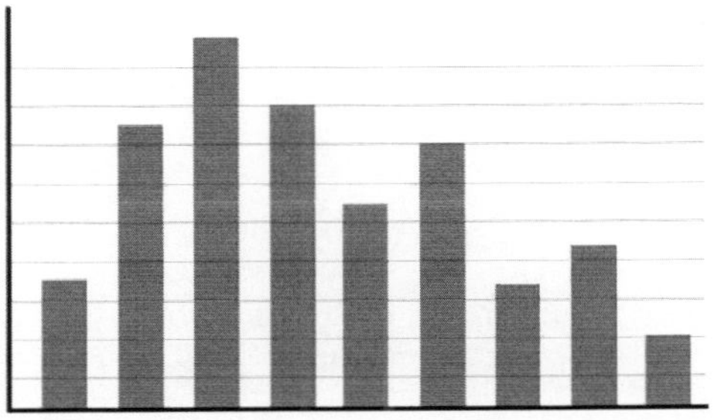

A **line graph** is used to display data or information that changes continuously over time.

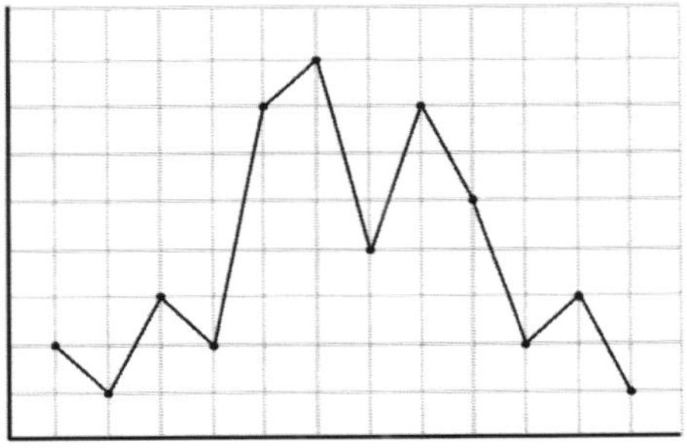

A **pie graph** or **circle graph** shows how the parts of something relate to the whole. It is divided into sectors, where each sector represents a particular category. The sections of this type of graph are usually represented by fractions.

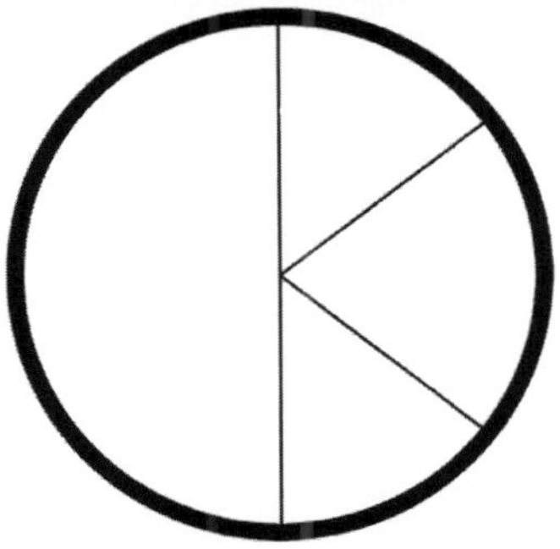

Lesson 1

Reading a Bar Graph 1

Our soccer team did well this year. Here is a graph of the points we scored each game.

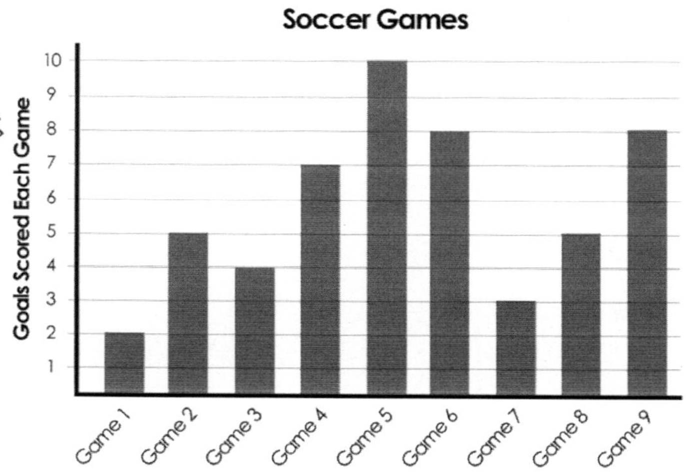

Use the bar graph to answer the questions below.

1. In which game did we score the highest number of goals? ________________
2. In which game did we score the lowest number of goals? ________________
3. How many goals did we score this entire season? ________________
4. In game 9 we scored how many more goals than in game 3? ________________
5. In game 5 we scored how many more goals than in game 7? ________________
6. In games 2, 3 and 4 we scored how many goals in total? ________________
7. In games 4, 5 and 6 we scored how many goals in total? ________________
8. In which games did we score the same number of goals? ________________

Reading a Bar Graph 2

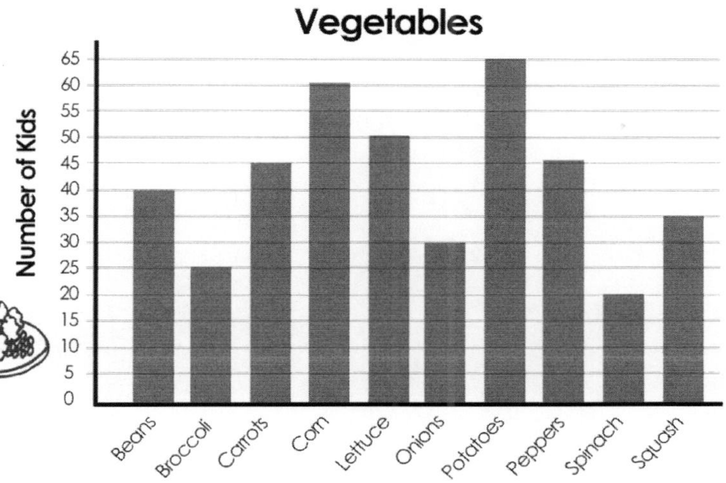

Use the bar graph to answer the questions below.

1. How many kids eat corn? _____

2. How many kids eat squash? _____

3. How many kids eat carrots? _____

4. How many kids eat onions? _____

5. How many kids eat peppers? _____

6. How many kids eat lettuce? _____

7. How many kids eat potatoes? _____

8. How many kids eat broccoli? _____

9. How many kids eat beans? _____

10. How many kids eat spinach? _____

11. How many kids prefer corn over squash? _____

12. How many kids prefer broccoli over spinach? _____

13. How many kids prefer potatoes over beans? _____

14. How many kids prefer lettuce over peppers? _____

15. How many kids prefer carrots over broccoli? _____

16. How many kids prefer corn over onions? _____

17. How many kids prefer potatoes over spinach? _____

18. How many kids prefer beans over onions? _____

Lesson 2

Creating a Bar Graph

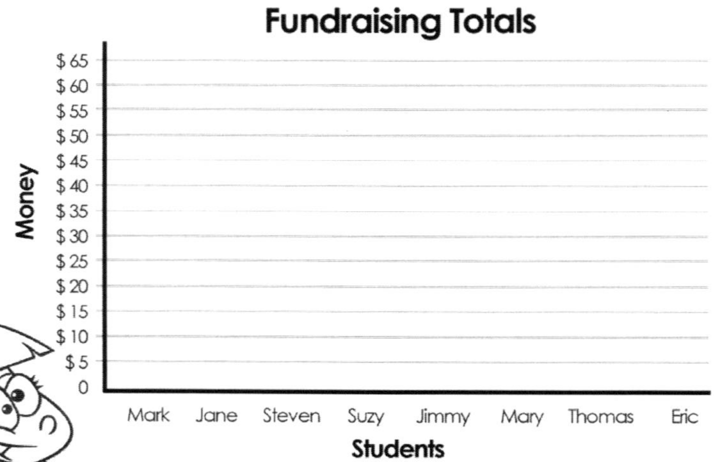

Money raised by each student	
Students	**Money**
Mark	$ 50
Jane	$ 15
Steven	$ 60
Suzy	$ 20
Jimmy	$ 35
Mary	$ 65
Thomas	$ 45
Eric	$ 5

Use the table above to draw the bar graph, then answer the questions below.

1. How much money did Thomas raise? $______

2. How much money did Suzy raise? $______

3. How much money did Jane raise? $______

4. How much money did Jimmy raise? $______

5. How much money did Mark raise? $______

6. How much money did Steven raise? $______

7. How much money did Mary raise? $______

8. How much money did Eric raise? $______

9. Steven raised how much more money than Eric? $______

10. Suzy needs to raise how much more money to catch up with Jimmy? $______

11. Mark needs to raise how much more money to catch up with Mary? $______

12. Steven raised how much more money than Jane ? $______

13. Suzy needs to raise how much more money to catch up with Mary? $______

14. Thomas raised how much more money than Jane? $______

Lesson 3

Comparing Line Graphs

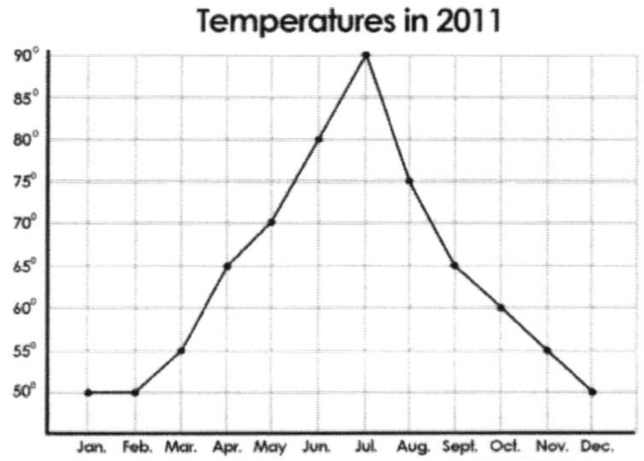

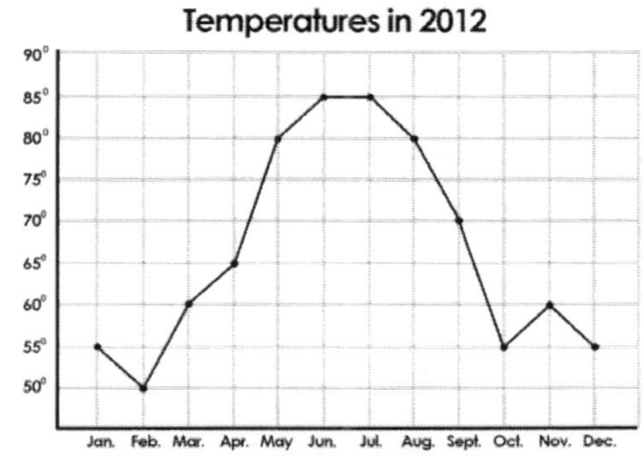

Use the graphs above to answer the questions below.

1. In which year was August hotter? ____________________
2. In which year was December colder? ____________________
3. What was the hottest temperature in 2012? ____________________
4. In 2011 what was the temperature in January? ____________________
5. In 2012 what was the temperature in January? ____________________
6. What was the coldest month in 2012? ____________________
7. What was the hottest month in 2011? ____________________
8. How much cooler was it in January 2011 than it was January in 2012? ____________________
9. What was the hottest temperature in 2011? ____________________
10. In 2011 what was the temperature in October? ____________________
11. In 2012 what was the temperature in October? ____________________
12. How much hotter was it in May 2012 than it was May in 2011? ____________________
13. Compared to April 2011, did the temperature rise, fall, or stay the same in April 2012? ____________________
14. Which year had the highest temperature? ____________________

Lesson 4

Creating a Line Graph

Line graphs use points and lines to show data visually.

Use the data on the left to draw your own line graph.
First plot the points, then draw a line connecting the points

Numbers of People in Museum	
Time	**People**
9 am	20
10 am	55
11 am	30
12 pm	10
1 pm	45
2 pm	65
3 pm	60
4 pm	40
5 pm	55
6 pm	15

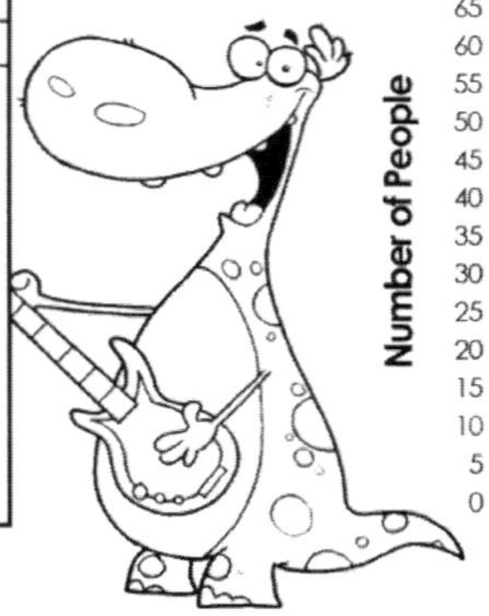

Museum Attendance

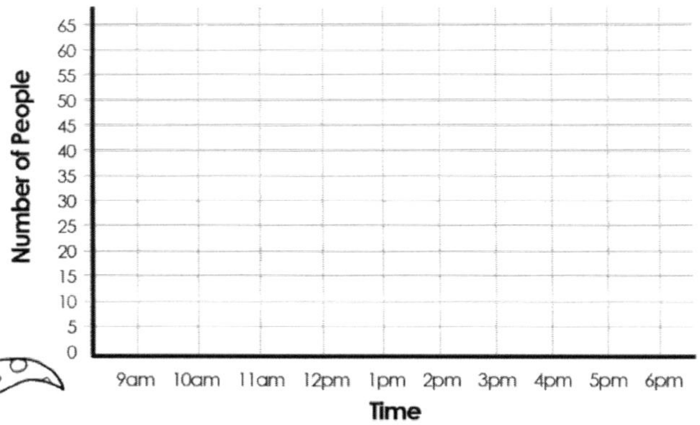

Use the line graph you just drew to answer the questions below.

1. At what time was the attendance in the museum the highest? _______________
2. At what time was the attendance in the museum the lowest? _______________
3. How many people were in the museum at noon? _______________
4. How many people were in the museum at 9am? _______________
5. How many people were in the museum at 4pm? _______________
6. How many more people were the in the museum at 5pm compared to 11am? _______________
7. From 1pm to 2pm, how many people showed up at the museum? _______________
8. From 5pm to 6pm, how many people left the museum? _______________
9. During what one-hour time period did the attendance increase the most? _______________
10. During what one-hour time period did the attendance decrease the most? _______________

Lesson 5

Identifying Points on a Graph

Graphs are used to show information in a visual form.

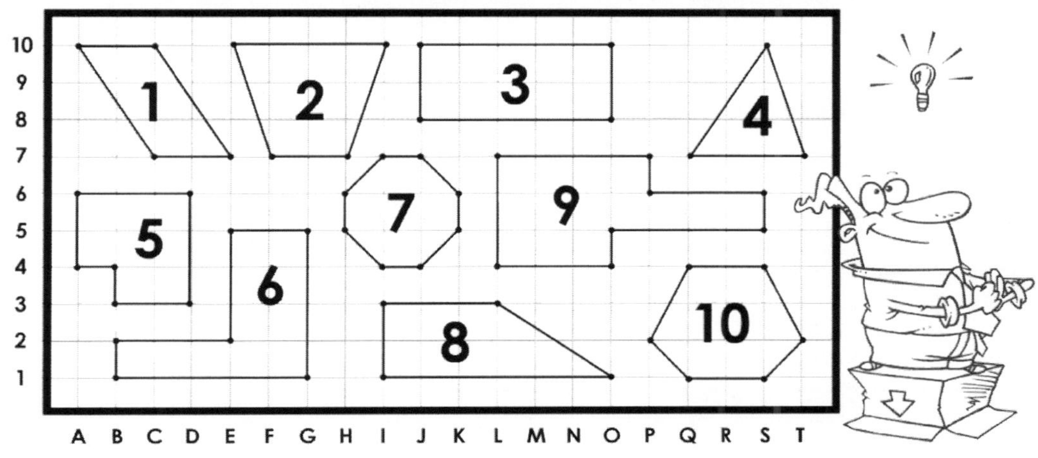

Using the graph above, write out the points that make up each shape.

1. A10, C10, C7, E7 ______________ **2.** ______________

3. ______________ **4.** ______________

5. ______________ **6.** ______________

7. ______________ **8.** ______________

9. ______________ **10.** ______________

Lesson 6

Plotting Points on a Graph

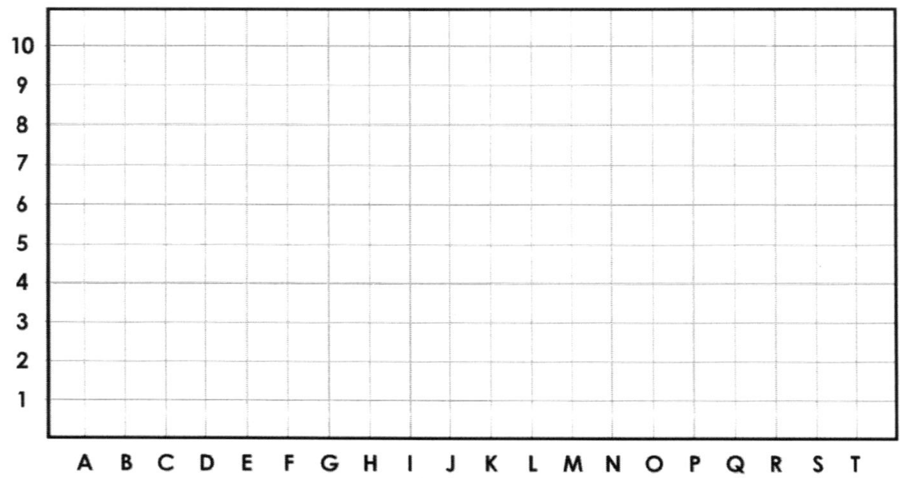

Using the coordinates below, plot the points on the graph above.
Draw a line between the points on the graph to create geometric shapes and the write the name for each shape in the blanks.

1. A4, B1, E1, F4 trapezoid
2. G3, i3, G1, i1 ____________
3. H6, L6, H4, L4 ____________
4. P7, R10, T7 ____________
5. F7, i10, L10, i7 ____________
6. N8, M5, N2, O5 ____________
7. P4, R5, T4, Q1, S1 ____________

Lesson 7

Reading a Pie Chart 1

A **pie graph** shows how the parts of something relate to the whole.
It is divided into sectors. Each sector represents a particular category.

Use the graphs below to answer the questions.

Students' Favorite Classes

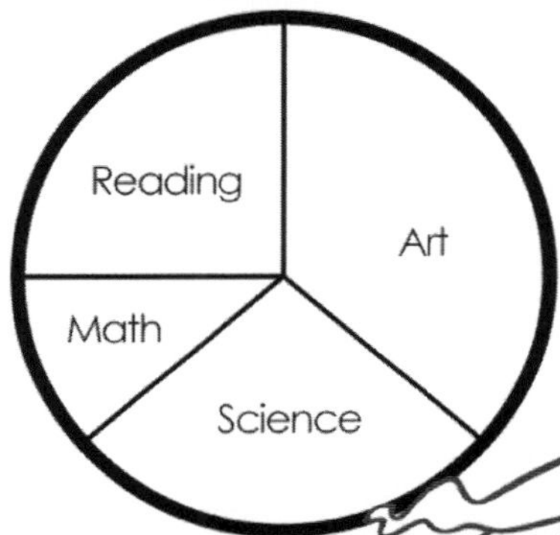

1. Which class do the students like most?

____

2. Which class do the students like the least?

____

3. What is the second-favorite class?

____

4. Which class do the students like more, math or reading?

____

Kids' Favorite Pets

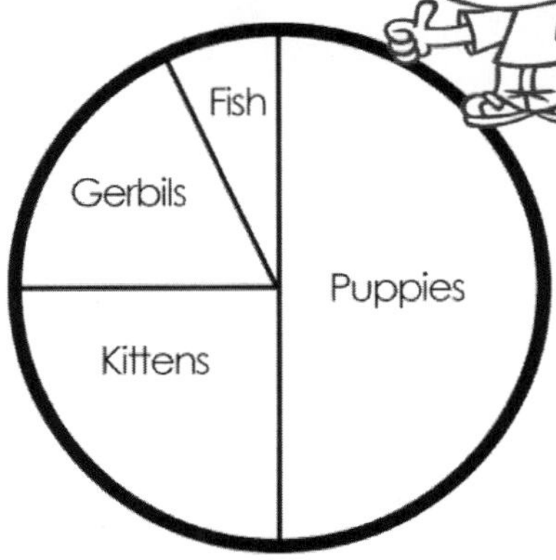

5. What is the kids' favorite pet?

____

6. What is the kids' least favorite pet?

____

7. What is the kids' second favorite pet?

____

8. Do more kids' want a gerbil or fish?

____

Lesson 8

Reading a Pie Chart 2a

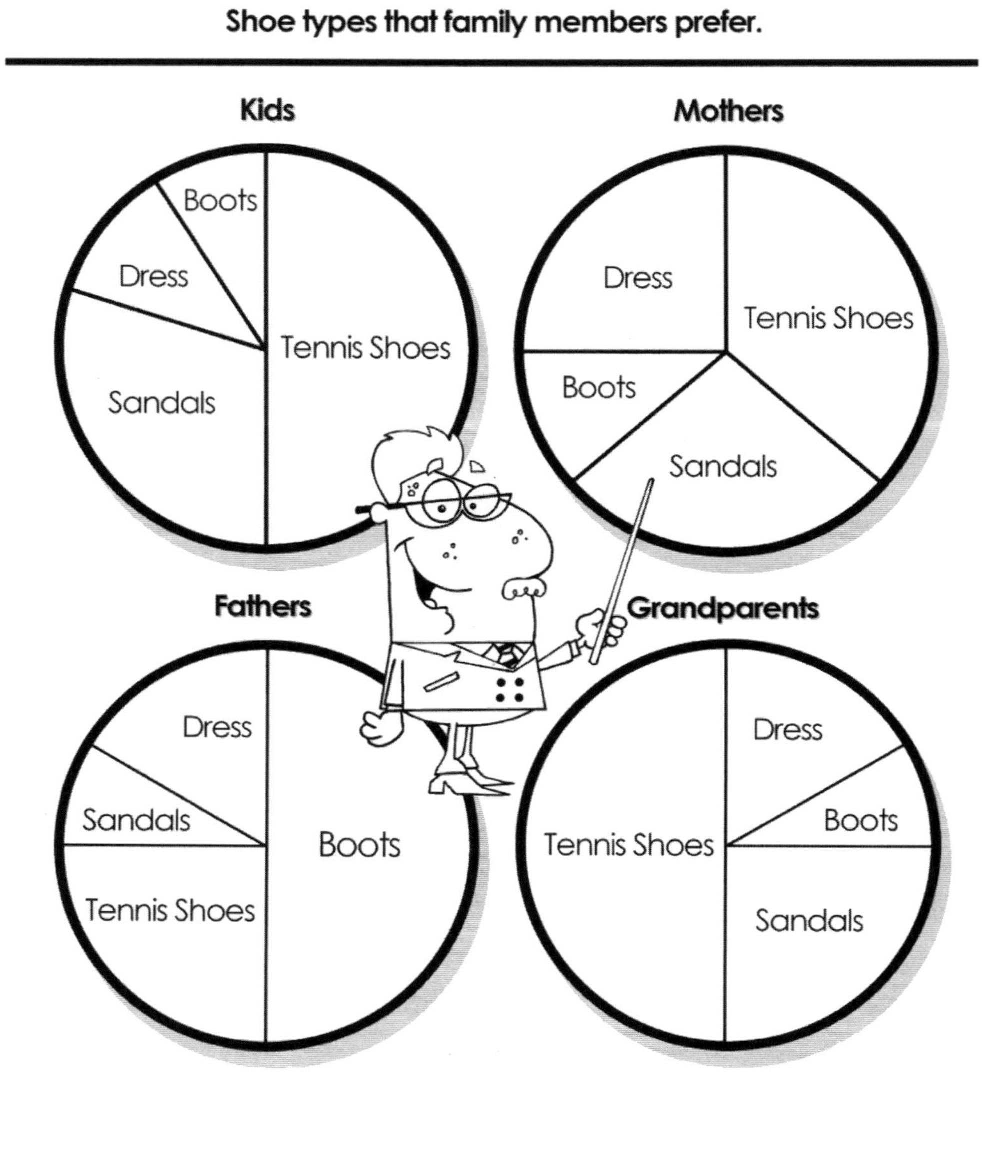

Lesson 9

Reading a Pie Chart 2b

Use the pie charts on the last page to answer the questions below.

1. Which shoes do kids like the most? ________________________
2. Which shoes do grandparents like the most? ________________________
3. Which shoes do mothers like the most? ________________________
4. Which shoes do fathers like the most? ________________________
5. What is the kids' second favorite shoes? ________________________
6. What is the fathers' second favorite shoes? ________________________
7. Which shoes do kids like least? ________________________
8. Which shoes do grandparents like least? ________________________
9. Which shoes do mothers like least? ________________________
10. Which shoes do fathers like least? ________________________

Lesson 10

Creating a Pie Chart

A **pie graph** shows how the parts of something relate to the whole. It is divided into sectors. Each sector represents a particular category. The sum of all the parts will always equal 100%.

Using the information below, fill in the pie graphs with the correct numbers.

Most Studied Planets

1. Mars - 50%
2. Mercury - 6%
3. Venus - 10%
4. Neptune - 34%

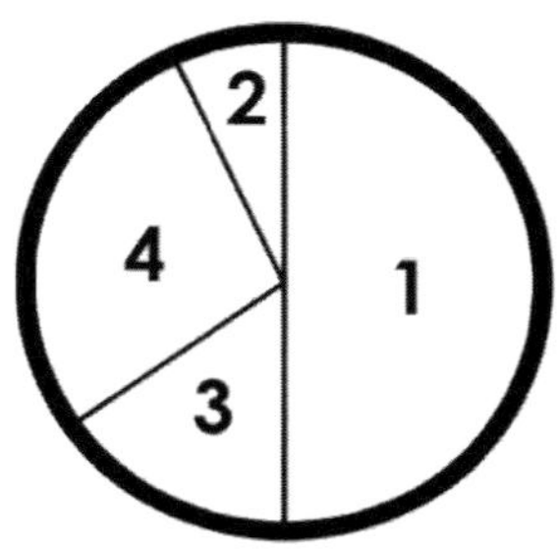

How Students Get to School

1. School Bus - 42%
2. Car - 35%
3. Bike - 15%
4. Walk - 8%

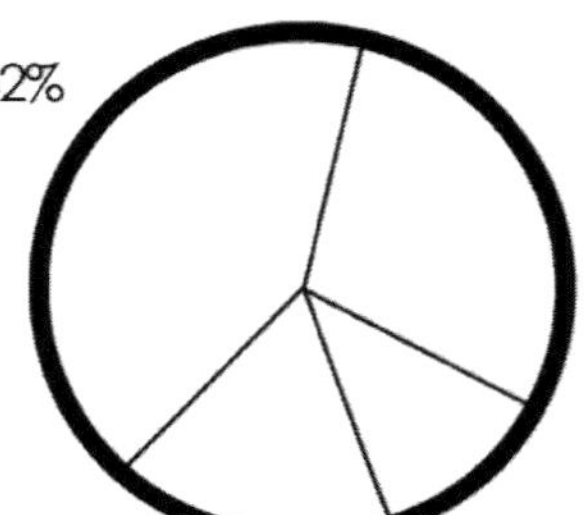

Favorite Movie Types in Schools

1. Comedy - 35%
2. Action - 18%
3. Drama - 8%
4. Animation - 24%
5. Science Fiction- 15%

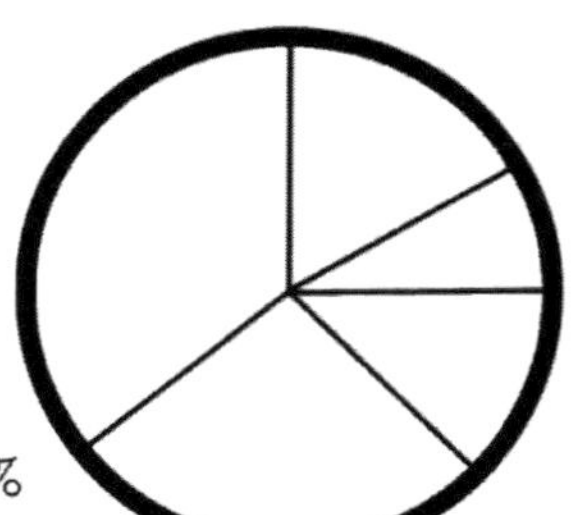

Fish Population in the Pond

1. Bass - 20%
2. Catfish - 27%
3. Trout - 14%
4. Guppies - 32%
5. Turtles - 7%

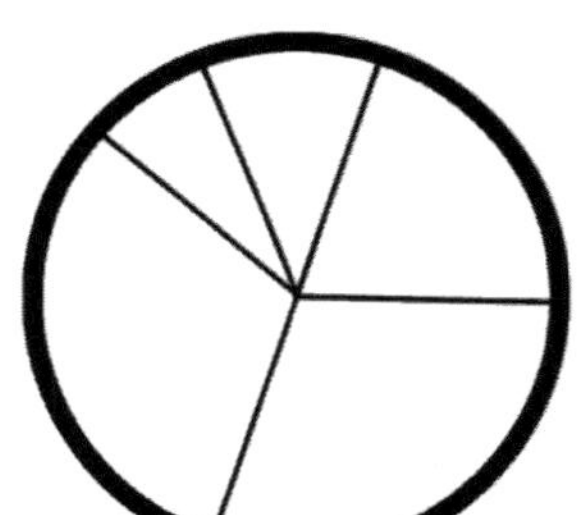

Practice Test #1

Practice Questions

1. What is the value of the digit 5 in the number 3,456,789?

Ⓐ Fifty thousand

Ⓑ Five thousand

Ⓒ Five-hundred thousand

Ⓓ Five million

2. In ice hockey, the number of points a player scores is defined as the sum of the number of goals and the number of assists. Which hockey player listed in the table below has the highest number of points?

Player	Goals	Assists
Phillips	2	23
Jackson	5	17
Robinson	13	15
Miller	8	19

Ⓐ Phillips

Ⓑ Jackson

Ⓒ Robinson

Ⓓ Miller

3. A recipe calls for $3\frac{3}{4}$ cups of flour. Which fraction below is equivalent to this amount?

Ⓐ $\frac{5}{2}$

Ⓑ $\frac{15}{4}$

Ⓒ $\frac{3}{2}$

Ⓓ $\frac{9}{4}$

4. One morning a total of 151 eggs are collected from a henhouse. The eggs are packed in cartons of 12 for shipment. How many eggs are remaining after as many cartons as possible are packed?

Ⓐ 3

Ⓑ 9

Ⓒ 7

Ⓓ 1

5. Which numeral is in the thousandths place in 0.3874?

Ⓐ 3

Ⓑ 8

Ⓒ 7

Ⓓ 4

6. A rectangular plot in a garden is three times longer than it is wide. What is the perimeter of the garden if it has a width of 8 meters?

Ⓐ 32 meters

Ⓑ 192 meters

Ⓒ 24 meters

Ⓓ 64 meters

7. Part A: The number of customers in a new restaurant is given in the table below:

Week	Customers
1	155
2	180
3	205

How many customers should be expected in week 4?

Ⓐ 225

Ⓑ 230

Ⓒ 200

Ⓓ 255

Part B: The average meal at the restaurant is $12. How much money will they make in week 4?

____

8. The rectangular prism below has a volume of 144 cu. cm. The length and width are given below. What is the height of the rectangular prism?

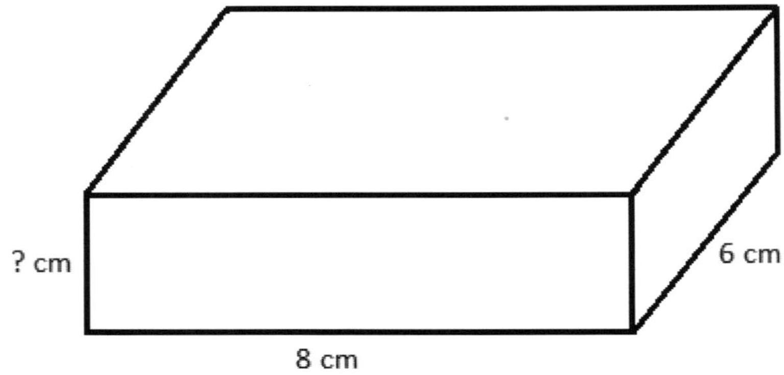

____

9. 0.58 - 0.39=

Ⓐ 0.19

Ⓑ 1.9

Ⓒ 0.29

Ⓓ 2.9

10. The recipe Mary is using to bake cupcakes requires 1 cup of milk and makes 8 cupcakes. If she needs to make 32 cupcakes for the party, how much milk is needed?

Ⓐ 1 pint

Ⓑ 1 gallon

Ⓒ 3 cups

Ⓓ 1 quart

11. Solve the equation: $\frac{2}{5}+\frac{3}{4}-\frac{1}{2}=?$

____

12. Which of the following is correct?

Ⓐ $\frac{4}{7}=\frac{12}{21}$

Ⓑ $\frac{3}{4}=\frac{12}{20}$

Ⓒ $\frac{5}{8}=\frac{15}{32}$

Ⓓ $\frac{7}{9}=\frac{28}{35}$

13. Donnie has a baseball card that is 4.2 inches tall and 2.6 inches wide. What is the area of the card?

____

14. An electronics store sells E Evercell brand batteries in packages of 4 and D Durapower brand batteries in packages of 6. Which expression represents the total number of batteries in the store?

Ⓐ $(4+E)\times(6+D)$

Ⓑ $(4\times E)+(6\times D)$

Ⓒ $(4+E)+(6+D)$

Ⓓ $(4\times E)\div(6\times D)$

15. At the park there is a walking trail that goes around the perimeter. One lap around the park is .28 miles. Samantha walks 11 laps. How far has she walked?

____

16. Solve the equations below:

$.3 \times 1.25 = ?$

$1.22 - .85 + .34 = ?$

$(.22 + 1.48) \times .5 = ?$

17. Given the figure of the parallelogram below, which side is parallel to side $\overline{RT}$?

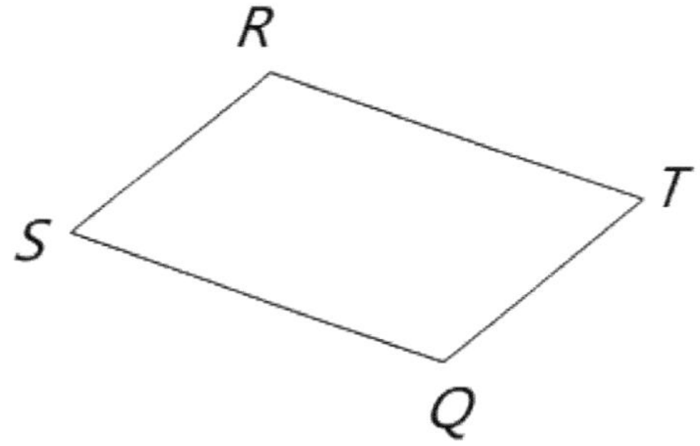

Ⓐ $\overline{RS}$

Ⓑ $\overline{QS}$

Ⓒ $\overline{QT}$

Ⓓ None of the above

18. A fish tank is a rectangular prism with a length of 7 inches and a width of 5 inches and can hold a volume of 210 cubic inches of water. What is the height of the tank?

Ⓐ 6 inches

Ⓑ 5 inches

Ⓒ 17.5 inches

Ⓓ 10 inches

19. The all-time rushing leader in professional football ran for 18,335 yards in his career. What is the best whole number approximation of the number of miles he ran?

____

20. A survey of a random sample of 100 drivers asked them the color of their car. The results of the survey are presented in the table below.

Color of car	Number of drivers
Blue	26
Red	14
Yellow	36
Silver	24

If the parking lot at the local store is filled with 25 cars, how many yellow cars would be expected to be in the lot?

Ⓐ 6

Ⓑ 9

Ⓒ 11

Ⓓ 12

21. Cindy earned \$100 one week at the ice cream stand. She put $\frac{1}{4}$ of the money in her savings account and kept the rest as cash. After this, she received a cash bonus of \$20 from the owner of the ice cream stand and didn't put any of it in the savings account. Which expression represents the amount of cash Cindy currently has?

Ⓐ $C = \frac{3}{4}(100) + 20$

Ⓑ $C = \frac{1}{4}(100) + 20$

Ⓒ $C = \frac{1}{4}(100) - 20$

Ⓓ $C = \frac{3}{4}(120)$

22. Mr. Thompson fills his 25.2 gallon gasoline tank with gas that costs \$2.98 a gallon. Which is the best approximation of the cost of the gasoline?

Ⓐ \$50

Ⓑ \$60

Ⓒ \$75

Ⓓ \$90

23. Using the order of operations solve the problem below.

$8 \times (5 - 2) + (4 + 5) =$ __________________

24. Janice gets home from school at 2:45 PM. She does homework for 1 hour and 30 minutes, then goes out and plays for 1 hour and 45 minutes before returning home for dinner. What time is it when Janice returns home for dinner?

Ⓐ 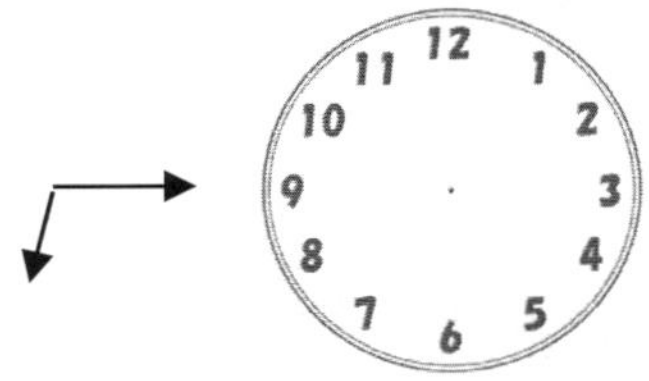

Ⓑ 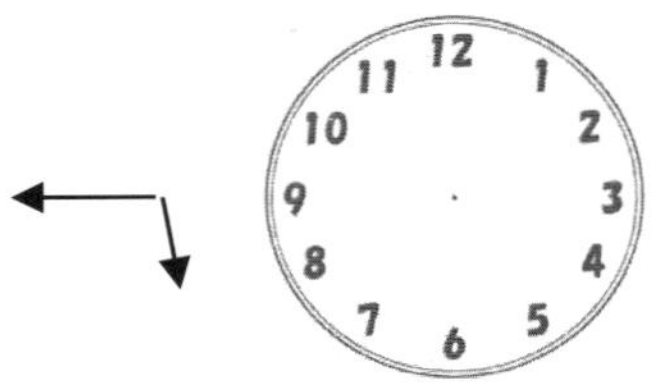

Ⓒ 

Ⓓ 

25. Two sisters were arguing who could have a larger piece of pie. Their mother told the older daughter she could have 2/5 of the pie. She told the younger daughter she could have 1/3 of the pie. Which daughter received a larger piece of pie?

Ⓐ The older daughter.

Ⓑ The younger daughter

Ⓒ Same size piece for each daughter

Ⓓ Not enough information to determine

26. It takes Jack 14.67 minutes to get to school in the morning. It only takes Clayton 10.24 minutes to get to school. How much less time does it take Jack to get to school?

____

27. A ship is located on the map at coordinates (4, 9). If the radar indicates the lighthouse is 5 units east and 4 units south of the ship, what is the location of the lighthouse?

Ⓐ (9, 5)

Ⓑ (9, 4)

Ⓒ (8, 3)

Ⓓ (9, 13)

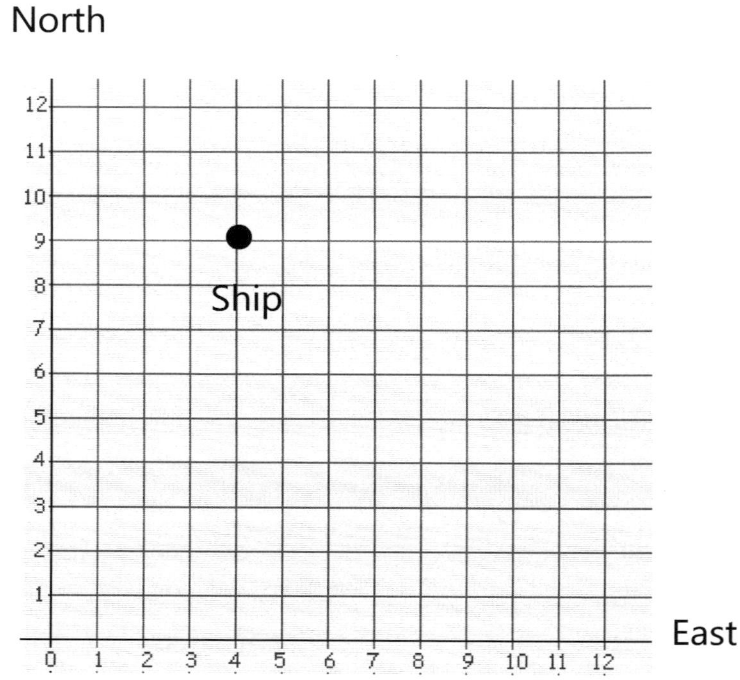

28. When taking a person's temperature with an oral thermometer, temperatures between $96.9°$ and $99.5°$ are considered normal. Which temperature below is outside of the normal range?

Ⓐ 97.2°

Ⓑ 99.3°

Ⓒ 98.9°

Ⓓ 96.3°

29. The high temperatures in degrees Celsius for a work week are given on the table below:

Day	Monday	Tuesday	Wednesday	Thursday	Friday
High Temp.	9	16	13	20	22

What was the mean high temperature for the week?

Ⓐ 14

Ⓑ 16

Ⓒ 13

Ⓓ 22

30. On the graph below plot the points (6,9), (3,8), and (-2,4).

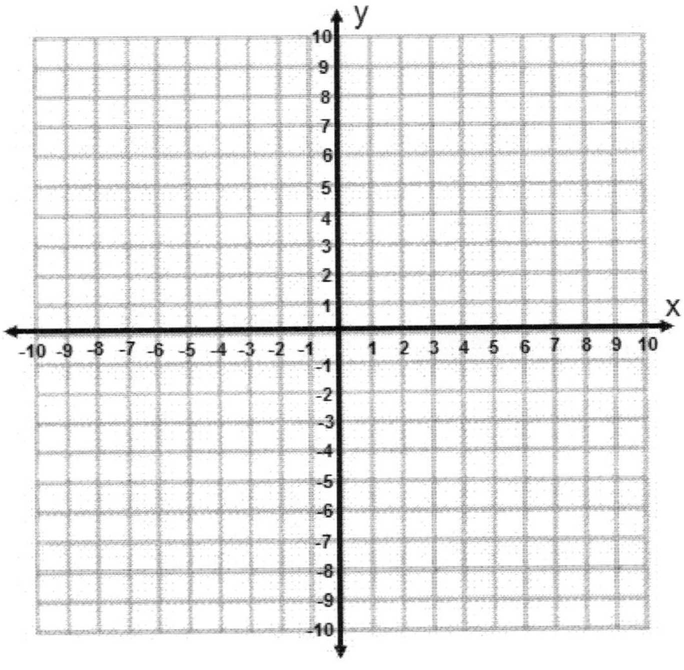

31. A little league has 92 children sign up for baseball season. If each team needs at least 14 players, how many complete baseball teams can be formed?

Ⓐ 5

Ⓑ 6

Ⓒ 7

Ⓓ 8

32. Part A: Given the isosceles trapezoid PQRS below, which two sides are congruent?

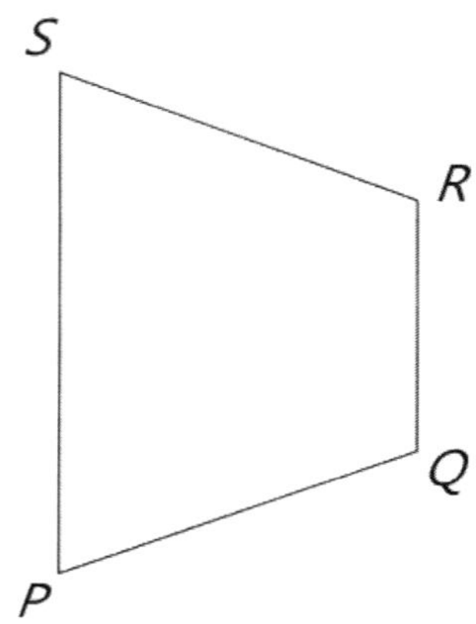

Ⓐ $\overline{PS}$ and $\overline{QR}$

Ⓑ $\overline{RS}$ and $\overline{QF}$ P

Ⓒ $\overline{QP}$ and $\overline{RQ}$

Ⓓ $\overline{PS}$ and $\overline{RS}$

Part B: Which two sides are parallel?

Ⓐ $\overline{PS}$ and $\overline{QR}$

Ⓑ $\overline{RS}$ and $\overline{QF}$ P

Ⓒ $\overline{QP}$ and $\overline{RQ}$

Ⓓ $\overline{PS}$ and $\overline{RS}$

33. A length of string is measured to be $\frac{31}{8}$ inches. Between which two points on the ruler below will this length lie?

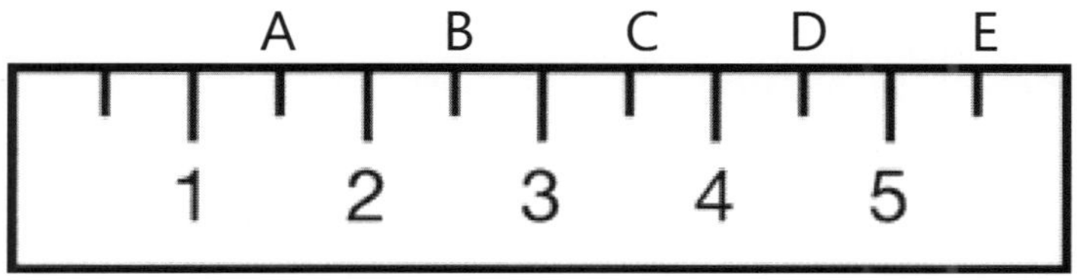

Ⓐ Between points A and B

Ⓑ Between points B and C

Ⓒ Between points C and D

Ⓓ Between points D and E

34. Which point lies within the shaded region below?

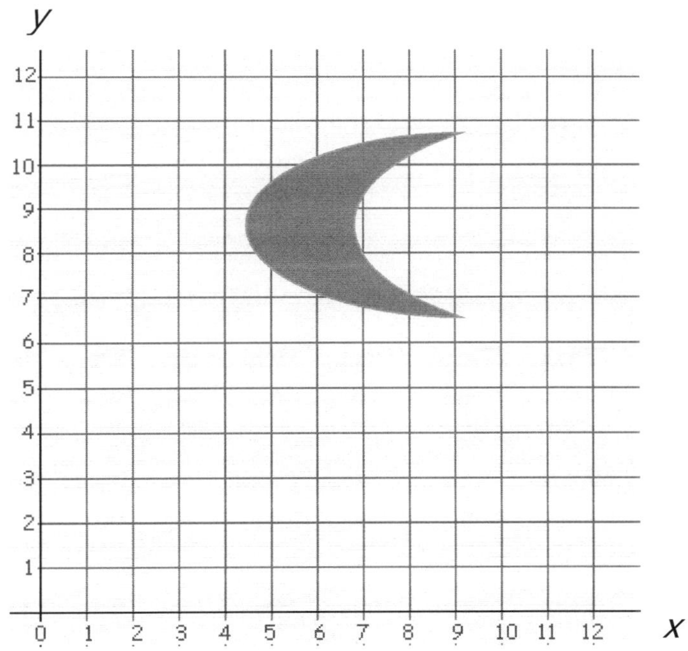

Ⓐ (5, 6)

Ⓑ (8, 6)

Ⓒ (7, 10)

Ⓓ (9, 9)

35. The model shown below represents $1\frac{7}{10}$

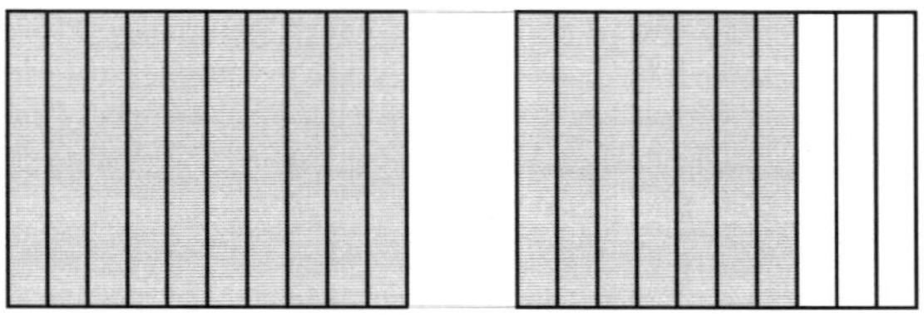

Which decimal does this also represent?

Ⓐ 0.7

Ⓑ 0.07

Ⓒ 1.7

Ⓓ 1.07

36. An electronics store sells T.V.'s for $525 and game systems for $250. If 36 people buy T.V. and 29 people buy a game system how much money would the store make?

____

37. Of the 20 people in Joan's class, 4 of them have birthdays in the winter, 7 have birthdays in the spring, 3 have birthdays in the summer, and 6 have birthdays in the fall. What is the probability a student chosen at random will have a birthday in either the spring or the summer?

Ⓐ $\frac{7}{20}$

Ⓑ $\frac{1}{2}$

Ⓒ $\frac{3}{20}$

Ⓓ $\frac{3}{10}$

38. Phil is going to school overseas for 9 weeks and 5 days. How many days will Phil be gone?

Ⓐ 95

Ⓑ 44

Ⓒ 59

Ⓓ 68

39. Julie shopped for first-aid cream. One large tube held 1.5 fluid ounces and the smallest tube held 0.33 fluid ounces. What is the difference in the number of fluid ounces of cream in the two tubes?

Ⓐ 1.8

Ⓑ 1.27

Ⓒ 1.23

Ⓓ 1.17

40. Jan played a game which used a fair spinner like the one shown here. Jan needs the arrow to land on green on her next turn.

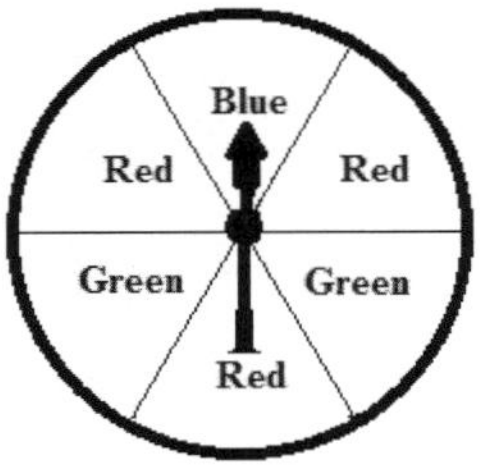

What is the probability that the arrow lands on green when Jan spins one time?

Ⓐ $\frac{1}{6}$

Ⓑ $\frac{1}{3}$

Ⓒ $\frac{1}{2}$

Ⓓ $\frac{2}{3}$

Practice Test #2

Practice Questions

1. Which number represents "fifty-seven thousand three hundred and forty"?

Ⓐ 570,340

Ⓑ 573,400

Ⓒ 5,734

Ⓓ 57,340

2. Four students were given a typing test measuring their speed in words per minute and then given the same typing test several weeks later. Which student had the greatest improvement?

Student	First score (words per minute)	Second score (words per minute)
Alexander	22	39
Betty	39	48
Carolyn	27	43
David	22	42

Ⓐ Alexander

Ⓑ Betty

Ⓒ Carolyn

Ⓓ David

3. A bookshelf is to be $7\frac{5}{8}$ inches wide. Which fraction below is equivalent to this measurement?

Ⓐ $\frac{35}{8}$

Ⓑ $\frac{75}{8}$

Ⓒ $\frac{61}{8}$

Ⓓ $\frac{43}{8}$

4. Toasty Donut Shop makes 141 donuts one morning. The donuts are packaged in boxes of 12 for delivery. How many single donuts are left over?

Ⓐ 3

Ⓑ 9

Ⓒ 6

Ⓓ 1

5. Which numeral is in the thousandths place in .5643?

Ⓐ 5

Ⓑ 6

Ⓒ 4

Ⓓ 3

6. Dennis weighs 56 pounds. His little brother Donny weighs 23 pounds less than him. What is Donny's weight in ounces?

____

7. A square flower garden has an area of 81 feet. What is the length of one side of the garden?

Ⓐ 9 feet

Ⓑ 20.25 feet

Ⓒ 40.5 feet

Ⓓ 324 feet

8. Which of the following is correct?

Ⓐ $\frac{2}{3} = \frac{18}{24}$

Ⓑ $\frac{4}{5} = \frac{16}{20}$

Ⓒ $\frac{1}{9} = \frac{4}{18}$

Ⓓ $\frac{3}{8} = \frac{9}{16}$

9. Round each of the decimals below to the nearest hundredth.

$3.116 \approx$ ________

$3.081 \approx$ ________

$3.006 \approx$ ________

$3.107 \approx$ ________

10. Which of the following figures is a trapezoid?

Ⓐ 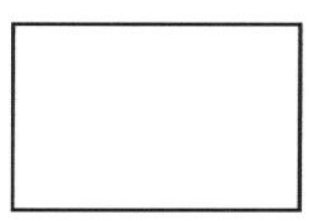

Ⓑ 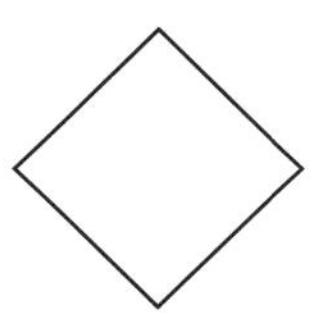

Ⓒ 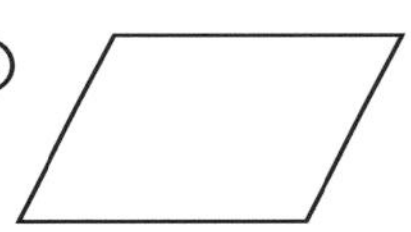

Ⓓ 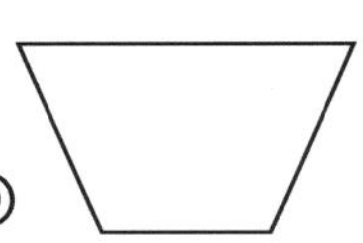

11. A gallon of cooking oil is used to make popcorn for 256 people. How much cooking oil is needed to make popcorn for 96 people?

Ⓐ 2 quarts

Ⓑ 3 pints

Ⓒ 1 quart

Ⓓ 1 cup

12. Jodi made a sum of money yesterday at a bake sale. She spent half of the money to buy more ingredients for next week's bake sale, and then spent $12 to go to the movies. Jodi has $17 remaining. How much did she make yesterday at the bake sale?

Ⓐ $36

Ⓑ $58

Ⓒ $46

Ⓓ $41

13. Express $99/14$ as a mixed fraction.

Ⓐ $7\frac{1}{14}$

Ⓑ $7\frac{3}{14}$

Ⓒ $7\frac{11}{14}$

Ⓓ $7\frac{5}{14}$

14. A little boy decides to give away all of his marbles. Each of his 4 friends is to receive an equal share. Which of the statements below describes how this can be done?

Ⓐ Multiply his marbles by 4 and give this amount to each of his friends

Ⓑ Multiply his marbles by 2 and give this amount to each of his friends

Ⓒ Multiply his marbles by 1/2 and give this amount to each of his friends

Ⓓ Multiply his marbles by 1/4 and give this amount to each of his friends

15. Part A: A store receives regular shipments of paper towels. Each shipment contains 26 boxes. Each box contains 6 packages and each package has 8 rolls of paper towels. How many rolls of paper towels come in one shipment?

____

Part B: If the store sells 6100 rolls each month how many shipments will it need in one month?

____

16. Part A: A zoo has three different lion enclosures. The first one is $\frac{5}{8}$ of an acre. The second one is $\frac{5}{6}$ of an acre. How much bigger is the second one than the first one?

____

Part B: If the third one is $\frac{7}{12}$, what is the total number of acres in all three enclosures?

____

17. Given the figure of the parallelogram below, which side is congruent to side $\overline{RT}$?

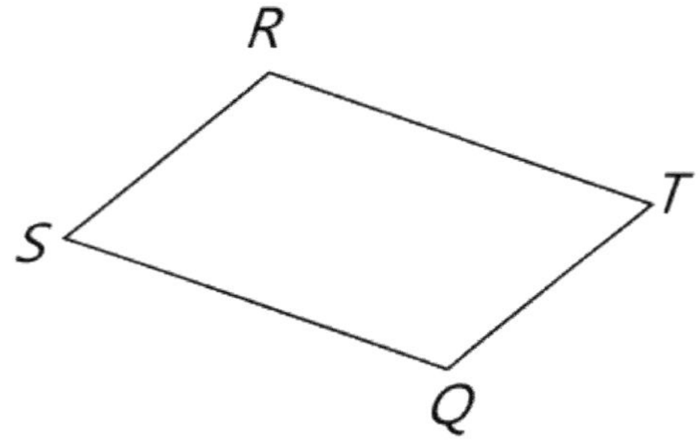

Ⓐ $\overline{RS}$

Ⓑ $\overline{QS}$

Ⓒ $\overline{QT}$

Ⓓ None of the above

18. A large rectangular-prism-shaped tank at the zoo is 8 feet wide and 5 feet high. How long is the tank if it holds a volume of 200 cubic feet of water?

Ⓐ 8 feet

Ⓑ 6 feet

Ⓒ 13 feet

Ⓓ 5 feet

19. Mount McKinley, the tallest mountain in North America, is 20,320 feet high. Approximately how many miles tall is the Mount?

Ⓐ 6

Ⓑ 5

Ⓒ 4

Ⓓ 3

20. Mrs. Jackson records the hair color of the 20 children in her room and obtains the following results:

Hair color	Number of students
Black	6
Brown	8
Blonde	4
Red	2

If the school has a total of 240 children, how many children with brown hair should be expected?

____

21. A grocery store determines the price of a gallon milk, *P*, in dollars will be determined by multiplying the wholesale price, *W*, in dollars by 1.5 and adding 25 cents. Which expression below represents this relationship?

Ⓐ $P = 1.5 + W + 0.25$

Ⓑ $P = 0.25W + 1.5$

Ⓒ $P = 1.75W$

Ⓓ $P = 1.5W + 0.25$

22. The movie Laura went to see ended at 8:15 PM. The movie she saw was 2 hours and 45 minutes long. What time did the movie start?

Ⓐ 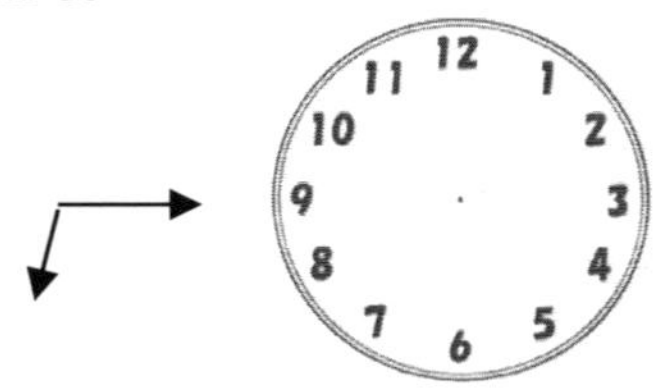

Ⓑ 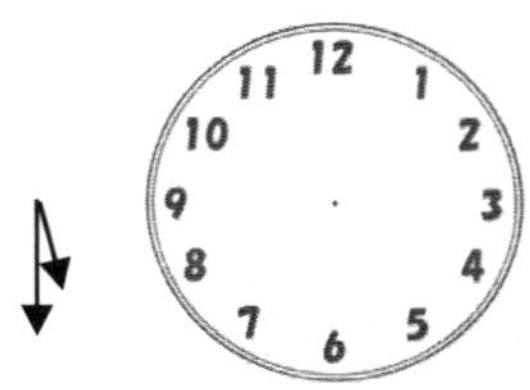

Ⓒ 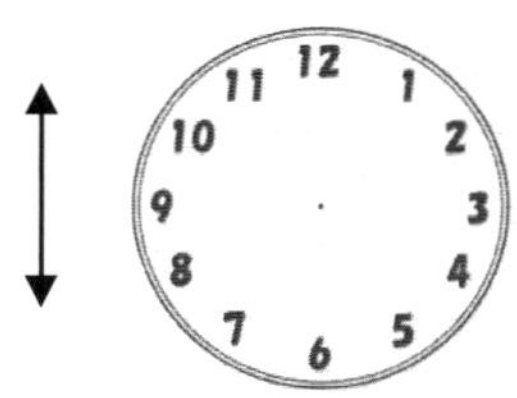

Ⓓ 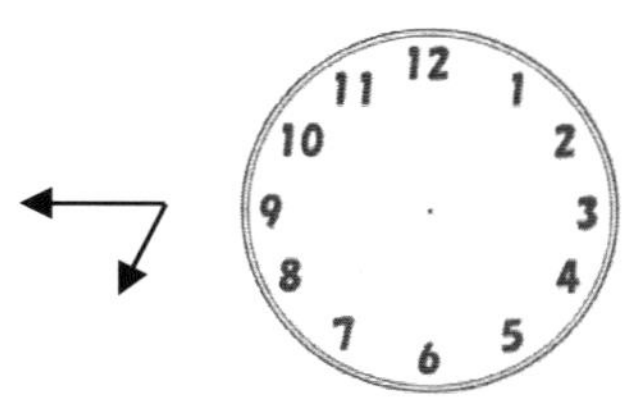

23. Using order of operations solve the problem below.

$3 + (9 - 4) \times (4 + 5) = ?$

____

24. On Saturday Allen spent 73 minutes mowing the grass. He spent 42 minutes washing his car, another 56 minutes repairing a fence, and 31 minutes trimming the shrubs. How much time did he spend doing chores on Saturday?

Ⓐ 2 hours 51 minutes

Ⓑ 3 hours 22 minutes

Ⓒ 3 hours 18 minutes

Ⓓ 3 hours 28 minutes

25. Which one of the statements about the rectangular prism below is FALSE?

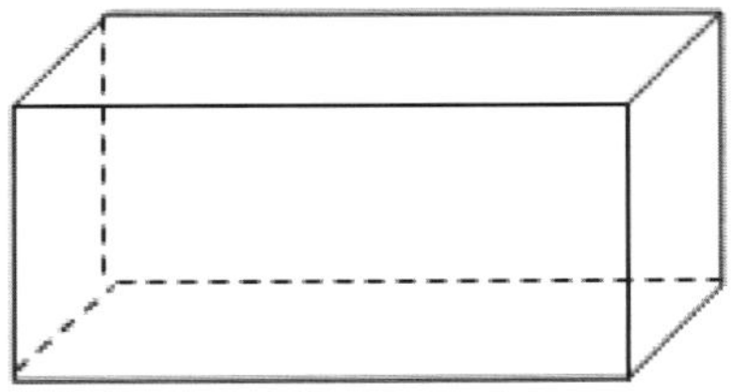

Ⓐ There are 12 edges on the rectangular prism.

Ⓑ The six sides of the rectangular prism all have the same area.

Ⓒ Some of the edges are parallel.

Ⓓ There are 8 vertices on the rectangular prism.

26. **The model shown below represents $1\frac{5}{10}$**

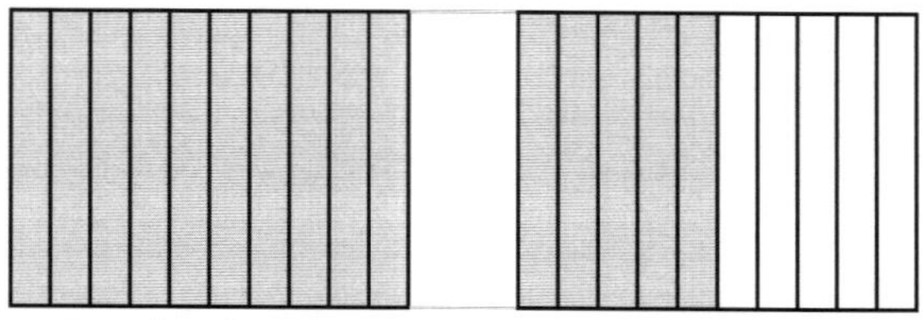

Which decimal does this also represent?

Ⓐ 0.5

Ⓑ 1.5

Ⓒ 1.05

Ⓓ 1.005

27. **An observation tower is located at point (8, 5) on the map grid below. A fire is observed from a location 4 units west and 2 units north of the tower. What is the location of the fire?**

Ⓐ (12, 7)

Ⓑ (4, 7)

Ⓒ (6, 9)

Ⓓ (4, 5)

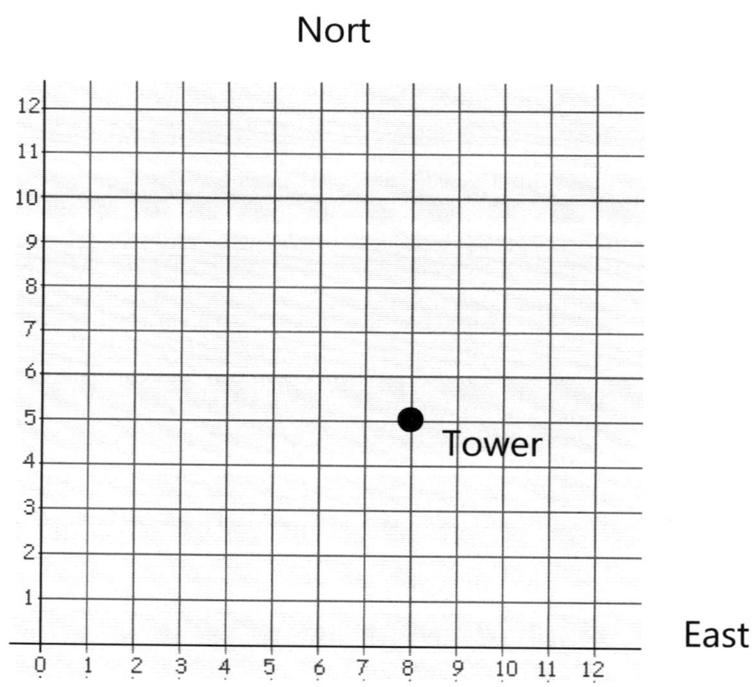

28. Maria is moving and needs a box to pack books in. The box needs to be 416 cubic inches. Which of the following boxes is the right size?

Ⓐ a box that is $8\ in. \times 12\ in. \times 5\ in.$

Ⓑ a box that is $12\ in. \times 4\ in. \times 9\ in.$

Ⓒ a box that is $13\ in. \times 5\ in. \times 7\ in.$

Ⓓ a box that is $13\ in. \times 4\ in. \times 8\ in.$

29. The number of washes the Squeaky Clean car wash made last week is given in the table below:

Day	Monday	Tuesday	Wednesday	Thursday	Friday
Car Washes	22	28	38	47	45

What is the mean number of car washes for the week?

Ⓐ 44

Ⓑ 47

Ⓒ 36

Ⓓ 31

30. 0.28 × 0.17

Ⓐ 0.2260

Ⓑ 0.4760

Ⓒ 0.0226

Ⓓ 0.0476

31. Jim brings two ice chests to the beach. Ice chest A has two compartments, while Ice Chest B just has one. Ice chest B can hold 24 drinks while Ice chest A can hold twice as many. If the larger compartment in Ice Chest A holds 34, how many does the smaller one hold?

____

32. Mandy's Farmer's Market sells pears in boxes of 18. A shipment of 417 pears arrives that morning. How many full boxes of pears can Mandy sell using that shipment?

Ⓐ 25

Ⓑ 23

Ⓒ 18

Ⓓ 20

33. The side length of a regular pentagon is 6.5 centimeters. What is the perimeter of this figure?

Ⓐ 26.0 cm.

Ⓑ 42.25 cm.

Ⓒ 39.0 cm.

Ⓓ 32.5 cm.

34. A length of yarn is measured to be $\frac{35}{8}$ inches. Between which points on the ruler will this length lie?

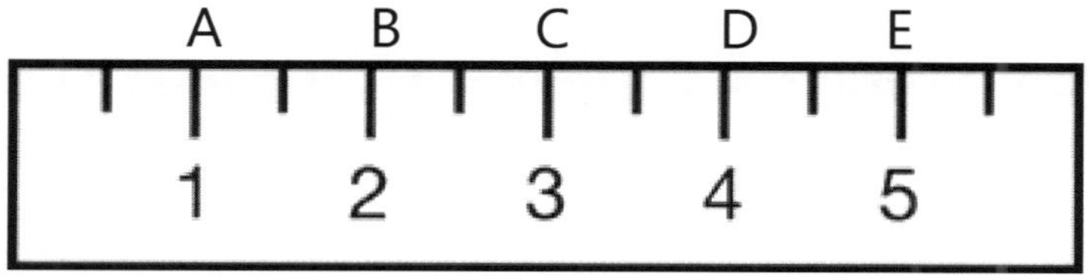

Ⓐ Between points A and B

Ⓑ Between points B and C

Ⓒ Between points C and D

Ⓓ Between points D and E

25. Which point lies within the shaded region below?

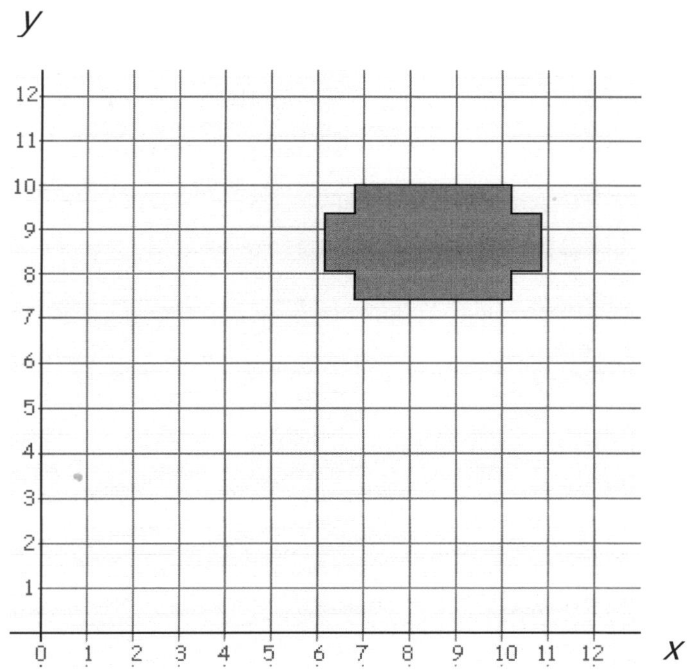

Ⓐ (5, 8)

Ⓑ (8, 9)

Ⓒ (7, 11)

Ⓓ (9, 7)

26. The workers at a large construction site were made up of 11 plumbers, 7 electricians, 13 carpenters, 8 concrete finishers and 11 laborers. What is the probability that a worker chosen at random will be either a carpenter or an electrician?

Ⓐ $\frac{13}{50}$

Ⓑ $\frac{9}{25}$

Ⓒ $\frac{2}{5}$

Ⓓ $\frac{7}{25}$

27. Which line graph correctly reflects the data shown in the table?

Time	Number of Customers
2:00 pm	20
4:00 pm	30
6:00 pm	50
8:00 pm	10

Ⓐ

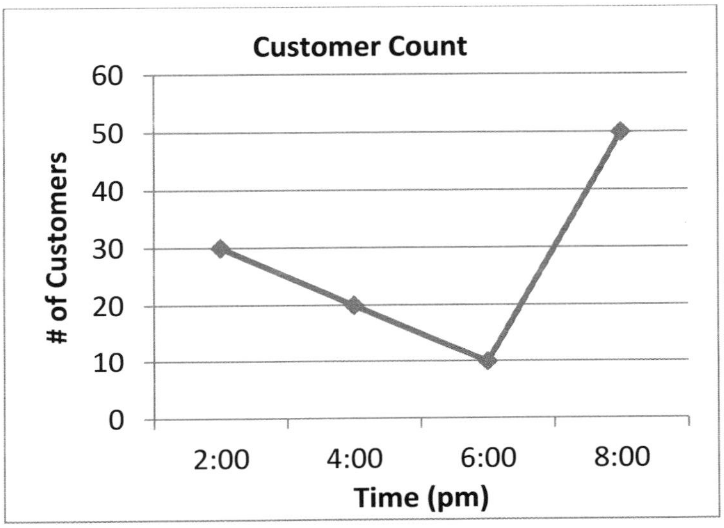

Ⓑ

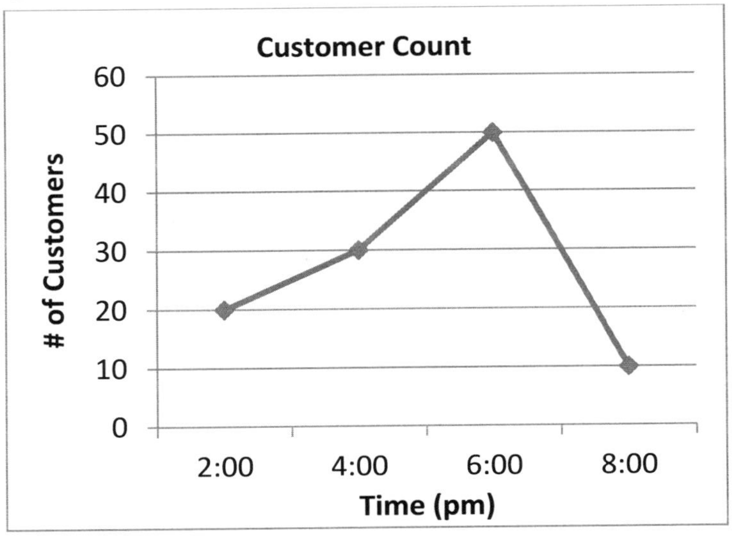

Ⓒ

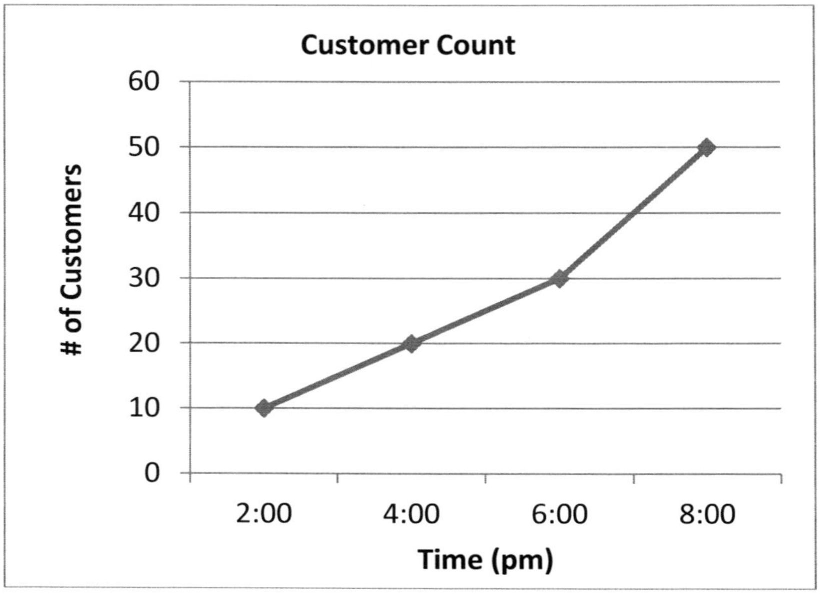
Customer Count
60
50
40
30
20
10
0
# of Customers
2:00
4:00
6:00
8:00
Time (pm)

Ⓓ

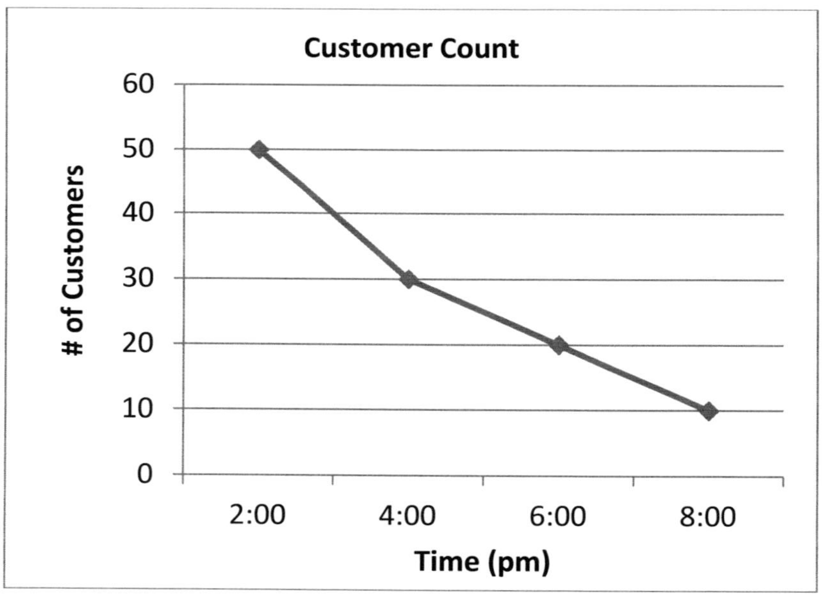
Customer Count
60
50
40
30
20
10
0
# of Customers
2:00
4:00
6:00
8:00
Time (pm)

28. Four students measured the length of the pencil each was using. The list shows the lengths, in centimeters, of the four pencils.

17.03 cm, 17.4 cm, 17.31 cm, 17.09 cm

Which list shows the lengths of the pencils in order, from shortest to longest?

Ⓐ *17.4 cm, 17.31 cm, 17.09 cm, 17.03 cm*

Ⓑ *17.03 cm, 17.09 cm, 17.4 cm, 17.31 cm*

Ⓒ *17.4 cm, 17.03 cm, 17.09 cm, 17.31 cm*

Ⓓ *17.03 cm, 17.09 cm, 17.31 cm, 17.4 cm*

29. What is the equivalent decimal number for five hundred twelve thousandths?

Ⓐ 0.512

Ⓑ 0.0512

Ⓒ 5120.

Ⓓ 0.00512

40. Reduce $\frac{14}{98}$ to lowest terms.

Ⓐ $\frac{7}{49}$

Ⓑ $\frac{2}{14}$

Ⓒ $\frac{1}{7}$

Ⓓ $\frac{3}{8}$

Thank You

We at Mometrix would like to extend our heartfelt thanks to you, our friend and patron, for allowing us to play a part in your journey. It is a privilege to serve people from all walks of life who are unified in their commitment to building the best future they can for themselves.

The preparation you devote to these important testing milestones may be the most valuable educational opportunity you have for making a real difference in your life. We encourage you to put your heart into it—that feeling of succeeding, overcoming, and yes, conquering will be well worth the hours you've invested.

We want to hear your story, your struggles and your successes, and if you see any opportunities for us to improve our materials so we can help others even more effectively in the future, please share that with us as well. **The team at Mometrix would be absolutely thrilled to hear from you!** So please, send us an email (support@mometrix.com) and let's stay in touch.

Online Resources

Due to our efforts to try to keep this book to a manageable length, we've created a link that will give you access to all of your online resources:

mometrix.com/resources719/ssnystg5mathwb

It's Your Moment, Let's Celebrate It!

Share your story @mometrixtestpreparation

TABLE OF CONTENTS

Workbook Answers

Chapter 1 - Whole Numbers

Pg 6

1.

1	5	6	3	2	7	8	2
Ten Millions	Millions	Hundred Thousands	Ten Thousands	Thousands	Hundreds	Tens	Ones

2.

2	4	8	7	9	3	6	0
Ten Millions	Millions	Hundred Thousands	Ten Thousands	Thousands	Hundreds	Tens	Ones

3.

6	2	1	5	8	5	2	4
Ten Millions	Millions	Hundred Thousands	Ten Thousands	Thousands	Hundreds	Tens	Ones

4.

3	0	6	7	1	2	3	4
Ten Millions	Millions	Hundred Thousands	Ten Thousands	Thousands	Hundreds	Tens	Ones

5.

5	2	1	9	7	3	0	5
Ten Millions	Millions	Hundred Thousands	Ten Thousands	Thousands	Hundreds	Tens	Ones

6.

8	3	4	9	8	1	4	7
Ten Millions	Millions	Hundred Thousands	Ten Thousands	Thousands	Hundreds	Tens	Ones

Pg 7

#									
1.	7 Hundred Millions	4 Ten Millions	8 Millions	4 Hundred Thousands	2 Ten Thousands	2 Thousands	7 Hundreds	1 Tens	9 Ones
2.	3 Hundred Millions	2 Ten Millions	9 Millions	6 Hundred Thousands	0 Ten Thousands	8 Thousands	1 Hundreds	1 Tens	4 Ones
3.	1 Hundred Millions	2 Ten Millions	4 Millions	3 Hundred Thousands	7 Ten Thousands	5 Thousands	2 Hundreds	7 Tens	7 Ones
4.	7 Hundred Millions	4 Ten Millions	1 Millions	5 Hundred Thousands	8 Ten Thousands	8 Thousands	3 Hundreds	7 Tens	9 Ones
5.	5 Hundred Millions	0 Ten Millions	4 Millions	2 Hundred Thousands	6 Ten Thousands	7 Thousands	3 Hundreds	3 Tens	2 Ones
6.	9 Hundred Millions	7 Ten Millions	2 Millions	1 Hundred Thousands	1 Ten Thousands	4 Thousands	0 Hundreds	8 Tens	9 Ones

Pg 8		Pg 9		Pg 10	
No.	Answer	No.	Answer	No.	Answer
1	3,000	1	24,453	1	900 + 400 = 1,300
2	9,000	2	55,718	2	500 + 500 = 1,000
3	1,000	3	19,554	3	100 + 600 = 700
4	8,000	4	28,132	4	400 + 700 = 1,100
5	3,000	5	12,966	5	900 - 500 = 400
6	4,000	6	93,359	6	800 - 200 = 600
7	6,000	7	96,591	7	600 - 500 = 100
8	8,000	8	56,772	8	400 - 200 = 200
9	6,000	9	83,297		
10	2,000	10	27,915		
11	40,000	11	35,212		
12	20,000	12	62,689		
13	90,000	13	49,212		
14	60,000	14	79,359		
15	70,000	15	93,756		
16	80,000	16	41,328		
17	30,000	17	43,957		
18	40,000	18	14,161		
19	20,000	19	93,564		
20	50,000	20	39,817		
21	300,000				
22	600,000				
23	200,000				
24	500,000				
25	200,000				
26	300,000				
27	900,000				
28	600,000				
29	800,000				
30	100,000				

Pg 11		Pg 12		Pg 13	
No.	Answer	No.	Answer	No.	Answer
1	6,000 + 4,000 = 10,000	1	1,225	1	6,515
2	5,000 + 1,000 = 6,000	2	1,024	2	12,834
3	9,000 + 7,000 = 16,000	3	1,580	3	12,670
4	5,000 + 5,000 = 10,000	4	742	4	11,229
5	3,000 + 6,000 = 9,000	5	1,261	5	16,342
6	8,000 + 7,000 = 15,000	6	1,111	6	8,877
7	2,000 + 5,000 = 7,000	7	1,353	7	5,300
8	4,000 + 5,000 = 9,000	8	1,632	8	11,866
9	9,000 + 500 = 9,500	9	1,236	9	13,940
10	4,000 - 2,000 = 2,000	10	1,430	10	9,715
11	9,000 - 5,000 = 4,000			11	15,009
12	7,000 - 6,000 = 1,000			12	5,461
13	5,000 - 3,000 = 2,000			13	4,177
14	9,000 - 8,000 = 1,000			14	15,408
15	4,000 - 2,000 = 2,000			15	13,512
16	4,000 - 800 = 3,200			16	24,745
17	6,000 - 2,000 = 4,000			17	10,693
18	8,000 - 6,000 = 2,000			18	14,319
				19	14,792
				20	14,112

Pg 14		Pg 15		Pg 16	
No.	Answer	No.	Answer	No.	Answer
1	23,795	1	104,654	1	596,052
2	16,340	2	188,944	2	977,698
3	16,891	3	144,072	3	1,160,308
4	23,486	4	189,476	4	1,097,102
5	18,748	5	104,323	5	1,089,063
6	22,475	6	103,894	6	1,283,759
7	20,531	7	156,084	7	1,336,765
8	13,385	8	140,874	8	845,509
9	13,938	9	184,913	9	1,051,175
10	19,146	10	147,781	10	1,085,891
11	17,264	11	57,012	11	1,975,054
12	17,039	12	183,425	12	841,668
13	16,951	13	131,969	13	1,410,112
14	14,558	14	101,039	14	1,518,639
15	22,189	15	184,161	15	2,240,839
16	14,766	16	115,576	16	720,411
17	21,953	17	83,250	17	1,776,777
18	13,765	18	68,871	18	1,577,184
19	8,331	19	174,540	19	1,304,447
20	18,795	20	264,261	20	1,662,926

Pg 17		Pg 18		Pg 19	
No.	**Answer**	**No.**	**Answer**	**No.**	**Answer**
1	12,052,629	1	443	1	1,112
2	7,888,122	2	452	2	1,111
3	17,265,467	3	143	3	3,781
4	21,709,039	4	284	4	2,779
5	14,622,984	5	539	5	1,756
6	11,129,457	6	118	6	6,487
7	19,771,741	7	861	7	7,511
8	17,143,156	8	451	8	2,264
9	10,170,485	9	252	9	524
10	14,603,355	10	129	10	5,685
11	23,268,932	11	291	11	327
12	13,589,274	12	450	12	2,047
13	15,296,451	13	288	13	4,635
14	17,280,455	14	457	14	2,059
15	12,562,642	15	432	15	5,475
16	15,576,391			16	2,889
17	15,540,467			17	1,454
18	15,214,301			18	916
19	22,688,631			19	2,755
20	20,429,648			20	2,747

Pg 20		Pg 21		Pg 22	
No.	**Answer**	**No.**	**Answer**	**No.**	**Answer**
1	2,786	1	131,482	1	592,288
2	25,038	2	507,851	2	1,409,294
3	21,376	3	277,758	3	5,730,630
4	36,508	4	34,013	4	2,437,389
5	20,756	5	778,375	5	2,113,834
6	16,804	6	191,436	6	5,220,339
7	20,507	7	411,246	7	7,314,169
8	4,557	8	352,113	8	2,876,907
9	37,509	9	221,963	9	3,135,552
10	38,809	10	232,179	10	5,127,660
11	18,499	11	47,078	11	1,801,944
12	26,055	12	181,244	12	4,683,052
13	15,864	13	426,781	13	3,125,607
14	43,464	14	151,044	14	4,587,627
15	45,132	15	374,747	15	3,670,658
16	46,172	16	96,861	16	3,371,113
17	18,489	17	189,668	17	6,478,871
18	21,529	18	412,017	18	2,359,169
19	57,435	19	199,681	19	3,467,162
20	76,939	20	619,306	20	2,282,335

Pg 23	
No.	**Answer**
1	13,138,506
2	30,680,207
3	22,547,298
4	35,657,655
5	7,593,206
6	46,473,155
7	55,559,777
8	89,277,747
9	34,798,707
10	19,262,091
11	86,135,587
12	29,474,647
13	64,926,012
14	43,864,964
15	30,236,771
16	37,778,627
17	81,291,709
18	37,006,688
19	56,327,553
20	38,185,370
21	66,798,298
22	75,126,679
23	15,285,265
24	32,454,367

Pg 26

Multiplication Table

x	1	2	3	4	5	6	7	8	9	10
1	1	2	3	4	5	6	7	8	9	10
2	2	4	6	8	10	12	14	16	18	20
3	3	6	9	12	15	18	21	24	27	30
4	4	8	12	16	20	24	28	32	36	40
5	5	10	15	20	25	30	35	40	45	50
6	6	12	18	24	30	36	42	48	54	60
7	7	14	21	28	35	42	49	56	63	70
8	8	16	24	32	40	48	56	64	72	80
9	9	18	27	36	45	54	63	72	81	90
10	10	20	30	40	50	60	70	80	90	100

Pg 27

1.

X	4	5	6
6	24	30	36
5	20	25	30
4	16	20	24
3	12	15	18
2	8	10	12

2.

X	0	6	8	4	9
5	0	30	40	20	45
4	0	24	32	16	36
3	0	18	24	12	27

3.

X	2	3	4	5	6
10	20	30	40	50	60
11	22	33	44	55	66
12	24	36	48	60	72

4.

X	5	4	3
6	30	24	18
5	25	20	15
4	20	16	12
3	15	12	9
2	10	8	6

Pg 28		Pg 29		Pg 30	
No.	**Answer**	**No.**	**Answer**	**No.**	**Answer**
1	260	1	1,968	1	735
2	147	2	3,168	2	1,536
3	108	3	432	3	1,944
4	552	4	1,944	4	3,216
5	456	5	2,088	5	5,525
6	392	6	1,036	6	3,404
7	116	7	935	7	3,354
8	160	8	2,046	8	1,015
9	476	9	1,656	9	3,196
10	747	10	288	10	1,800
				11	2,916
				12	5,568
				13	2,666
				14	8,740
				15	1,638
				16	7,200
				17	1,260
				18	6,566
				19	2,128
				20	3,705

Pg 31		Pg 32		Pg 33	
No.	Answer	No.	Answer	No.	Answer
1	42	1	7,383	1	25,532
2	640	2	4,921	2	28,896
3	57	3	22,016	3	36,096
4	72	4	16,524	4	11,713
		5	15,200	5	41,724
		6	24,999	6	40,807
		7	33,418	7	8,668
		8	5,640	8	15,876
		9	21,204	9	9,164
		10	53,952	10	31,178
		11	74,036	11	9,924
		12	37,905	12	18,278
		13	23,970	13	63,264
		14	50,007	14	45,689
		15	47,288	15	37,944
		16	45,045	16	22,743
		17	60,800	17	67,425
		18	57,072	18	14,314
		19	26,826	19	52,500
		20	83,040	20	63,624

Pg 34		Pg 35		Pg 36	
No.	**Answer**	**No.**	**Answer**	**No.**	**Answer**
1	3,381	1	77,532	1	31,572
2	956	2	102,915	2	68,740
3	1,536	3	167,684	3	152,875
4	608	4	253,425	4	32,147
		5	90,364	5	134,096
		6	376,467	6	174,801
		7	296,472	7	59,496
		8	230,278	8	226,023
		9	156,581	9	51,940
		10	254,910	10	128,808
		11	238,908	11	465,519
		12	404,247	12	382,932
		13	174,135	13	207,900
		14	606,268	14	641,056
		15	291,712	15	579,198
		16	260,559	16	269,244
		17	718,650	17	196,174
		18	524,688	18	793,945
		19	116,795	19	561,000
		20	488,166	20	885,024

Pg 37		Pg 38		Pg 39	
No.	Answer	No.	Answer	No.	Answer
1	157,680	1	66,794	1	418,284
2	222,221	2	69,689	2	250,355
3	79,530	3	258,937	3	584,168
4	269,346	4	128,853	4	826,428
5	63,784	5	230,955	5	1,660,480
6	120,825	6	130,104	6	1,604,106
7	568,874	7	180,048	7	785,436
8	182,400	8	103,170	8	588,707
9	145,148	9	350,966	9	1,668,172
10	616,710	10	247,648	10	1,940,352
11	110,670	11	140,140	11	3,672,774
12	106,524	12	101,106	12	1,145,224
13	308,355	13	203,109	13	555,182
14	445,060	14	285,950	14	3,315,922
15	473,324	15	104,328	15	3,198,804
		16	273,456	16	2,714,376
		17	180,560	17	4,070,924
		18	193,400	18	5,319,210
		19	87,269	19	5,624,400
		20	582,556	20	6,151,680

Pg 40		Pg 41	
No.	Answer	No.	Answer
1	2,133,216	1	6^4
2	345,555	2	3^3
3	1,143,539	3	5^3
4	1,110,444	4	7^4
5	2,901,440	5	9^5
6	2,880,279	6	8^6
7	1,093,680	7	2^6
8	855,218	8	4^4
9	1,770,131	9	5^3
10	1,327,798	10	6^5
11	4,844,560	11	7^7
12	1,395,384	12	2^3
13	3,455,694	13	3^4
14	630,343	14	9^6
15	1,953,252		
16	1,192,296		
17	5,038,836		
18	782,760		
19	8,052,375		
20	3,588,480		

Pg 42	
No.	Answer
1	9 x 9 x 9 = 729
2	5 x 5 x 5 x 5 x 5 = 3,125
3	8 x 8 x 8 x 8 = 4,096
4	2 x 2 x 2 x 2 x 2 x 2 x 2 x 2 x 2 = 512
5	6 x 6 x 6 x 6 = 1,296
6	4 x 4 x 4 x 4 x 4 = 1,024

Pg 43	
No.	**Answer**
1	8 x 8 = 64
2	6 x 6 x 6 x 6 x 6 = 7,776
3	7 x 7 x 7 x 7 = 2,401
4	3 x 3 x 3 x 3 x 3 x 3 x 3 x 3 = 6,561
5	4 x 4 x 4 = 64
6	5 x 5 x 5 x 5 x 5 = 3,125

Pg 44	
No.	**Answer**
1	9 < 16
2	64 > 9
3	16 < 25
4	7,776 > 64
5	27 > 25
6	125 > 49
7	4,096 > 125
8	216 < 729
9	256 < 4,096
10	25 < 81
11	343 > 4
12	256 > 9
13	512 > 16
14	81 < 729
15	36 < 49

Chapter 3 – Division

Pg 47		Pg 48		Pg 49		Pg 50	
No.	**Answer**	**No.**	**Answer**	**No.**	**Answer**	**No.**	**Answer**
1	16 r 1	1	13 r 2	1	8 trips	1	367 r 1
2	7 r 3	2	12 r 3	2	5 days	2	297 r 1
3	12 r 5	3	17 r 2	3	7 apples	3	134
4	45 r 1	4	10 r 2	4	9 cookies		
5	24 r 3	5	39				
6	14 r 2	6	11 r 3				
7	11 r 3	7	14 r 3				
8	33 r 1	8	21 r 1				
		9	15 r 1				
		10	41 r 1				
		11	10 r 7				
		12	12 r 5				

Pg 51		Pg 52		Pg 53	
No.	**Answer**	**No.**	**Answer**	**No.**	**Answer**
1	153 r 2	1	65 r 7	1	1,241 r 2
2	32	2	68 r 4	2	569 r 5
3	196	3	129 r 4	3	1,522 r 1
4	139 r 2	4	338 r 1	4	630 r 1
5	90 r 5	5	21 r 2	5	1,325 r 3
6	148 r 4	6	250	6	2,178 r 3
7	188	7	104 r 1	7	632
8	148 r 1	8	122 r 6	8	968 r 1
9	207 r 1	9	37 r 4	9	450 r 4
10	232 r 2	10	275 r 2	10	1,867 r 1
11	111 r 1	11	113 r 1	11	1,142 r 2
12	140 r 6	12	368	12	999 r 3
13	423	13	84 r 12		
14	44 r 2	14	25		
15	204	15	87 r 1		
16	138	16	95 r 3		
17	192 r 2	17	453 r 1		
18	69 r 4	18	83 r 3		
19	75 r 6	19	97 r 2		
20	149 r 3	20	157		

Pg 54		Pg 55		Pg 56	
No.	**Answer**	**No.**	**Answer**	**No.**	**Answer**
1	8,447 r 3	1	4540 r 3	1	52 Hours
2	21,624	2	15,337 r 3	2	13 Days
3	7,325 r 1	3	2,160 r 3	3	51 Hours
4	44,652 r 1	4	8,502 r 4	4	119 Sections
5	7,338 r 6	5	32,380 r 1		
6	18,027 r 4	6	10,381 r 4		
7	9,025	7	24,623 r 2		
8	18,327	8	10,136 r 7		
9	19,560 r 1	9	13,302		
10	4,050 r 6	10	8,324 r 3		
11	16,634 r 3	11	3,439 r 5		
12	7,800 r 7	12	14,152 r 4		

Pg 57		Pg 58		Pg 59	
No.	**Answer**	**No.**	**Answer**	**No.**	**Answer**
1	21 r 8	1	22 r 5	1	207
2	19 r 10	2	24 r 18	2	148 r 6
3	20 r 9	3	20 r 9	3	137 r 40
4	37 r 5	4	5 r 4	4	111 r 27
5	15 r 24	5	43 r 1	5	226 r 12
6	13 r 24	6	22 r 7	6	259 r 11
7	16 r 16	7	22 r 4	7	213 r 14
8	12 r 9	8	22 r 9	8	291 r 3
9	10 r 53	9	21 r 20	9	203 r 30
10	19 r 19	10	17 r 8	10	118 r 3
		11	10 r 22	11	161 r 17
		12	10 r 26	12	205 r 10
		13	28 r 9		
		14	38 r 5		
		15	23 r 8		
		16	15 r 15		
		17	3		
		18	18 r 3		
		19	7 r 5		
		20	2 r 63		

Pg 60		Pg 61	
No.	Answer	No.	Answer
1	3,229 r 8	1	2,280 r 6
2	2,502 r 29	2	2,268 r 10
3	1,686 r 32	3	1,278 r 3
4	2,237 r 20	4	1,055 r 13
5	2,122 r 17	5	1,357 r 21
6	585 r 7	6	1,189 r 81
7	3,018 r 23	7	459 r 12
8	1,791 r 26	8	1,029 r 5
9	543 r 35	9	1,345 r 15
10	1,057 r 63	10	942 r 87
11	1,128 r 11	11	1,050 r 35
12	1,629 r 9	12	1,113 r 9

Pg 63		Pg 64	
No.	Answer	No.	Answer
1	$\frac{13}{15}$	1	$\frac{21}{73}$
2	$\frac{23}{37}$	2	$\frac{7}{28}$
3	$\frac{49}{80}$	3	$\frac{22}{89}$
4	$\frac{100}{109}$	4	$\frac{20}{146}$
5	$\frac{30}{64}$	5	$\frac{114}{634}$
6	$\frac{14}{21}$	6	$\frac{4}{12}$
7	$\frac{383}{865}$	7	$\frac{283}{759}$
8	$\frac{33}{55}$	8	$\frac{26}{56}$
9	$\frac{10}{13}$	9	$\frac{79}{207}$
10	$\frac{45}{74}$	10	$\frac{13}{49}$
11	$\frac{238}{250}$	11	$\frac{167}{277}$
12	$\frac{7}{94}$	12	$\frac{238}{534}$
		13	$\frac{66}{88}$
		14	$\frac{39}{129}$
		15	$\frac{189}{952}$

Pg 65	
No.	**Answer**
1	Tomatoes: $\frac{13}{28}$ Eggplants: $\frac{6}{28}$ Potatoes: $\frac{9}{28}$
2	Blue Jays: $\frac{3}{15}$ Sparrows: $\frac{9}{15}$ Ducks: $\frac{6}{15}$ Eagles: $\frac{1}{15}$
3	Bass: $\frac{2}{17}$ Trout: $\frac{6}{17}$ Guppies: $\frac{5}{17}$ Goldfish: $\frac{4}{17}$
4	Hamburgers: $\frac{15}{76}$ Chicken Wings: $\frac{22}{76}$ Sausages: $\frac{39}{76}$

Chapter 4 - Fractions

Pg 66

$\frac{1}{4}$ 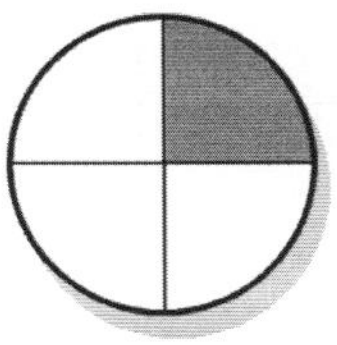 = $\frac{2}{8}$ 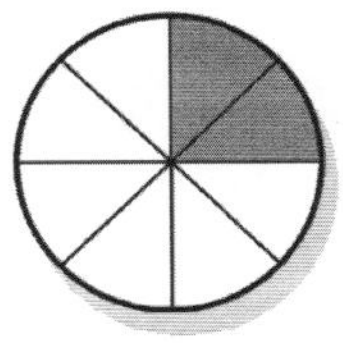

$\frac{2}{4}$ 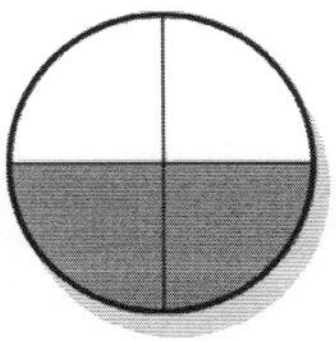 = $\frac{4}{8}$ 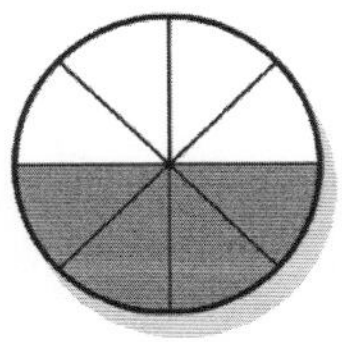

$\frac{3}{8}$ 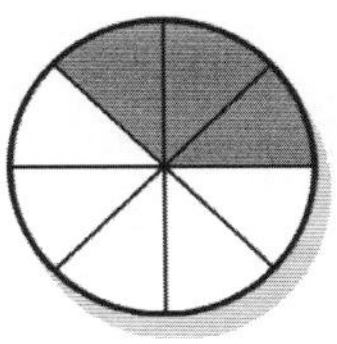 = $\frac{6}{16}$ 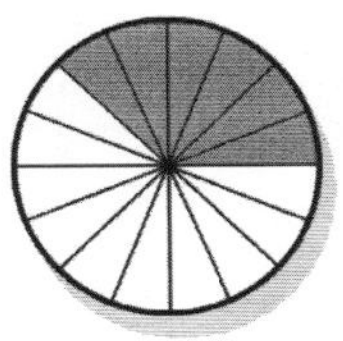

$\frac{5}{8}$ 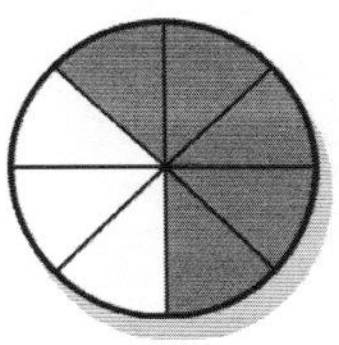 = $\frac{10}{16}$ 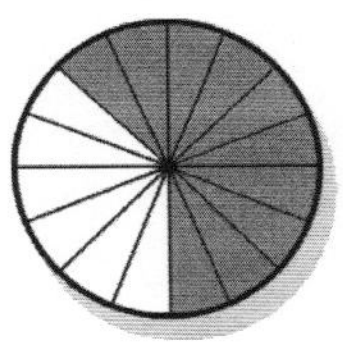

Pg 67		Pg 68		Pg 69	
No.	Answer	No.	Answer	No.	Answer
1	$\frac{9}{9}, \frac{2}{3}$	1	$\frac{3}{5}, \frac{4}{5}$	1	$\frac{5}{7} + \frac{2}{7} = \frac{7}{7}$
2	$\frac{4}{4}, \frac{1}{3}$	2	$\frac{4}{6}, \frac{5}{6}$	2	$\frac{1}{5} + \frac{2}{5} = \frac{3}{5}$
3	$\frac{5}{5}, \frac{4}{7}$	3	$\frac{3}{7}, \frac{5}{7}$	3	$\frac{7}{10} + \frac{2}{10} = \frac{9}{10}$
4	$\frac{3}{3}, \frac{3}{8}$	4	$\frac{3}{8}, \frac{6}{8}$	4	$\frac{10}{12} + \frac{2}{12} = \frac{12}{12}$
5	$\frac{3}{3}, \frac{5}{7}$	5	$\frac{3}{5}, \frac{2}{5}$	5	$\frac{2}{9} + \frac{3}{9} = \frac{5}{9}$
6	$\frac{8}{8}, \frac{2}{5}$	6	$\frac{3}{4}, \frac{2}{4}$	6	$\frac{5}{7} + \frac{2}{7} = \frac{7}{7}$
7	$\frac{5}{5}, \frac{2}{5}$	7	$\frac{5}{7}, \frac{2}{7}$	7	$\frac{6}{9} + \frac{1}{9} = \frac{7}{9}$
8	$\frac{4}{4}, \frac{4}{9}$	8	$\frac{8}{9}, \frac{4}{9}$	8	$\frac{9}{12} + \frac{2}{12} = \frac{11}{12}$
9	$\frac{6}{6}, \frac{2}{5}$			9	$\frac{6}{7} + \frac{4}{7} = \frac{10}{7}$
10	$\frac{9}{9}, \frac{1}{3}$			10	$\frac{7}{8} + \frac{1}{8} = \frac{8}{8}$
11	$\frac{2}{2}, \frac{4}{7}$			11	$\frac{3}{9} + \frac{5}{9} = \frac{8}{9}$
12	$\frac{16}{16}, \frac{1}{2}$			12	$\frac{9}{10} + \frac{7}{10} = \frac{16}{10}$

Pg 70		Pg 71		Pg 72	
No.	Answer	No.	Answer	No.	Answer
1	$\frac{12}{18}-\frac{4}{18}=\frac{8}{18}$	1	$\frac{2}{2}$	1	12
2	$\frac{4}{7}-\frac{1}{7}=\frac{3}{7}$	2	$\frac{3}{3}$	2	12
3	$\frac{7}{9}-\frac{4}{9}=\frac{3}{9}$	3	$\frac{4}{4}$	3	10
4	$\frac{4}{5}-\frac{3}{5}=\frac{1}{5}$	4	$\frac{3}{3}$	4	40
5	$\frac{3}{7}-\frac{2}{7}=\frac{1}{7}$	5	$\frac{8}{8}$	5	5
6	$\frac{6}{7}-\frac{5}{7}=\frac{1}{7}$	6	$\frac{5}{5}$	6	90
7	$\frac{9}{9}-\frac{6}{9}=\frac{3}{9}$	7	$\frac{3}{3}$	7	80
8	$\frac{8}{9}-\frac{3}{9}=\frac{5}{9}$	8	$\frac{11}{11}$	8	16
9	$\frac{6}{7}-\frac{3}{7}=\frac{3}{7}$	9	$\frac{9}{9}$	9	28
10	$\frac{8}{9}-\frac{2}{9}=\frac{6}{9}$			10	90
11	$\frac{5}{6}-\frac{2}{6}=\frac{3}{6}$			11	14
12	$\frac{8}{9}-\frac{5}{9}=\frac{3}{9}$			12	55
				13	128
				14	15
				15	50
				16	80
				17	12
				18	15
				19	6
				20	16

Pg 73		Pg 74	
No.	Answer	No.	Answer
1	$\frac{4}{8}+\frac{1}{8}=\frac{5}{8}$	1	$\frac{10}{20}-\frac{6}{20}=\frac{4}{20}$
2	$\frac{4}{12}+\frac{6}{12}=\frac{10}{12}$	2	$\frac{14}{15}-\frac{12}{15}=\frac{2}{15}$
3	$\frac{6}{21}+\frac{5}{21}=\frac{11}{21}$	3	$\frac{13}{18}-\frac{6}{18}=\frac{7}{18}$
4	$\frac{4}{28}+\frac{21}{28}=\frac{25}{28}$	4	$\frac{35}{40}-\frac{20}{40}=\frac{15}{40}$
5	$\frac{30}{50}+\frac{12}{50}=\frac{42}{50}$	5	$\frac{40}{48}-\frac{29}{48}=\frac{11}{48}$
6	$\frac{6}{24}+\frac{15}{24}=\frac{21}{24}$	6	$\frac{16}{24}-\frac{15}{24}=\frac{1}{24}$
7	$\frac{21}{48}+\frac{16}{48}=\frac{37}{48}$	7	$\frac{36}{49}-\frac{21}{49}=\frac{15}{49}$
8	$\frac{45}{81}+\frac{12}{81}=\frac{57}{81}$	8	$\frac{45}{54}-\frac{29}{54}=\frac{16}{54}$
9	$\frac{9}{36}+\frac{18}{36}=\frac{27}{36}$	9	$\frac{63}{81}-\frac{54}{81}=\frac{9}{81}$
10	$\frac{28}{63}+\frac{5}{63}=\frac{33}{63}$	10	$\frac{54}{63}-\frac{35}{63}=\frac{19}{63}$
11	$\frac{39}{72}+\frac{24}{72}=\frac{63}{72}$	11	$\frac{27}{48}-\frac{24}{48}=\frac{3}{48}$
12	$\frac{17}{56}+\frac{35}{56}=\frac{52}{56}$	12	$\frac{70}{100}-\frac{50}{100}=\frac{20}{100}$

Pg 75	
No.	**Answer**
1	$5\frac{10}{12}$
2	$6\frac{4}{9}$
3	$7\frac{4}{5}$
4	$2\frac{20}{23}$
5	$13\frac{6}{8}$
6	$13\frac{10}{15}$
7	$13\frac{30}{39}$
8	$12\frac{9}{10}$
9	$4\frac{5}{19}$
10	$3\frac{5}{8}$
11	$3\frac{6}{16}$
12	$5\frac{4}{6}$
13	$5\frac{4}{25}$
14	$11\frac{1}{10}$
15	$8\frac{27}{44}$

Pg 76		Pg 77	
No.	Answer	No.	Answer
1	$5\frac{5}{10} = 5\frac{1}{2}$	1	$\frac{13}{3}$
2	$9\frac{9}{12} = 9\frac{3}{4}$	2	$\frac{38}{4}$
3	$9\frac{6}{18} = 9\frac{1}{3}$	3	$\frac{13}{2}$
4	$8\frac{4}{8} = 8\frac{1}{2}$	4	$\frac{32}{5}$
5	$12\frac{12}{24} = 12\frac{1}{2}$	5	$\frac{95}{10}$
6	$15\frac{18}{36} = 15\frac{1}{2}$	6	$\frac{21}{5}$
7	$11\frac{21}{56} = 11\frac{3}{8}$	7	$\frac{25}{7}$
8	$14\frac{45}{81} = 14\frac{5}{9}$	8	$\frac{14}{3}$
9	$3\frac{8}{16} = 3\frac{1}{2}$	9	$\frac{26}{5}$
10	$12\frac{4}{12} = 12\frac{1}{3}$	10	$\frac{30}{3}$
11	$8\frac{14}{28} = 8\frac{1}{2}$	11	$\frac{27}{5}$
12	$12\frac{6}{9} = 12\frac{2}{3}$	12	$\frac{18}{8}$
13	$39\frac{28}{42} = 39\frac{2}{3}$	13	$\frac{52}{5}$
14	$18\frac{18}{63} = 18\frac{2}{7}$	14	$\frac{27}{3}$
15	$25\frac{12}{21} = 25\frac{4}{7}$	15	$\frac{69}{11}$
16	$11\frac{20}{50} = 11\frac{2}{5}$	16	$\frac{16}{3}$
		17	$\frac{37}{22}$
		18	$\frac{24}{9}$
		19	$\frac{34}{4}$
		20	$\frac{32}{3}$

Pg 78	
No.	Answer
1	7
2	4
3	3
4	9
5	8
6	31
7	5
8	42
9	$2\frac{3}{6}$
10	$2\frac{2}{4}$
11	$3\frac{1}{2}$
12	$2\frac{3}{8}$
13	$5\frac{3}{4}$
14	$8\frac{2}{3}$
15	$5\frac{5}{9}$
16	$5\frac{6}{8}$

Chapter 5 – Decimals

Pg 80		Pg 81		Pg 82		Pg 83	
No.	**Answer**	**No.**	**Answer**	**No.**	**Answer**	**No.**	**Answer**
1	10.83	1	19.44	1	40.365	1	971.2
2	11.55	2	17.82	2	16.728	2	522.16
3	17.01	3	18.61	3	108.352	3	233.49
4	74.83	4	22.83	4	13.774	4	480.18
5	71.38	5	264.57	5	68.174	5	1,535.15
6	71.22	6	85.62	6	131.437	6	856.17
		7	93.31	7	109.184	7	839.27
		8	115.88	8	116.236	8	829.72
		9	1,000.77	9	77.166	9	1,019.78

Pg 84		Pg 85	
No.	**Answer**	**No.**	**Answer**
1	points: 75.4 rebounds: 16.2	1	165.93
2	18.5	2	130.62
3	19.55	3	337.26
4	40.34	4	443.47
		5	898.79
		6	1,328.24
		7	913.05
		8	1,676.61
		9	98.011
		10	47.257
		11	134.537
		12	110.116
		13	752.03
		14	1,591.924
		15	1,292.80
		16	675.154
		17	1,161.326
		18	1,130.321
		19	1,107.368
		20	1,526.574

Pg 86		Pg 87		Pg 88		Pg 89	
No.	**Answer**	**No.**	**Answer**	**No.**	**Answer**	**No.**	**Answer**
1	2,292.203	1	8,947.33	1	4.55	1	49.97
2	1,024.508	2	14,437.96	2	13.45	2	27.68
3	2,369.367	3	10,098.36	3	27.4	3	13.89
4	1,589.946	4	9,065.53	4	559.93	4	15.96
5	1,602.404	5	20,055.64	5	88.65	5	1.17
6	2,443.596	6	14,216.45	6	298.91	6	30.6
7	2,241.336	7	12,316.47			7	18.17
8	1,953.052	8	8,814.81			8	46.75
9	1,862.583	9	10,754.98			9	17.56
10	2,328.303	10	13,061.62				
11	1,192.89	11	10,903.89				
12	2,315.809	12	11,889.87				
13	3,293.375	13	23,148.84				
14	2,686.997	14	12,299.29				
15	2,241.406	15	10,762.47				
16	2,921.589	16	23,018.72				

Pg 90		Pg 91		Pg 92		Pg 93	
No.	**Answer**	**No.**	**Answer**	**No.**	**Answer**	**No.**	**Answer**
1	592.45	1	79.312	1	49.33	1	883.23
2	802.22	2	36.252	2	326.39	2	2,100.45
3	293.5	3	55.411	3	105.26	3	4,459.81
4	37.64	4	60.407	4	123.73	4	2,713.83
5	112.21	5	11.221	5	241.84	5	5,062.25
6	466.93	6	338.301	6	341.48	6	7,294.40
7	499.62	7	16.151	7	347.08	7	5,944.50
8	103.94	8	6.905	8	169.62	8	1,416.89
9	279.49	9	579.732	9	534.35	9	2,339.55
				10	465.36	10	4,778.22
				11	87.14	11	2,424.61
				12	33.44	12	1,172.31
				13	44.791	13	452.891
				14	20.014	14	632.574
				15	13.269	15	626.454
				16	5.9	16	316.231
				17	21.28	17	94.845
				18	36.574	18	202.634
				19	42.545	19	153.408
				20	25.487	20	561.034

Pg 94		Pg 95		Pg 96		Pg 97	
No.	**Answer**	**No.**	**Answer**	**No.**	**Answer**	**No.**	**Answer**
1	17.3123	1	1.35	1	$152.40	1	$519.58
2	39.8811	2	26.82	2	$328.14	2	$333.97
3	21.4554	3	53.96	3	$387.76	3	$777.29
4	45.6271	4	2.41	4	$227.07	4	$642.55
5	164.069			5	$447.00	5	$928.53
6	168.894			6	$1,433.61	6	$1,528.24
7	20.514			7	$585.61	7	$1,213.41
8	109.208			8	$1,281.75	8	$1,605.84
9	10,213.10			9	$889.47	9	$702.13
10	1,588.44			10	$1,343.92	10	$1,236.92
11	6,203.53			11	$771.90	11	$1,142.83
12	5.35945			12	$1,076.38	12	$978.09
13	2,176.26			13	$1,452.60	13	$2,496.52
14	202.851			14	$1,132.89	14	$2,007.13
15	2.03419			15	$1,109.55	15	$2,701.26
16	12.2159			16	$882.25	16	$2,751.54
17	74,083.40					17	1,364.77
18	20,618.30					18	$1,139.83
19	13,601.50					19	$1,405.49
20	1,078.77					20	$1,875.55

Pg 98		Pg 99		Pg 100		Pg 101	
No.	Answer	No.	Answer	No.	Answer	No.	Answer
1	$2.38	1	$167.57	1	53.12	1	22.737
2	$3.35	2	$235.72	2	9.57	2	5.891
3	$1.85	3	$221.39	3	29.48	3	4.446
4	$2.47	4	$205.16	4	21.24	4	34.368
5	$5.31	5	$335.66	5	13.05	5	19.032
6	$1.79	6	$685.64	6	56.95	6	27.36
7	$3.82	7	$141.12	7	13.23	7	35.336
8	$4.63	8	$65.73	8	60.76	8	1,440.60
9	$2.86	9	$213.18	9	44.66	9	8.2917
10	$2.14	10	$508.08	10	77.9	10	194.88
11	$1.75	11	$62.57	11	65.12	11	.24153
12	$4.22	12	$671.71	12	33.63	12	995.9
13	$59.09	13	$275.12	13	30.38	13	32.074
14	$104.35	14	$488.63	14	10.75	14	293.26
15	$76.62	15	$34.40	15	33.93	15	6.6744
16	$222.33	16	$524.21			16	185.52
17	$451.09	17	$212.65			17	2.058
18	$321.63	18	$175.49			18	223.29
19	$441.51	19	$248.53			19	5,603.40
20	$82.86	20	$216.79			20	4.0736
						21	31.524
						22	395.34
						23	26.978
						24	19.91
						25	442.96

Pg 102		Pg 103	
No.	Answer	No.	Answer
1	124.576	1	938.448
2	14.5497	2	357.7665
3	1,656.86	3	449.709
4	167.678	4	1.831536
5	42.526	5	5696.46
6	14.1327	6	1,242.448
7	340.548	7	318.8694
8	110.451	8	304.3408
9	927.5	9	1,371.806
10	24.2934	10	404.9125
11	7303.12	11	248.5998
12	1,762.18	12	27,895.43
13	360.549	13	86.8795
14	509.819	14	185.8618
15	270.338	15	257.2271
16	262.145	16	54,917.25
17	1,653.75	17	624.9639
18	78.4101	18	6,041.386
19	55.062	19	107.1348
20	192.576	20	41,661.18
21	8,360.52		
22	8,045.73		
23	35.1978		
24	27.6216		
25	745.129		

Chapter 6 – Geometry

Pg 108		Pg 109	
No.	**Answer**	**No.**	**Answer**
1	74 x 74 = 5,476 in.^{2}	1	11in. x 6in. ÷ 2 = 33 in.^{2}
2	134ft. x 749ft. = 100,366 ft.^{2}	2	12ft. x 17ft. ÷ 2 = 102 ft.^{2}
3	205in. x 205in. = 42,025 in.^{2}	3	5in. x 14in. ÷ 2 = 35 in.^{2}
4	299ft. x 436ft. = 130,364 ft.^{2}	4	75in. x 46in. ÷ 2 =1,72 5in.^{2}
5	637in. x 637in. = 405,769 in.^{2}	5	94in. x 89in. ÷ 2 = 4,183 in.^{2}
6	507yd. x 1,262yd. = 639,834 yd.^{2}	6	112ft. x 156ft. ÷ 2 = 8,736 ft.^{2}

Pg 110		Pg 111	
No.	**Answer**	**No.**	**Answer**
1	6 x 6 = 36 ft.^{2}	1	6 + 9 x 6 ÷ 2 = 45 yds.^{2}
2	13 x 5 = 65 in.^{2}	2	24 + 16 x 8 ÷ 2 = 160 ft.^{2}
3	15 x 17 = 255 ft.^{2}	3	20 + 32 x 12 ÷ 2 = 312 in.^{2}
4	75 x 45 = 3,375 ft.^{2}	4	55 + 110 x 40 ÷ 2 = 3,300 ft.^{2}
5	136 x 115 = 15,640 in.^{2}	5	136 + 175 x 212 ÷ 2 = 32,966 in.^{2}
6	563 x 599 = 337,237 ft.^{2}	6	250 + 210 x 88 ÷ 2 = 20,240 in.^{2}

Pg 112		Pg 113	
No.	Answer	No.	Answer
1	55 + 36 + 42 + 67 = 197 yd.	1	12 + 4 + 4 + 6 + 8 + 10 = 44 yd.
2	125 + 89 + 89 + 125 = 428 ft.	2	4 + 13 + 1 + 12 + 15 = 45 ft.
3	123 + 215 + 107 + 324 = 769 in.	3	88 + 200 + 96 + 88 + 105 + 88 + 411 = 1,076 in.
4	75 + 347 + 62 + 289 +101 = 874 ft.	4	8 + 8 + 8 + 8 + 8 + 8 + 8 + 8 = 64 ft.
5	572 + 635 + 468 = 1,675 in.	5	20 + 20 + 5 + 15 + 15 + 5 = 80 in.
6	917 + 234 + 705 + 917 = 2,773 yd.	6	35 + 4 + 17 + 20 + 19 + 15 + 4 = 114 in.
		7	60 + 55 + 34 + 27 + 10 = 186 ft.
		8	7 + 18 + 19 + 7 + 22 + 8 + 23 = 104 in.
		9	100 + 100 + 25 + 25 + 27 + 50 + 25 = 352 yd.

Pg 114	
No.	**Answer**
1	vertex- 1, ray- 2, point- 3
2	vertex-1, line segment-2, point -5
3	line-1, ray-2, point-2
4	line-1, ray-2, vertex-1, point-2
5	ray-3, vertex-2, point-4
6	ray-1, line segment-1, vertex-1, point-4
7	ray- 3, vertex-2, point-4
8	ray-2, line-2, point-2

Pg 115			
No.	**Answer**		
1	Angle: ABC	Vertex: B	Rays: AB, CB
2	Angle: 123	Vertex: 2	Rays: 12, 23
3	Angle: QRS	Vertex: R	Rays: SR, QR
4	Angle: XYZ	Vertex: Y	Rays: XY, YZ
5	Angle: 456	Vertex: 5	Rays: 45, 56
6	Angle: EFG	Vertex: F	Rays: EF, EG
7	Angle: MNO	Vertex: N	Rays: MN, NO
8	Angle: 678	Vertex: 7	Rays: 67, 78
9	Angle: DEF	Vertex: E	Rays: FE, DE
10	Angle: 789	Vertex: 8	Rays: 78, 89
11	Angle: 012	Vertex: 1	Rays: 01, 12
12	Angle: UVW	Vertex: V	Rays: UV, VW

Pg 117

1. Pyramid
   a. 4
   b.6
   c. 4

2. Cylinder
   a. 0
   b. 2
   c. 3

3. Cube
   a. 8
   b. 12
   c. 6

Pg 118

1. Cone
   a. 1
   b. 1
   c. 2

2. Cuboid
   a. 8
   b. 12
   c. 6

3. Pyramid
   a. 5
   b. 8
   c. 5

Pg 120			
No.	**Answer**		
1	Circle: A	Radius: AB, AC, AD	Diameter: BC
2	Circle: E	Radius: EF, EH, EG	Diameter: FG
3	Circle: X	Radius: XW, XZ, XY	Diameter: WY
4	Circle: R	Radius: RQ, RS,RT	Diameter: QT
5	Circle: M	Radius: ML, MN, MO	Diameter: LO
6	Circle: X	Radius: XR, XA, XP	Diameter: AR

Pg 121		Pg 122	
No.	**Answer**	**No.**	**Answer**
1	18 ÷ 2 = 9 cm.	1	12 x 2 = 24 in.
2	36 ÷ 2 = 18 in.	2	29 x 2 = 58 cm.
3	112 ÷ 2 = 56 ft.	3	89 x 2 = 178 ft.
4	388 ÷ 2 = 194 in.	4	113 x 2 = 226 cm.
5	956 ÷ 2 = 478 ft.	5	624 x 2 = 1,24 in.
6	3,624 ÷ 2 = 1,812 cm.	6	2,935x 2 = 5,870 ft.

Pg 123	
No.	**Answer**
1	345.4 in.
2	226.08 cm.
3	942 ft.
4	120.89 ft.
5	3,337.192 in.
6	21.64716 cm.

Chapter 7 - Graphs

Pg 126		Pg 127	
No.	**Answer**	**No.**	**Answer**
1	Game 5	1	60
2	Game 1	2	35
3	52 Goals	3	45
4	4 Goals	4	30
5	7 Goals	5	45
6	16 Goals	6	50
7	25 Goals	7	65
8	Games 2 and 8	8	25
		9	40
		10	20
		11	25
		12	5
		13	25
		14	5
		15	20
		16	30
		17	45
		18	10

Pg 128

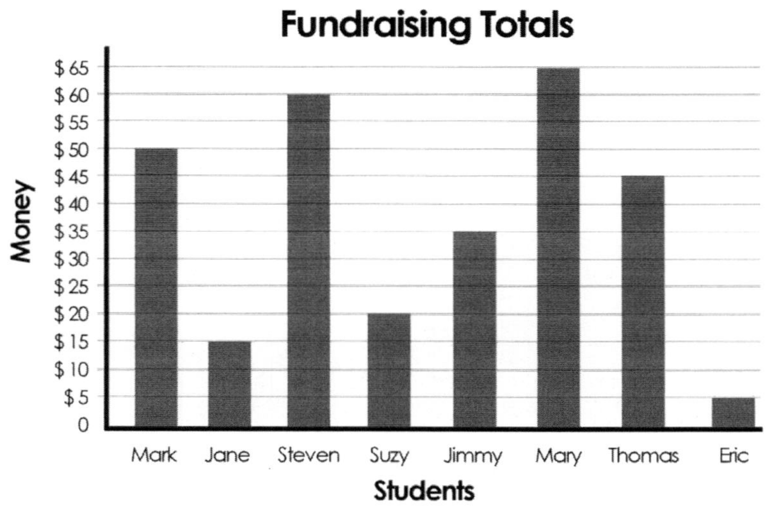

Pg 128	
No.	**Answer**
1	$45
2	$20
3	$15
4	$35
5	$50
6	$60
7	$65
8	$5
9	$55
10	$15
11	$15
12	$45
13	$45
14	$30

Pg 129	
No.	**Answer**
1	2012
2	2011
3	85 degrees
4	50 degrees
5	55 degrees
6	Feb
7	July
8	5 degrees
9	90 degrees
10	60 degrees
11	55 degrees
12	10 degrees
13	Stayed the same
14	2011

Pg 130

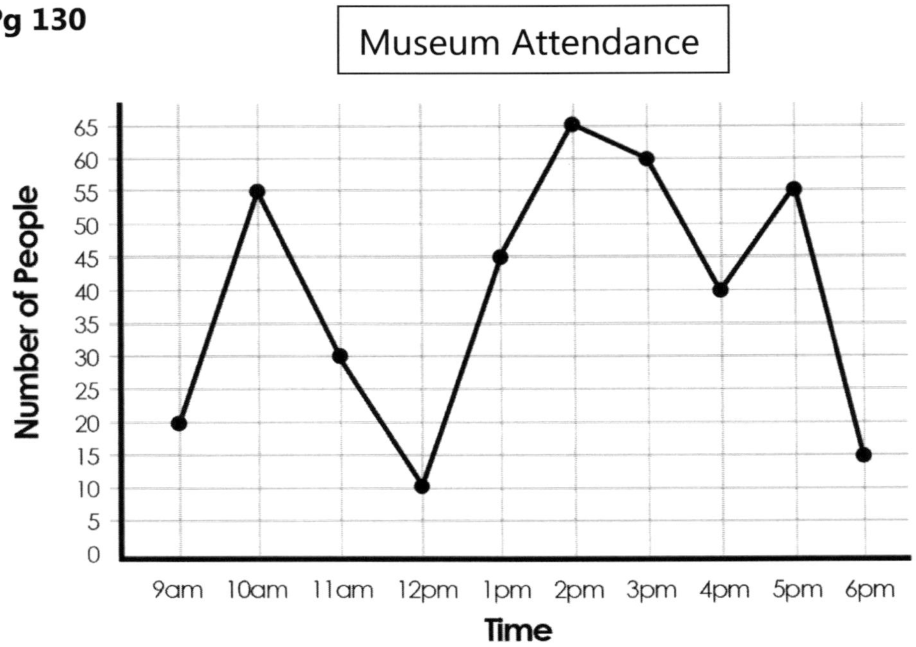

Pg 130	
No.	**Answer**
1	2pm
2	12pm
3	10
4	20
5	40
6	25
7	20
8	40
9	12pm - 1pm
10	5pm - 6pm

Pg 131	
No.	**Answer**
1	A10, C10, C7, E7
2	E10, I10, F7, H7
3	J10, J8, O10, O8
4	Q7, S10, T7
5	A6, A4, B4, B3, D3, D6
6	B2, B1, E5, E2, G5, G1
7	H6, H5, I7, I4, J7, J4, K6, K5
8	I3, I1, L3, O1
9	L7, L4, O5, O4, P7, P6, S6, S5
10	P2, Q4, Q1, S4, S1, T2

Pg 132

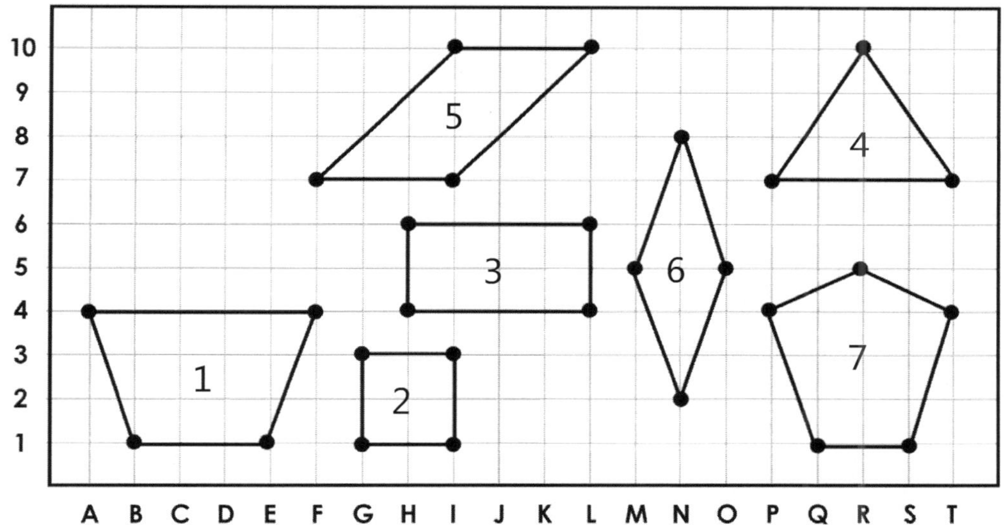

Pg 132	
No.	**Answer**
1	trapezoid
2	square
3	rectangle
4	triangle
5	parallelogram
6	rhombus
7	pentagon

Pg 133		Pg 135	
No.	**Answer**	**No.**	**Answer**
1	Art	1	Tennis shoes
2	Math	2	Tennis shoes
3	Science	3	Tennis shoes
4	Reading	4	Boots
5	Puppies	5	Sandals
6	Fish	6	Tennis shoes
7	Kittens	7	Boots
8	Gerbil	8	Boots
		9	Boots
		10	Sandals

Pg 136

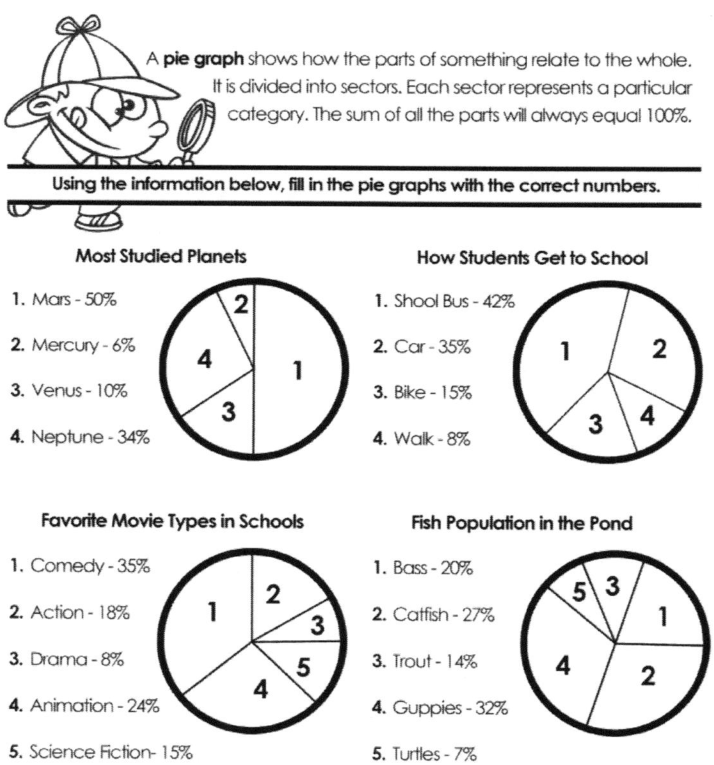
A **pie graph** shows how the parts of something relate to the whole. It is divided into sectors. Each sector represents a particular category. The sum of all the parts will always equal 100%.

Using the information below, fill in the pie graphs with the correct numbers.

Most Studied Planets

1. Mars - 50%
2. Mercury - 6%
3. Venus - 10%
4. Neptune - 34%

How Students Get to School

1. Shool Bus - 42%
2. Car - 35%
3. Bike - 15%
4. Walk - 8%

Favorite Movie Types in Schools

1. Comedy - 35%
2. Action - 18%
3. Drama - 8%
4. Animation - 24%
5. Science Fiction- 15%

Fish Population in the Pond

1. Bass - 20%
2. Catfish - 27%
3. Trout - 14%
4. Guppies - 32%
5. Turtles - 7%

Practice Test Answers

Practice Test #1

Answers and Explanations

1. A: The digit 5 is in the 5th column, which is the ten thousands column. Therefore the digit represents the value 50,000.

2. C: Robinson has the highest number of points. The number of goals and assists need to be added to determine this.

Player	Goals	Assists	Points
Phillips	2	23	25
Jackson	5	17	22
Robinson	13	15	28
Miller	8	19	27

3. B: $\frac{15}{4}$. The value of 3 is equivalent to $\frac{12}{4}$. Therefore, $3\frac{3}{4} = \frac{12}{4} + \frac{3}{4} = \frac{15}{4}$. Another way of
of finding this is sometimes called the "C" method. $3\frac{3}{4}$ equals $\frac{4\times3+3}{4} = \frac{15}{4}$.

4. C: The largest multiple of 12 less than 151 is 144. This means there are $151 - 144 = 7$ eggs left over.

5. C: Count from the 3: tenths, hundredths, thousandths.

6. D: A diagram of the plot would look like this:

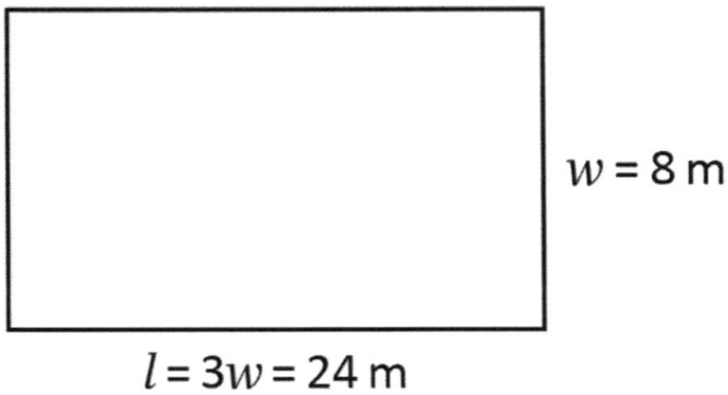

The perimeter of a rectangle is the formula $P = 2L + 2W$ which produces $2(24) + 2(8) = 48 + 16 = 64\ m$.

7. Part A: B: The pattern in the table is that the number of customers is increasing by 25 each week. This means that there should be $205 + 25 = 230$ customers expected in week 4.

Week	Customers
1	155
2	180
3	205
4	230

+25

+25

+25

Part B: $2760: From Part A you know there will be 230 people in week 4. If each meal is $12 then just multiply to get the answer. $230 \times 12 = 2760$

8. 3: The area of a rectangular prism is $A = L \times W \times H$. The problem gives *L, W,* and *A*. To get *H* just divide *A* by *L* and *W.* $144 \div 8 = 18 \div 6 = 3$. So *H*=3.

9. A: This is a simple subtraction problem with decimals. Line up the decimals and subtract 9 from 8. Since this can't be done, borrow 10 from the 5. Cross out the 5 and make it 4. Now subtract 9 from 18 to get 9. Subtract 3 from 4 and get 1. Place the decimal point before the 1.

10. D: The recipe is being multiplied by 4 in this problem, therefore $\frac{1}{8} = \frac{4}{32}$ so a total of 4 cups of milk are needed. Since this is not one of the choices, a conversion is needed. 1 pint = 2 cups and 1 quart = 2 pints, therefore 1 quart = 4 cups.

11. A: To solve a problem like this first find a least common denominator. For 2, 4, and 5 that would be 20. Then convert each fraction to twentieths. $\frac{2}{5} = \frac{8}{20}, \frac{3}{4} = \frac{15}{20}, and\ \frac{1}{2} = \frac{10}{20}$. Next perform the operations that were given. $\frac{8}{20} + \frac{15}{20} - \frac{10}{20} = \frac{13}{20}$.

12. A: To solve, test each answer. Notice that in (A), the numerator has been multiplied by 3 to get 12. The denominator has been multiplied by 3 to get 21. In (B) the numerator has been multiplied by 4 and the denominator has been multiplied by 5. In (C), the numerator has been multiplied by 3 and the denominator has been multiplied by 4. In (D), the numerator has been multiplied by 4 and the denominator has been multiplied by a number less than 4.

13. 10.92: $A = L \times W$, so multiplying $4.2 \times 2.6 = 10.92$. The area of the card is 10.92 sq inches.

14. B: The total number of Evercell batteries is $(4 \times E)$ and the total number of Durapower batteries is $(6 \times D)$. The sum of the two is the total number of batteries in the store.

15. 3.08: To find the total distance multiply the number of laps times the distance of one lap. $11 \times .28 = 3.08$

16. .375, .71, .85: $.3 \times 1.25 = .375$

$1.22 - .85 + .34 = .37 + .34 = .71$

$(.22 + 1.48) \times .5 = (1.7) \times .5 =..85$

17. B: One property of parallelograms is that the opposite sides are parallel. This means $\overline{QS} \parallel \overline{RT}$.

18. A: The rectangular prism volume formula $V = l \times w \times h$ is used here. $210 = 7 \times 5 \times h$. Dividing both sides by 35 gives the answer $h = 6$ inches.

19. Divide the number of yards by 1760, the number of yards in 1 mile. $\frac{18335}{1760} \approx \mathbf{10.42}$ miles.

20. B: There are 36 out of 100 yellow cars in the sample. Since the parking lot has $\frac{1}{4}$ as many cars as the sample, $\frac{1}{4}$ as many yellow cars should be expected.

21. A: $C = \frac{3}{4}(100) + 20$. Since $\frac{1}{4}$ of the original \$100 was sent to the savings account, $\frac{3}{4}$ of the money was kept in cash. The bonus was then added afterward.

22. C: Use approximation to solve this problem quickly: $25 \times \$3 = \$75$. The actual cost to fill the tank was $25.2 \times \$2.98 = \$75.10$.

23. D: The order of operations is parentheses, exponents, multiply, divide, add, subtract. So for this problem it would be: $8 \times (5 - 2) + (4 + 5) = 8 \times 3 + 9 = 24 + 9 = 33$

24. C: Add the 1 hour and 30 minutes to find that Janice finishes her homework at 4:15 PM. Next, add 1 hour and 45 minutes to find that Janice returns home at 6:00 PM.

25. A: The simplest way to compare the two pieces of pie is to find a common dominator for both fractions. The older daughter was given 2/5 of the pie, while the younger daughter was given 1/3 of the pie. The least common dominator for the two fractions is 15. Therefore, the older daughter received 6/15 of the pie and the younger daughter received 5/15 of the pie. 6/15 is larger than 5/15; therefore, the older daughter received a larger slice of the pie.

26. 4.43: When a problem asks for the difference use subtraction. $14.67 - 10.24 = 4.43$.

27. A: Translate the point 5 units to the right and 4 units down to find the location of the lighthouse.

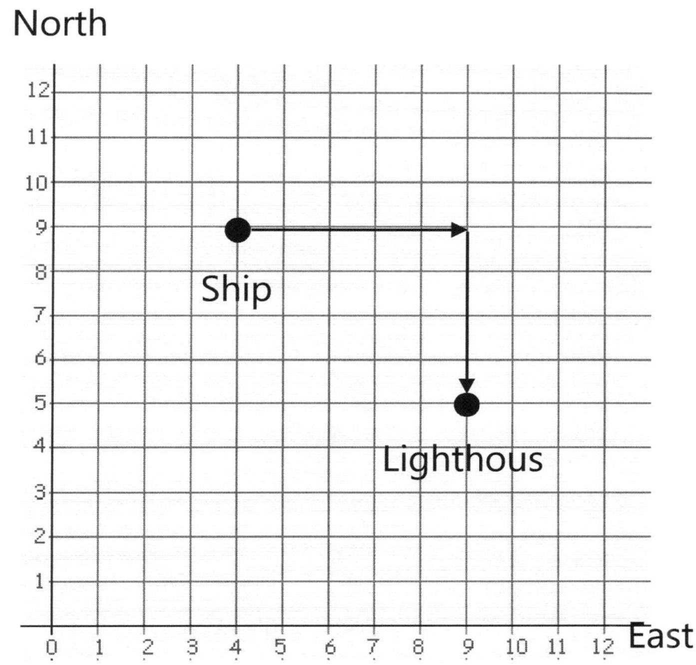

28. D: Plotting the values on a number line demonstrates that this is the only value not in the normal range.

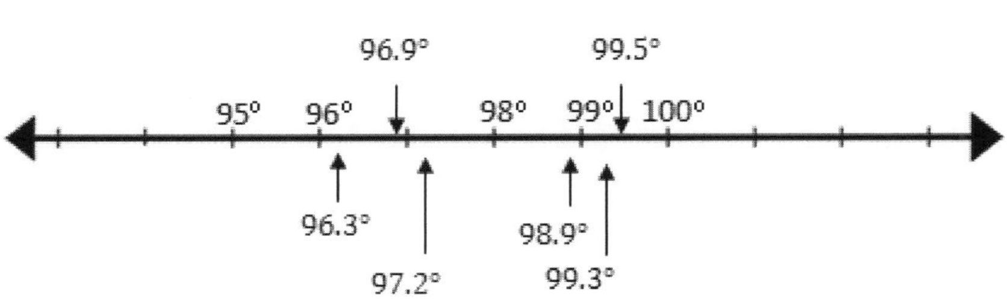

29. B: Use the formula for finding the mean: $\frac{sum\ of\ values}{number\ of\ values}$.

$$\frac{9+16+13+20+22}{5} = \frac{80}{5} = 16.$$

30.

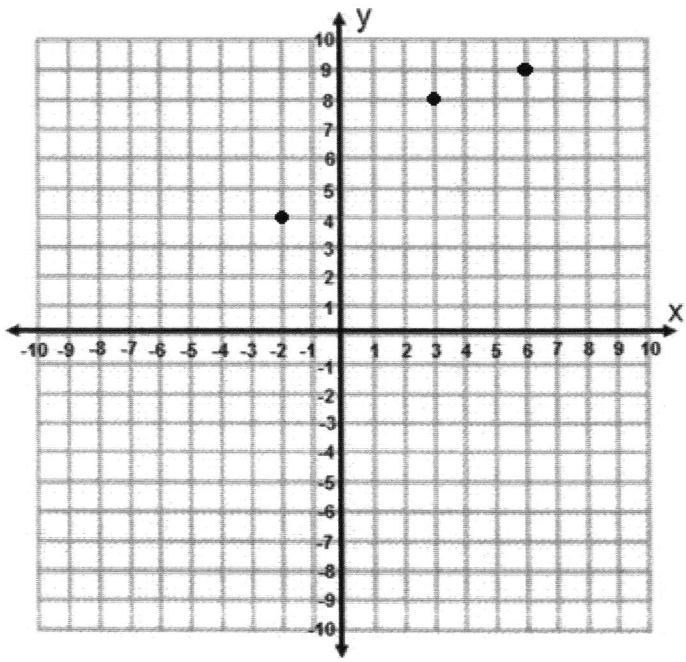

31. B: Divide 92 by 14. $92 \div 14 = 6\,R\,8$. Since 8 is not enough for another team, a total of 6 teams can be formed.

32. Part A: B: By the definition of an isosceles trapezoid, the legs (non-parallel sides) are congruent.

Part B: A: Since the figure is defined as an isosceles, it is known that $\overline{PS}$ and $\overline{QR}$ are parallel and not congruent in length.

33. C:
Expressing $\frac{31}{8} = 3\frac{7}{8}$ makes this easier to see.

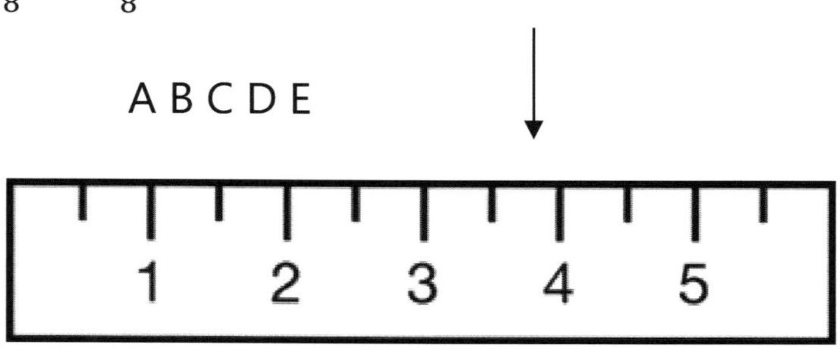

34. C: The points are marked on the figure below.

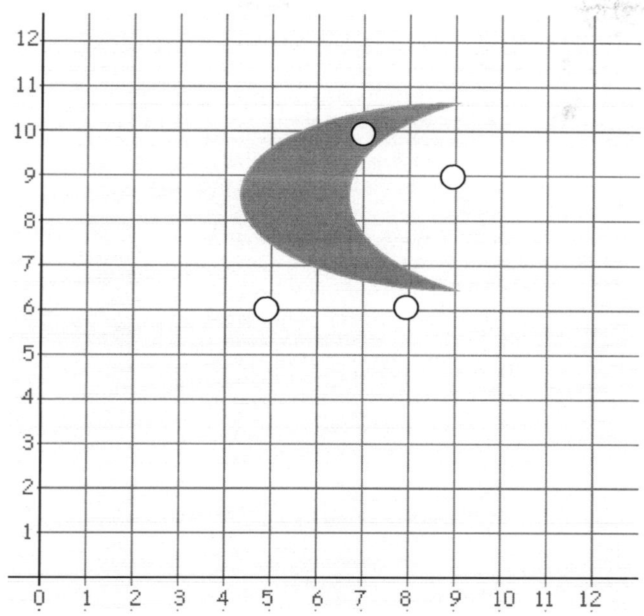

35. C: $1\frac{7}{10}$ is read as one and seven tenths. The 1 can be converted to an equivalent fraction of

$\frac{10}{10}$ and is shown as all ten parts of the first ten section are shaded. $\frac{7}{10}$ indicates that only seven of the ten parts are shaded in the second set of ten. Since the 7 is over the denominator of a ten and read as seven tenths, the seven should be placed in the tenths location when in decimal form. This is the first location to the right of the decimal. The correct decimal form for this is 1.7.

36. $26,150: The total amount they made from T.V.'s is $\$525 \times 36 = \$18{,}900$. The total that they make from game systems is $\$250 \times 29 = \$7{,}250$. $\$18{,}900 + \$7{,}250 = \$26{,}150$

37. B: Since the probability of being born in the spring or summer is being calculated, the probabilities are added. $\frac{7}{20} + \frac{3}{20} = \frac{10}{20} = \frac{1}{2}$.

38. D: Multiplying the number of weeks by 7 and then adding 5 more days gives the desired result. $7 \times 9 + 5 = 68$.

39. D: To find the difference, subtract. It is important to align decimal places. Note, when subtracting here, the digit in the hundredths place in 0.33 has no digit aligned above it. We must add a zero to 1.5 so that we can align the hundredths places correctly. Now we can subtract 33 hundredths from the 50 hundredths to get 17 hundredths. So, we get 1.17 as our correct answer.

40. B: There are 2 green sections on the spinner and the spinner has 6 sections in all. The probability of spinning green is 2 out of 6, when expressed as a fraction is $\frac{2}{6}$. Written in simplest terms, the fraction is $\frac{1}{3}$.

Practice Test #2

Answers and Explanations

1. D: Fifty-seven thousand is 57,000; adding the three hundred forty to that amount gives the correct answer: 57,340.

2. D: Construct a 3rd column representing improvement. This would be the second score minus the first score for each of the students. David has the greatest improvement of 20 words per minute between the two tests.

Student	First score (words per minute)	Second score (words per minute)	Improvement Second – First scores
Alexander	22	39	17
Betty	39	48	9
Carolyn	27	43	16
David	22	42	20

3. C: The value of 7 is equivalent to $\frac{56}{8}$. Therefore, $7\frac{5}{8} = \frac{56}{8} + \frac{5}{8} = \frac{61}{8}$. Another way of finding this is sometimes called the "C" method: $7\frac{5}{8}$ equals $\frac{8\times7+5}{8} = \frac{61}{8}$.

4. B: The largest multiple of 12 less than 141 is $12 \times 11 = 132$. This leaves $141 - 132 = 9$ donuts remaining.

5. C: Count from the 5: tenths, hundredths, thousandths.

6. 528: First find Donny's weight in pounds. So, 56-23=33, then it can be converted to ounces by multiplying times 16. $33 \times 16 = 528$.

7. A: Use the area formula for a square: $A = s^2$. Solve the equation: $81 = s^2$, $s = \pm 9$. Since the side of the garden is a length, it must be positive, $s = 9$ feet.

8. B: To solve, test each answer. Notice that in (A), the numerator has been multiplied by 9 to get 18. The denominator has been multiplied by 8. These are not equal fractions. In (C) the numerator has been multiplied by 4 and the denominator has been multiplied by 2. These are not equal fractions. In (D) the numerator has been multiplied by 3 and the denominator has been multiplied by 2. These are not equal fractions. In (B), both numerator and denominator have been multiplied by 4.

9. The hundredths place is the second number after the decimal point. When rounding 1-4 rounds down and 5-9 rounds up.

$3.116 \approx 3.12$

$3.081 \approx 3.08$

$3.006 \approx 3.01$

$3.107 \approx 3.11$

10. D: A trapezoid is a quadrilateral with only one pair of opposite sides parallel.
The other three figures in the problem are a rectangle, a rhombus, and a parallelogram (in that order).

11. B: The proportion given is that 1 gallon of cooking oil will make enough popcorn for 256 people, or 128 ounces serves 256 people. Notice that the amount of oil in ounces needed is exactly one half the number of people being served. This means 48 ounces are needed to serve 96 people. The equivalent amount listed in the choices is 3 pints.

12. B: Working the problem backwards, Jody had \$29 before she went to the movies. This was half of the money she made at the bake sale. This means $2 \times \$29 = \$58$ was made at the bake sale.

13. A: Since all the answers have a 7 as the whole number, multiply 7 x 14. The answer is 98. The remainder is 1.

14. D: Since the marbles are being equally distributed in 4 equal parts, each friend is simply receiving $\frac{1}{4}$ of the marbles.

15. Part A: 1248: To find the total number of rolls multiply the number of rolls in a package times the number of packages, then times the number of boxes. $8 \times 6 \times 26 = 1248$

Part B: 5: To find out how many shipments they need divide 6100 by 1248. $6100 \div 1248 \approx 4.89$. So they would need at least 5 shipments a month.

16. Part A: $\frac{5}{24}$: First you need like denominators. For 6 and 8 that would be 24. $\frac{5}{8} = \frac{15}{24}$ *and* $\frac{5}{6} = \frac{20}{24}$. So, the second one is $\frac{5}{24}$ bigger.

Part B: $2\frac{1}{24}$: To find the total you will also need to first find like denominators. In this case 24 will also work. So, $\frac{7}{12} = \frac{14}{24}$, then $\frac{15}{24} + \frac{20}{24} + \frac{14}{24} = \frac{49}{24} = 2\frac{1}{24}$

17. B: By definition, the opposite sides of a parallelogram are equal and congruent.

18. D: Use the volume of a rectangular prism formula $V = L \times W \times H$ to determine the length of the tank.

$200 = L \times 8 \times 5 \rightarrow 200 = 40L \rightarrow L = 5$ feet.

19. C: Dividing the height of Mt. McKinley by the number of feet in a mile gives the correct result. $\frac{20320}{5280} = 3.85$ miles. This rounds to the approximation of 4 miles high.

20. Using the ratio $8 : 20$ and noticing that the school has 12 times more students than the classroom. Multiplying the ratio by 12 gives: $\mathbf{96 : 240}$.

21. D: The other choices define A. Raising the wholesale price by $1.75. B. Multiplying the wholesale price by 0.25 and then adding $1.50. C. Multiplying the wholesale price by 1.75.

22. B: Since Laura was leaving the movies at 8:15, go backward 2:45 to get the start time of the movie. 2 hours prior was 6:15, and the additional 45 minutes moves the start time back to 5:30 PM.

23. 48: Order of operations are parentheses, exponents, multiplication, division, addition, and subtraction. The steps to solve this problem are:
$3 + (9 - 4) \times (4 + 5) =?$
$3 + 5 \times 9 =?$
$3 + 45 = 48$

24. B: If you add all of the minutes together you get 202. When converted to hours and minutes that is three hours and 22 minutes.

25. B: Unless the rectangular prism is a cube, some of the sides will have different areas than others. Opposite sides will be equal in area.

26. B: $1\frac{5}{10}$ is read as one and five tenths. The 1 can be converted to an equivalent fraction of

$\frac{10}{10}$ and is shown as all ten parts of the first ten section are shaded. $\frac{5}{10}$ indicates that only
five of the ten parts are shaded in the second set of ten. Since the 5 is over the denominator of a ten and read as five tenths, the five should be placed

in the tenths location when in decimal form. This is the first location to the right of the decimal. The correct decimal form for this is 1.5.

27. B: On the plane provided, north is up and west is to the left. Shift point (8, 5) up 2 and left 4 units to obtain the position of the fire.

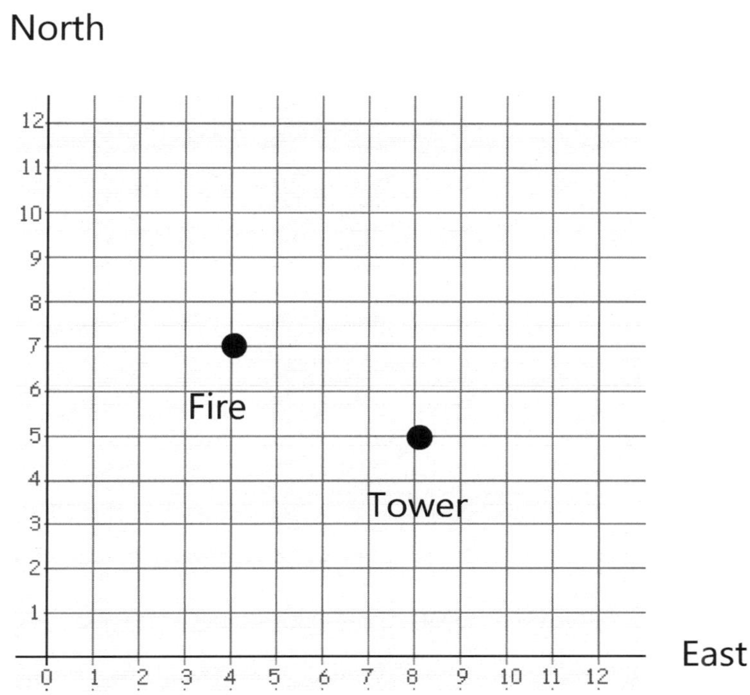

28. D: A box that is $13 \times 4 \times 8$ would be 416 cubic inches.

29. C: Use the formula for finding the mean, $mean = \frac{sum\ of\ values}{number\ of\ values}$.

$$\frac{22+28+38+48+45}{5} = \frac{180}{5} = 36$$

30. D: If Ice Chest A can hold twice as many drinks as B then that means it can hold 48 drinks. If the larger compartment holds 34 and 48-34=14, then the smaller one holds 14.

31. C: If the average weight of a horse is 1100 lbs, the weight of the horses in the race would be $8 \times 1100 = 8800$ lbs. Dividing this number by 2000 gives the total weight in tons. $8800\ lbs \times \frac{1\ ton}{2000\ lbs} = \frac{8800}{2000}\ tons = 4.4\ tons$.

32. The solution is found by finding the whole number part of the quotient when dividing 417 by 18: $417 \div 18 = \mathbf{23\ \mathit{R}\ 3}$. Therefore 23 full boxes can be made and 3 pears would be left over.

33. D: A regular pentagon is a 5 sided figure with all sides equal in length. Therefore the perimeter is $5 \times 6.5 = 32.5$ centimeters.

34. C: Convert $\frac{35}{8}$ to a mixed number using division: $\frac{35}{8} = 4\frac{3}{8}$. Point D is located at $4\frac{1}{2}$ inches, so the length is before D. C is 3 inches, so obviously the length is more than C.

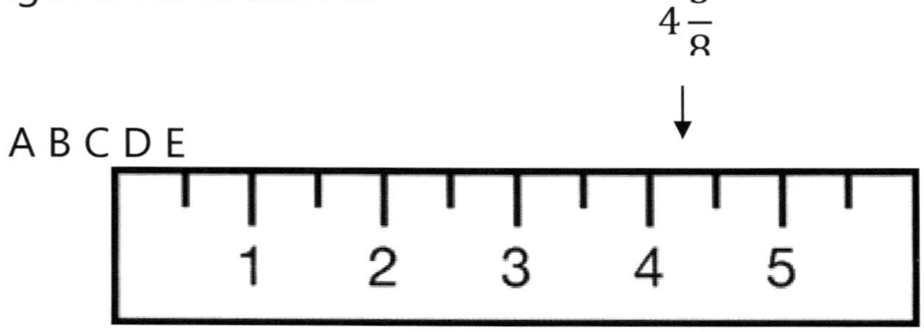

35. B: The four choices are marked on the diagram below.

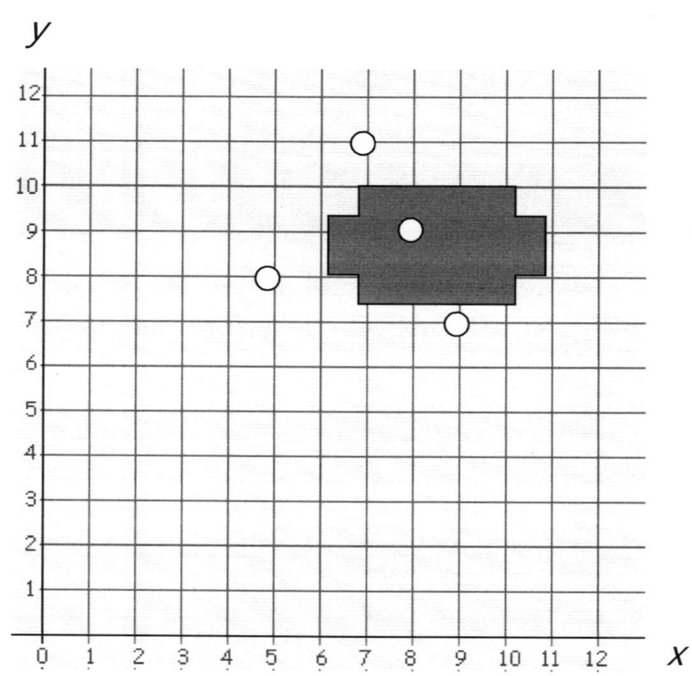

36. C: Since the probability of being either a carpenter or an electrician is being calculated, the probabilities are added. $\frac{13}{50} + \frac{7}{50} = \frac{20}{50} = \frac{2}{5}$.

37. B: This is the only line graph that correctly shows the increase in customers up to 6:00 pm and then the decrease in customers at 8:00 pm.

38. D: To correctly order the numbers in this question, making the decimals all have the same number of digits by adding as many zeros as necessary to the numbers with fewer digits makes them easier to compare. Here, only 17.4 has fewer digits than the others, so add one zero to make it 17.40 (this does not change the value). Now, by comparing place values from left to right of 17.03, 17.4, 17.31, and 17.09, we see that 17.03 is the shortest, 17.09 is the next longest, 17.31 is the third longest, and 17.4 is the longest. Notice the question asked for shortest to longest, not longest to shortest.

39. A: Write 512 then add the decimal in the thousandths place, the third place from the right.

40. C: Divide the numerator and denominator by 14.

Online Resources

Due to our efforts to try to keep this book to a manageable length, we've created a link that will give you access to all of your online resources:

mometrix.com/resources719/ssnystg5mathwb

It's Your Moment, Let's Celebrate It!

Share your story @mometrixtestpreparation

Mometrix
TEST PREPARATION

North Carolina
Grade 6
Mathematics

Dear Future Exam Success Story

First of all, **THANK YOU** for purchasing Mometrix study materials!

Second, congratulations! You are one of the few determined test-takers who are committed to doing whatever it takes to excel on your exam. **You have come to the right place.** We developed these study materials with one goal in mind: to deliver you the information you need in a format that's concise and easy to use.

In addition to optimizing your guide for the content of the test, we've outlined our recommended steps for breaking down the preparation process into small, attainable goals so you can make sure you stay on track.

We've also analyzed the entire test-taking process, identifying the most common pitfalls and showing how you can overcome them and be ready for any curveball the test throws you.

Standardized testing is one of the biggest obstacles on your road to success, which only increases the importance of doing well in the high-pressure, high-stakes environment of test day. Your results on this test could have a significant impact on your future, and this guide provides the information and practical advice to help you achieve your full potential on test day.

Your success is our success

We would love to hear from you! If you would like to share the story of your exam success or if you have any questions or comments in regard to our products, please contact us at **800-673-8175** or **support@mometrix.com**.

Thanks again for your business and we wish you continued success!

Sincerely,
The Mometrix Test Preparation Team

Written and edited by the Mometrix Test Preparation Team
Printed in the United States of America

TABLE OF CONTENTS

Introduction

Thank you for purchasing this resource! You have made the choice to prepare yourself for a test that could have a huge impact on your future, and this guide is designed to help you be fully ready for test day. Obviously, it's important to have a solid understanding of the test material, but you also need to be prepared for the unique environment and stressors of the test, so that you can perform to the best of your abilities.

For this purpose, the first section that appears in this guide is the **Success Strategies**. We've devoted countless hours to meticulously researching what works and what doesn't, and we've boiled down our findings to the most impactful steps you can take to improve your performance on the test. We start at the beginning with study planning and move through the preparation process, all the way to the testing strategies that will help you get the most out of what you know when you're finally sitting in front of the test.

We recommend that you start preparing for your test as far in advance as possible. However, if you've bought this guide as a last-minute study resource and only have a few days before your test, we recommend that you skip over the first two Success Strategies since they address a long-term study plan.

If you struggle with **test anxiety**, we strongly encourage you to check out our recommendations for how you can overcome it. Test anxiety is a formidable foe, but it can be beaten, and we want to make sure you have the tools you need to defeat it.

Strategy #1 – Plan Big, Study Small

There's a lot riding on your performance. If you want to ace this test, you're going to need to keep your skills sharp and the material fresh in your mind. You need a plan that lets you review everything you need to know while still fitting in your schedule. We'll break this strategy down into three categories.

Information Organization

Start with the information you already have: the official test outline. From this, you can make a complete list of all the concepts you need to cover before the test. Organize these concepts into groups that can be studied together, and create a list of any related vocabulary you need to learn so you can brush up on any difficult terms. You'll want to keep this vocabulary list handy once you actually start studying since you may need to add to it along the way.

Time Management

Once you have your set of study concepts, decide how to spread them out over the time you have left before the test. Break your study plan into small, clear goals so you have a manageable task for each day and know exactly what you're doing. Then just focus on one small step at a time. When you manage your time this way, you don't need to spend hours at a time studying. Studying a small block of content for a short period each day helps you retain information better and avoid stressing over how much you have left to do. You can relax knowing that you have a plan to cover everything in time. In order for this strategy to be effective though, you have to start studying early and stick to your schedule. Avoid the exhaustion and futility that comes from last-minute cramming!

Study Environment

The environment you study in has a big impact on your learning. Studying in a coffee shop, while probably more enjoyable, is not likely to be as fruitful as studying in a quiet room. It's important to keep distractions to a minimum. You're only planning to study for a short block of time, so make the most of it. Don't pause to check your phone or get up to find a snack. It's also important to **avoid multitasking**. Research has consistently shown that multitasking will make your studying dramatically less effective. Your study area should also be comfortable and well-lit so you don't have the distraction of straining your eyes or sitting on an uncomfortable chair.

The time of day you study is also important. You want to be rested and alert. Don't wait until just before bedtime. Study when you'll be most likely to comprehend and remember. Even better, if you know what time of day your test will be, set that time aside for study. That way your brain will be used to working on that subject at that specific time and you'll have a better chance of recalling information.

Finally, it can be helpful to team up with others who are studying for the same test. Your actual studying should be done in as isolated an environment as possible, but the work of organizing the information and setting up the study plan can be divided up. In between study sessions, you can discuss with your teammates the concepts that you're all studying and quiz each other on the details. Just be sure that your teammates are as serious about the test as you are. If you find that your study time is being replaced with social time, you might need to find a new team.

Strategy #2 – Make Your Studying Count

You're devoting a lot of time and effort to preparing for this test, so you want to be absolutely certain it will pay off. This means doing more than just reading the content and hoping you can remember it on test day. It's important to make every minute of study count. There are two main areas you can focus on to make your studying count.

Retention

It doesn't matter how much time you study if you can't remember the material. You need to make sure you are retaining the concepts. To check your retention of the information you're learning, try recalling it at later times with minimal prompting. Try carrying around flashcards and glance at one or two from time to time or ask a friend who's also studying for the test to quiz you.

To enhance your retention, look for ways to put the information into practice so that you can apply it rather than simply recalling it. If you're using the information in practical ways, it will be much easier to remember. Similarly, it helps to solidify a concept in your mind if you're not only reading it to yourself but also explaining it to someone else. Ask a friend to let you teach them about a concept you're a little shaky on (or speak aloud to an imaginary audience if necessary). As you try to summarize, define, give examples, and answer your friend's questions, you'll understand the concepts better and they will stay with you longer. Finally, step back for a big picture view and ask yourself how each piece of information fits with the whole subject. When you link the different concepts together and see them working together as a whole, it's easier to remember the individual components.

Finally, practice showing your work on any multi-step problems, even if you're just studying. Writing out each step you take to solve a problem will help solidify the process in your mind, and you'll be more likely to remember it during the test.

Modality

Modality simply refers to the means or method by which you study. Choosing a study modality that fits your own individual learning style is crucial. No two people learn best in exactly the same way, so it's important to know your strengths and use them to your advantage.

For example, if you learn best by visualization, focus on visualizing a concept in your mind and draw an image or a diagram. Try color-coding your notes, illustrating them, or creating symbols that will trigger your mind to recall a learned concept. If you learn best by hearing or discussing information, find a study partner who learns the same way or read aloud to yourself. Think about how to put the information in your own words. Imagine that you are giving a lecture on the topic and record yourself so you can listen to it later.

For any learning style, flashcards can be helpful. Organize the information so you can take advantage of spare moments to review. Underline key words or phrases. Use different colors for different categories. Mnemonic devices (such as creating a short list in which every item starts with the same letter) can also help with retention. Find what works best for you and use it to store the information in your mind most effectively and easily.

Strategy #3 – Practice the Right Way

Your success on test day depends not only on how many hours you put into preparing, but also on whether you prepared the right way. It's good to check along the way to see if your studying is paying off. One of the most effective ways to do this is by taking practice tests to evaluate your progress. Practice tests are useful because they show exactly where you need to improve. Every time you take a practice test, pay special attention to these three groups of questions:

- The questions you got wrong
- The questions you had to guess on, even if you guessed right
- The questions you found difficult or slow to work through

This will show you exactly what your weak areas are, and where you need to devote more study time. Ask yourself why each of these questions gave you trouble. Was it because you didn't understand the material? Was it because you didn't remember the vocabulary? Do you need more repetitions on this type of question to build speed and confidence? Dig into those questions and figure out how you can strengthen your weak areas as you go back to review the material.

Additionally, many practice tests have a section explaining the answer choices. It can be tempting to read the explanation and think that you now have a good understanding of the concept. However, an explanation likely only covers part of the question's broader context. Even if the explanation makes perfect sense, **go back and investigate** every concept related to the question until you're positive you have a thorough understanding.

As you go along, keep in mind that the practice test is just that: practice. Memorizing these questions and answers will not be very helpful on the actual test because it is unlikely to have any of the same exact questions. If you only know the right answers to the sample questions, you won't be prepared for the real thing. **Study the concepts** until you understand them fully, and then you'll be able to answer any question that shows up on the test.

It's important to wait on the practice tests until you're ready. If you take a test on your first day of study, you may be overwhelmed by the amount of material covered and how much you need to learn. Work up to it gradually.

On test day, you'll need to be prepared for answering questions, managing your time, and using the test-taking strategies you've learned. It's a lot to balance, like a mental marathon that will have a big impact on your future. Like training for a marathon, you'll need to start slowly and work your way up. When test day arrives, you'll be ready.

Start with the strategies you've read in the first two Success Strategies—plan your course and study in the way that works best for you. If you have time, consider using multiple study resources to get different approaches to the same concepts. It can be helpful to see difficult concepts from more than one angle. Then find a good source for practice tests. Many times, the test website will suggest potential study resources or provide sample tests.

Practice Test Strategy

If you're able to find at least three practice tests, we recommend this strategy:

UNTIMED AND OPEN-BOOK PRACTICE

Take the first test with no time constraints and with your notes and study guide handy. Take your time and focus on applying the strategies you've learned.

TIMED AND OPEN-BOOK PRACTICE

Take the second practice test open-book as well, but set a timer and practice pacing yourself to finish in time.

TIMED AND CLOSED-BOOK PRACTICE

Take any other practice tests as if it were test day. Set a timer and put away your study materials. Sit at a table or desk in a quiet room, imagine yourself at the testing center, and answer questions as quickly and accurately as possible.

Keep repeating timed and closed-book tests on a regular basis until you run out of practice tests or it's time for the actual test. Your mind will be ready for the schedule and stress of test day, and you'll be able to focus on recalling the material you've learned.

Strategy #4 – Pace Yourself

Once you're fully prepared for the material on the test, your biggest challenge on test day will be managing your time. Just knowing that the clock is ticking can make you panic even if you have plenty of time left. Work on pacing yourself so you can build confidence against the time constraints of the exam. Pacing is a difficult skill to master, especially in a high-pressure environment, so **practice is vital**.

Set time expectations for your pace based on how much time is available. For example, if a section has 60 questions and the time limit is 30 minutes, you know you have to average 30 seconds or less per question in order to answer them all. Although 30 seconds is the hard limit, set 25 seconds per question as your goal, so you reserve extra time to spend on harder questions. When you budget extra time for the harder questions, you no longer have any reason to stress when those questions take longer to answer.

Don't let this time expectation distract you from working through the test at a calm, steady pace, but keep it in mind so you don't spend too much time on any one question. Recognize that taking extra time on one question you don't understand may keep you from answering two that you do understand later in the test. If your time limit for a question is up and you're still not sure of the answer, mark it and move on, and come back to it later if the time and the test format allow. If the testing format doesn't allow you to return to earlier questions, just make an educated guess; then put it out of your mind and move on.

On the easier questions, be careful not to rush. It may seem wise to hurry through them so you have more time for the challenging ones, but it's not worth missing one if you know the concept and just didn't take the time to read the question fully. Work efficiently but make sure you understand the question and have looked at all of the answer choices, since more than one may seem right at first.

Even if you're paying attention to the time, you may find yourself a little behind at some point. You should speed up to get back on track, but do so wisely. Don't panic; just take a few seconds less on each question until you're caught up. Don't guess without thinking, but do look through the answer choices and eliminate any you know are wrong. If you can get down to two choices, it is often worthwhile to guess from those. Once you've chosen an answer, move on and don't dwell on any that you skipped or had to hurry through. If a question was taking too long, chances are it was one of the harder ones, so you weren't as likely to get it right anyway.

On the other hand, if you find yourself getting ahead of schedule, it may be beneficial to slow down a little. The more quickly you work, the more likely you are to make a careless mistake that will affect your score. You've budgeted time for each question, so don't be afraid to spend that time. Practice an efficient but careful pace to get the most out of the time you have.

Test-Taking Strategies

This section contains a list of test-taking strategies that you may find helpful as you work through the test. By taking what you know and applying logical thought, you can maximize your chances of answering any question correctly!

It is very important to realize that every question is different and every person is different: no single strategy will work on every question, and no single strategy will work for every person. That's why we've included all of them here, so you can try them out and determine which ones work best for different types of questions and which ones work best for you.

Question Strategies

✓ Read Carefully

Read the question and the answer choices carefully. Don't miss the question because you misread the terms. You have plenty of time to read each question thoroughly and make sure you understand what is being asked. Yet a happy medium must be attained, so don't waste too much time. You must read carefully and efficiently.

✓ Contextual Clues

Look for contextual clues. If the question includes a word you are not familiar with, look at the immediate context for some indication of what the word might mean. Contextual clues can often give you all the information you need to decipher the meaning of an unfamiliar word. Even if you can't determine the meaning, you may be able to narrow down the possibilities enough to make a solid guess at the answer to the question.

✓ Prefixes

If you're having trouble with a word in the question or answer choices, try dissecting it. Take advantage of every clue that the word might include. Prefixes can be a huge help. Usually, they allow you to determine a basic meaning. *Pre-* means before, *post-* means after, *pro-* is positive, *de-* is negative. From prefixes, you can get an idea of the general meaning of the word and try to put it into context.

✓ Hedge Words

Watch out for critical hedge words, such as *likely, may, can, often, almost, mostly, usually, generally, rarely*, and *sometimes*. Question writers insert these hedge phrases to cover every possibility. Often an answer choice will be wrong simply because it leaves no room for exception. Be on guard for answer choices that have definitive words such as *exactly* and *always*.

✓ Switchback Words

Stay alert for *switchbacks*. These are the words and phrases frequently used to alert you to shifts in thought. The most common switchback words are *but, although*, and *however*. Others include *nevertheless, on the other hand, even though, while, in spite of, despite*, and *regardless of*. Switchback words are important to catch because they can change the direction of the question or an answer choice.

⊘ Face Value

When in doubt, use common sense. Accept the situation in the problem at face value. Don't read too much into it. These problems will not require you to make wild assumptions. If you have to go beyond creativity and warp time or space in order to have an answer choice fit the question, then you should move on and consider the other answer choices. These are normal problems rooted in reality. The applicable relationship or explanation may not be readily apparent, but it is there for you to figure out. Use your common sense to interpret anything that isn't clear.

Answer Choice Strategies

⊘ Answer Selection

The most thorough way to pick an answer choice is to identify and eliminate wrong answers until only one is left, then confirm it is the correct answer. Sometimes an answer choice may immediately seem right, but be careful. The test writers will usually put more than one reasonable answer choice on each question, so take a second to read all of them and make sure that the other choices are not equally obvious. As long as you have time left, it is better to read every answer choice than to pick the first one that looks right without checking the others.

⊘ Answer Choice Families

An answer choice family consists of two (in rare cases, three) answer choices that are very similar in construction and cannot all be true at the same time. If you see two answer choices that are direct opposites or parallels, one of them is usually the correct answer. For instance, if one answer choice says that quantity *x* increases and another either says that quantity *x* decreases (opposite) or says that quantity *y* increases (parallel), then those answer choices would fall into the same family. An answer choice that doesn't match the construction of the answer choice family is more likely to be incorrect. Most questions will not have answer choice families, but when they do appear, you should be prepared to recognize them.

⊘ Eliminate Answers

Eliminate answer choices as soon as you realize they are wrong, but make sure you consider all possibilities. If you are eliminating answer choices and realize that the last one you are left with is also wrong, don't panic. Start over and consider each choice again. There may be something you missed the first time that you will realize on the second pass.

⊘ Avoid Fact Traps

Don't be distracted by an answer choice that is factually true but doesn't answer the question. You are looking for the choice that answers the question. Stay focused on what the question is asking for so you don't accidentally pick an answer that is true but incorrect. Always go back to the question and make sure the answer choice you've selected actually answers the question and is not merely a true statement.

⊘ Extreme Statements

In general, you should avoid answers that put forth extreme actions as standard practice or proclaim controversial ideas as established fact. An answer choice that states the "process should be used in certain situations, if..." is much more likely to be correct than one that states the "process should be discontinued completely." The first is a calm rational statement and doesn't even make a definitive, uncompromising stance, using a hedge word *if* to provide wiggle room, whereas the second choice is far more extreme.

⊘ BENCHMARK

As you read through the answer choices and you come across one that seems to answer the question well, mentally select that answer choice. This is not your final answer, but it's the one that will help you evaluate the other answer choices. The one that you selected is your benchmark or standard for judging each of the other answer choices. Every other answer choice must be compared to your benchmark. That choice is correct until proven otherwise by another answer choice beating it. If you find a better answer, then that one becomes your new benchmark. Once you've decided that no other choice answers the question as well as your benchmark, you have your final answer.

⊘ PREDICT THE ANSWER

Before you even start looking at the answer choices, it is often best to try to predict the answer. When you come up with the answer on your own, it is easier to avoid distractions and traps because you will know exactly what to look for. The right answer choice is unlikely to be word-for-word what you came up with, but it should be a close match. Even if you are confident that you have the right answer, you should still take the time to read each option before moving on.

General Strategies

⊘ TOUGH QUESTIONS

If you are stumped on a problem or it appears too hard or too difficult, don't waste time. Move on! Remember though, if you can quickly check for obviously incorrect answer choices, your chances of guessing correctly are greatly improved. Before you completely give up, at least try to knock out a couple of possible answers. Eliminate what you can and then guess at the remaining answer choices before moving on.

⊘ CHECK YOUR WORK

Since you will probably not know every term listed and the answer to every question, it is important that you get credit for the ones that you do know. Don't miss any questions through careless mistakes. If at all possible, try to take a second to look back over your answer selection and make sure you've selected the correct answer choice and haven't made a costly careless mistake (such as marking an answer choice that you didn't mean to mark). This quick double check should more than pay for itself in caught mistakes for the time it costs.

⊘ PACE YOURSELF

It's easy to be overwhelmed when you're looking at a page full of questions; your mind is confused and full of random thoughts, and the clock is ticking down faster than you would like. Calm down and maintain the pace that you have set for yourself. Especially as you get down to the last few minutes of the test, don't let the small numbers on the clock make you panic. As long as you are on track by monitoring your pace, you are guaranteed to have time for each question.

⊘ DON'T RUSH

It is very easy to make errors when you are in a hurry. Maintaining a fast pace in answering questions is pointless if it makes you miss questions that you would have gotten right otherwise. Test writers like to include distracting information and wrong answers that seem right. Taking a little extra time to avoid careless mistakes can make all the difference in your test score. Find a pace that allows you to be confident in the answers that you select.

✓ Keep Moving

Panicking will not help you pass the test, so do your best to stay calm and keep moving. Taking deep breaths and going through the answer elimination steps you practiced can help to break through a stress barrier and keep your pace.

Final Notes

The combination of a solid foundation of content knowledge and the confidence that comes from practicing your plan for applying that knowledge is the key to maximizing your performance on test day. As your foundation of content knowledge is built up and strengthened, you'll find that the strategies included in this chapter become more and more effective in helping you quickly sift through the distractions and traps of the test to isolate the correct answer.

Now that you're preparing to move forward into the test content chapters of this book, be sure to keep your goal in mind. As you read, think about how you will be able to apply this information on the test. If you've already seen sample questions for the test and you have an idea of the question format and style, try to come up with questions of your own that you can answer based on what you're reading. This will give you valuable practice applying your knowledge in the same ways you can expect to on test day.

Good luck and good studying!

Mathematics

Ratio

A ratio is a direct comparison of two parts of a whole. This is not the same as comparing each part to the whole, as in the case of fractions. For example, for every 3 girls in Maggie's class there are 5 boys. The ratio of girls to boys is a direct comparison of the number of girls and boys, and is therefore 3:5. (Note how this is different from a fraction: 3/8 of the students in Maggie's class are girls, which relates the number of one part, girls, to the whole, students.) Any ratio can be written in three ways: with a colon, as a fraction, or with the word "to". For example, the ratio of girls to boys in Maggie's class can be written as either "3:5", "$\frac{3}{5}$", or "3 to 5". All three ways are read as "three to five".

The following shows how ratios can describe various situations:

- Every car in the parking lot has four wheels. - "Every car in the parking lot has four wheels," means the ratio of cars to wheels is 1:4, because for every one car there are four wheels.
- There are two eyes on every face. - "There are two eyes on every face," means the ratio of eyes to faces is 2:1, because for every two eyes there is one face.
- Every full deck of cards has four aces. - "Every full deck of cards has four aces," means either that the ratio of decks to aces is 1:4, because for each deck there are four aces, or that the ratio of cards to aces is 52:4, because for every set of 52 cards (1 deck), there are 4 aces.
- A recipe calls for two cups of flour for every two dozen cookies. - "A recipe calls for two cups of flour for every two dozen cookies," means the ratio of cups of flour to cookies is 2:24, because for every two cups of flour used 24 (two dozen) cookies will be made.

Unit Rate

Unit rate expresses a quantity of one thing in terms of one unit of another. For example, if you travel 30 miles every two hours, a unit rate expresses this comparison in terms of one hour: in one hour you travel 15 miles, so your unit rate is 15 miles per hour. Other examples are how much one ounce of food costs (price per ounce), or figuring out how much one egg costs out of the dozen (price per 1 egg, instead of price per 12 eggs). The denominator of a unit rate is always 1. Unit rates are used to compare different situations to solve problems. For example, to make sure you get the best deal when deciding which kind of soda to buy, you can find the unit rate of each. If Soda #1 costs $1.50 for a 1-liter bottle, and soda #2 costs $2.75 for a 2-liter bottle, it would be a better deal to buy Soda #2, because its unit rate is only $1.375 per 1-liter, which is cheaper than Soda #1. Unit rates can also help determine the length of time a given event will take. For example, if you can paint 2 rooms in 4.5 hours, you can determine how long it will take you to paint 5 rooms by solving for the unit rate per room and then multiplying that by 5.

Example Problem 1

<u>At the store you see two different bags of candy for sale. Bag A has 32 pieces of candy in it and costs $2.10. Bag B has 50 pieces of candy in it and costs $3.50. Find the unit cost per one piece of candy from each bag and determine which is the better deal.</u>

One piece of candy in Bag A costs about $0.065, or 6.5 cents. This can be found be taking the total price, $2.10, and dividing it by the number of pieces of candy, 32, to determine the cost for one piece of candy: $\frac{2.10}{32} = 0.06562$, or about $0.065. One piece of candy in Bag B costs $0.07, or 7 cents. This can be found in the same way, dividing the total cost, \$3.50, by the number of pieces of candy, 50: $\frac{3.5}{50} = 0.07$, or \$0.07. Since a piece of candy in Bag B is slightly more expensive, it is the better deal to buy Bag A.

Example Problem 2

You decide to bake oatmeal cookies for a bake sale. Your recipe calls for 5 cups of flour, 2 cups of sugar, 1 cup of butter, and 3 cups of oats. However, you only have 1 cup of oats. You decide to make as many cookies as you can with the 1 cup of oats that you have. Find how much of each ingredient you will need to make that many cookies.

You will need to use $1\,{}^{2}/_{3}$ cups of flour, ${}^{2}/_{3}$ cup of sugar, and ${}^{1}/_{3}$ cup of butter. These can be found by finding the unit rate of each per 1 cup of oats. If there are 5 cups of flour needed for every 3 cups of oats, then $\frac{5}{3} = 1\,{}^{2}/_{3}$ cups of flour needed for every 1 cup of oats. Similarly, if there needs to be 2 cups of sugar for every 3 cups of oats, then there needs to be ${}^{2}/_{3}$ cup of sugar for every 1 cup of oats. And finally, if there is 1 cup of butter needed for every 3 cups of oats, then there will need to be ${}^{1}/_{3}$ cup of butter for every 1 cup of oats.

Example Problem 3

Janice made \$40 during the first 5 hours she spent babysitting. She will continue to earn money at this rate until she finishes babysitting in 3 more hours. Find how much money Janice earned babysitting and how much she earns per hour.

Janice will earn \$64 babysitting in her 8 total hours (adding the first 5 hours to the remaining 3 gives the 8 hour total). This can be found by setting up a proportion comparing money earned to babysitting hours. Since she earns \$40 for 5 hours and since the rate is constant, she will earn a proportional amount in 8 hours: $\frac{40}{5} = \frac{x}{8}$. Cross-multiplying will yield $5x = 320$, and division by 5 shows that $x = 64$.

Janice earns \$8 per hour. This can be found by taking her total amount earned, \$64, and dividing it by the total number of hours worked, 8. Since $\frac{64}{8} = 8$, Janice makes \$8 in one hour. This can also be found by finding the unit rate, money earned per hour: $\frac{64}{8} = \frac{x}{1}$.Since cross-multiplying yields $8x = 64$, and division by 8 shows that $x = 8$, Janice earns \$8 per hour.

Example Problem 4

The McDonalds are taking a family road trip, driving 300 miles to their cabin. It took them 2 hours to drive the first 120 miles. They will drive at the same speed all the way to their cabin. Find the speed at which the McDonalds are driving and how much longer it will take them to get to their cabin.

The McDonalds are driving 60 miles per hour. This can be found by setting up a proportion to find the unit rate, the number of miles they drive per one hour: $\frac{120}{2} = \frac{x}{1}$. Cross-multiplying yields $2x = 120$ and division by 2 shows that $x = 60$.

Since the McDonalds will drive this same speed for the remaining miles, it will take them another 3 hours to get to their cabin. This can be found by first finding how many miles the McDonalds have left to drive, which is 300 – 120 = 180. The McDonalds are driving at 60 miles per hour, so a proportion can be set up to determine how many hours it will take them to drive 180 miles: $\frac{180}{x} = \frac{60}{1}$. Cross-multiplying yields $60x = 180$, and division by 60 shows that $x = 3$. This can also be found by using the formula $D = r \times t$ (or $Distance = rate \times time$), where $180 = 60 \times t$, and division by 60 shows that $t = 3$.

Example Problem 5

It takes Andy 10 minutes to read 6 pages of his book. He has already read 150 pages in his book that is 210 pages long. Find how long it takes Andy to read 1 page and also find how long it will take him to finish his book if he continues to read at the same speed.

It takes Andy 1 minute and 40 seconds to read one page in his book. This can be found by finding the unit rate per one page, by dividing the total time it takes him to read 6 pages by 6. Since it takes him 10 minutes to read 6 pages, $\frac{10}{6} = 1\,^2/_3$ minutes, which is 1 minute and 40 seconds.

It will take Andy another 100 minutes, or 1 hour and 40 minutes to finish his book. This can be found by first figuring out how many pages Andy has left to read, which is 210-150 = 60. Since it is now known that it takes him $1\,^2/_3$ minutes to read each page, then that rate must be multiplied by however many pages he has left to read (60) to find the time he'll need: $60 \times 1\,^2/_3 = 100$, so it will take him 100 minutes, or 1 hour and 40 minutes, to read the rest of his book.

Example Problem 6

Find the unit rate in the situations given:

A. *Pizza Place is offering a deal for $40 for 8 pizzas. What is the cost of each pizza?*
B. *The ratio of flight attendants to airplanes is 42:14. How many flight attendants are on each airplane?*
C. *Milo has a pledge of $100 for the 25 mile walk-a-thon. How much will Milo earn for each mile?*
D. *It takes the cleaning service 8 hours to clean 20 garages. How long does it take to clean 1 garage?*

A. The unit rate is $5 per pizza. This is found by $\frac{\$40}{8} = \$5$.
B. The unit ratio is 3:1 which means there are 3 flight attendants for each airplane. This is found by $\frac{42}{14} = 3$.
C. The unit rate is $4 per mile. This is found by $\frac{\$100}{25} = \$4$.
D. The unit rate is 0.4 hours, or 24 minutes, to clean one garage. This is found by $\frac{8\ hours}{20} = 0.4$ hours. This can be converted to minutes multiplying by a conversion factor: $0.4\ hours \times \frac{60\ minutes}{1\ hour} = 24\ minutes$.

Percent

Percent is one way of expressing what portion something is out of a whole. You can think of it like dividing the whole into 100 equal parts, called percents. The whole, all 100 parts, is called 100% (read as "one hundred percent"). Half of the whole is half (50) of the parts, so we say it is 50%, and so on. (Percent compares one quantity to another; sometimes neither number is necessarily 'whole' or 'all' of something.) To find what percent one number is of another, divide the first by the second, and multiply the answer by 100. For example, we can use percent to compare a part to a whole by asking how much money someone spends on their housing payment each month out of his or her total amount of money that month. If someone earns $2000 every month and spends

\$800 of that on their housing payment, then that person spends $\frac{800}{2000} \times (100) = 0.4 \times 100 = 40\%$ of his or her income on housing payments. Another example showing how percent can simply relate two numbers is comparing your age to your mother's age. If you are 12 years old and your mother is 40 years old, then you are $\frac{12}{40} \times 100 = 0.3 \times 100 = 30\%$ of her age.

Example Problem 1

Johnny got 80% of the questions correct on his math test. Find how many questions Johnny answered correctly if the test had 75 questions on it. Also, find what Johnny's new score would be if he was able to earn an extra 10% of his original score by doing corrections on the questions he missed.

Johnny got 60 questions correct. To find this, set up the percent calculation, leaving the number Johnny got right as *x*: $(\frac{x}{75} \times 100 = 80\%$. Multiply both sides by 75 and then divide both sides by 100 to solve for $x = \frac{80 \times 75}{100} = 60$. We say we are finding 80% of 75, which we now know means simply multiplying 75 by 0.80, which is 60.

Johnny's new score would be $^{66}/_{75}$, which is a score of 88%. This can be found in two ways. One is finding what number of questions is 10% of Johnny's original number right, or 10% of 60, which is 6 questions. If Johnny gets those 6 questions added back to his score, he would then have a total of 66 questions correct out of 75, which is $\frac{66}{75}$, which is 0.88, or 88%. The other way is by finding 10% of Johnny's original score of 80% and adding that to his original score: 10% of 80% = $0.10 \times 80\% = 8\%$, and 80% + 8% = 88%.

Example Problem 2

A sweater at a local department store is on sale for \$33. Find the original price of the sweater if it is marked 40% off the original price.

The sweater was originally \$55. To find this, set up a proportion to determine what number 33 is 60% of. We use 60% because if the sweater is 40% *off* we *subtracted* 40% from the price, so we have 60% *left*. The proportion will compare the percent over 100 to 33 over the original price: $\frac{60}{100} = \frac{33}{x}$. Cross-multiplying yields $60x = 3300$, and division by 60 shows that $x = 55$.

Greater or Equal To

Examples

For each situation listed below, determine which quantity is greater or if they are equal:

3 yards and 20 feet

70 minutes and 1 hour

188 pennies and 2 dollars

2 feet and 24 inches

1 kilometer and 100 meters

20 feet is greater. Since there are 3 feet in each yard, there are 9 feet in 3 yards, and 20 feet is greater than 9 feet.

70 minutes is greater, since there are only 60 minutes in one hour.

2 dollars is greater. Since there are 100 pennies in each dollar, there are 200 pennies in 2 dollars, which is greater than 188 pennies.

These quantities are equal, since there are 12 inches in each foot, and therefore 24 inches in 2 feet.

1 kilometer is greater, because in each kilometer there are 1000 meters, which is greater than 100 meters.

Conversions

Example Problem 1

Tony is going to buy new carpet for two rooms in his house. One room is $12\ feet \times 12\ feet$*, and the other is* $10\ feet \times 18\ feet$*. The carpet Tony wants to buy is on sale for \$10 per square yard. How much will Tony pay for the amount of carpet he needs for both rooms?*

Tony will pay \$360 for his carpet. First figure out how much carpet Tony needs to buy in square yards and then multiply that by \$10 per square yard.

Since Tony's room dimensions are in feet, they must first be converted to yards. The first room is 12 feet × 12 feet, and since there are 3 feet in each yard, that room is 4 yards × 4 yards (because $^{12}/_3 = 4$). Similarly, the room that is 10 feet × 18 feet measures $3\ ^1/_3$ yards × 6 yards (because $^{10}/_3 = 3\ ^1/_3$, and $^{18}/_3 = 6$). So, the total square yardage of Tony's rooms is $4 \times 4 = 16$ square yards, plus $3\ ^1/_3 \times 6 = 20$ square yards, or 16 + 20 = 36 square yards. Since the carpet costs \$10 per square yard, then the total cost is $\$10 \times 36 = \$360$.

Example Problem 2

Tyson is driving home from work. He is driving 45 miles per hour and is 10 miles away from home. Find how many minutes it will take Tyson to get the rest of the way home if he continues to drive at the same speed.

It will take Tyson $13\ ^1/_3$ minutes to get home. Convert Tyson's speed to miles per minute, using a conversion factor of 60 minutes in 1 hour: $\frac{45\ miles}{1\ hour} \times \frac{1\ hour}{60\ minutes} = 0.75\ ^{miles}/_{minute}$. (The 'hours' units cancel and the answer is then in 'miles per minute'.) Because $distance = rate \times time$, $\frac{distance}{rate} = time$. Therefore, if Tyson has 10 miles left to go, dividing that by 0.75 miles per minute finds how many minutes it will take Tyson to get home. $\frac{10}{0.75} = 13\ ^1/_3$, so it will take Tyson $13\ ^1/_3$ minutes to get home.

Example Problem 3

When Mrs. Smith turned 50 years old she wanted to figure out how many minutes she had been alive. She determined that she had been alive for 25,000,000 minutes. Is she correct?

No, Mrs. Smith is not correct. She has been alive for 26,280,000 minutes. This is found by converting 50 years into minutes, using conversion factors from years to days to hours to minutes: $50\ years \times \frac{365\ days}{1\ year} \times \frac{24\ hours}{1\ day} \times \frac{60\ minutes}{1\ hour} =$ 26,280,000 minutes. The first multiplication operation will give 18,250, which is how many days Mrs. Smith has been alive (the 'years' units cancel). Multiplying that by $\frac{24\ hours}{1\ day}$ will cancel the 'days' units and yield 438,000 hours. Finally, multiplying that by $\frac{60\ minutes}{1\ hour}$ will cancel the 'hours' units and leave an answer of 26,280,000 minutes.

DIVISION

EXAMPLE PROBLEM

SOLVE THE FOLLOWING DIVISION PROBLEM:

$$9\overline{)9027}$$

The answer to the problem of 9027 divided by 9 is 1003.

$$\begin{array}{r} 1003 \\ 9\overline{)9027} \\ \underline{9000} \\ 0027 \\ \underline{0027} \\ 0 \end{array}$$

Of course, 9 divides into 9 exactly one time, so a 1 is placed on the answer line, and the product of 1 and 9 is placed under the thousands place of the dividend. (The remaining places are zero). 9 does not go into 0, so a 0 is placed on the answer line above 0. Since 9 also does not go into 2, another 0 is placed on the answer line. 9 goes into 27 three times, so a 3 is placed on the answer line above the 7. There is no remainder, because 9 goes into 27 exactly 3 times with nothing left over.

DECIMALS

EXAMPLE PROBLEM 1

ADD THE FOLLOWING DECIMALS:

$$\begin{array}{r} 13.48 \\ \underline{+2.5} \end{array}$$

The answer is 15.98.

$$\begin{array}{r} 13.48 \\ \underline{+\ \ 2.5} \\ 15.98 \end{array}$$

It is important to line up the digits correctly which can be done by making sure that the decimal points are lined up vertically, which results in lining up digits that have the same place values. Start by putting a decimal point in the answer line directly below the decimal points in the problem, and then add the digits in the column farthest to the right. There is no digit in 2.5 that lines up with the 8 in 13.48, so 0 is added to 8, and the answer, 8, is brought down below the addition line to the answer. Next, add the 4 and 5, as they are in the same place value (the tenths place in this case); put their sum, 9, in the tenths place of the answer. Adding the digits in the ones place puts a 5 in the ones place of the answer. Finally, the 1 in the tens place in 13.48 isn't added to any digit in 2.5, so the sum of 1 and 0 is put in the tens place of the answer, which makes the final answer 15.98.

Example Problem 2

Subtract the following decimals:

37.4

- 5.32

The answer is 32.08.

37.4

- 5.32

32.08

It is important to line up the digits correctly which can be done by making sure that the decimal points are lined up vertically, which results in lining up digits that have the same place values. Start by putting a decimal point in the answer line directly below the decimal points in the problem, and then subtract the digits in the column farthest to the right, the top minus the bottom. Since there is currently no digit above the 2, it is considered a 0, but since 2 cannot be subtracted from 0, borrow from the 4, making the 0 a 10 and making the 4 a 3. Since 2 can now be subtracted from 10, put the answer, 8, in the hundredths place of the answer. Now subtract 3 (remember: it's not a 4 anymore!) from 3, which is 0. In the ones place subtract 5 from 7, which is 2. And finally nothing is being subtracted from the 3 in the tens place in 37.4, so the 3 is brought down to the answer, making the final answer 32.08.

Prime Factorization

Prime Factorization is breaking a number down into a list of its prime factors. For example, the prime factorization of 60 is $2 \times 2 \times 3 \times 5$, because 2, 3, and 5 are all prime numbers and $2 \times 2 \times 3 \times 5 = 60$. This can be found by first breaking down 60 into any two factors, perhaps 30 and 2. Since 2 is a prime number, it's already a prime factor, but 30 needs to be broken down into factors. 30 can be broken into 2 and 15, 3 and 10, or 6 and 5, but it does not matter which we use. If 3 and 10 are used, the factorization of 60 is $2 \times 3 \times 10$. Since 2 and 3 are prime but 10 is not, we have to break 10 down into 2 and 5, which now makes the factorization of $60 = 2 \times 3 \times 2 \times 5$. This is the prime factorization of 60 because these numbers are all prime. To report the answer in proper form put the numbers in order from least to greatest: the final answer for the prime factorization of 60 is $2 \times 2 \times 3 \times 5$.

Greatest Common Factor

The greatest common factor is the greatest number that all numbers in a set are evenly divisible by. For example, the Greatest Common Factor of 36 and 48 is 12. One way to find this is by simply listing all the factors of 36 and 48; the common factors of 36 and 48 are 1, 2, 3, 4, 6, and 12, and 12 is the greatest of these. This can also be found using the prime factorization of both 36 and 48. The prime factorization of 36 is $2 \times 2 \times 3 \times 3$, and the prime factorization of 48 is $2 \times 2 \times 2 \times 2 \times 3$. Find how many of each prime factor these factorizations have in common: both factorizations have two 2's and one 3, so the Greatest Common Factor of 36 and 48 must be $2 \times 2 \times 3$, which equals 12.

Examples

The following sums can be expressed by factoring out a common factor:

15 + 21
16 + 20
50 + 80
27 + 63
6 + 52
18 + 66

'15 + 21' = 3(5 + 7)

'16 + 20' = 4(4 + 5)

'50 + 80' = 10(5 + 8)

'27 + 63' = 9(3 + 7)

'6 + 52' = 2(3 + 26)

'18 + 66' = 6(3 + 11)

These answers cannot be factored any further because there are no common factors left between the numbers inside the parentheses. In other words, the number that was factored out of each pair of numbers is that pair's greatest common factor.

Least common multiple

The least common multiple is the smallest number that is evenly divisible by all numbers in a given set. For example, the least common multiple of 6 and 8 is 24. One way to find this is to list the common multiples of 6 and 8, 24, 48, 72, ...etc, and the least of these is 24. This can also be found using the prime factorization of both 6 and 8. The prime factorization of 6 is 2×3, and the prime factorization of 8 is $2 \times 2 \times 2$. For each factor, count the number of times it occurs in each factorization. Find the greatest number of times each factor shows up, and multiply each factor that many times. Since 2 shows up three times in 8's factorization, and 3 shows up once in 6's prime factorization, multiply $2 \times 2 \times 2 \times 3$, which equals 24.

Highest and Lowest Temperature

Example Problem

At 1am in Anchorage, Alaska, it was -17° outside. The temperature fell a total of 10 degrees by sunrise, and then rose steadily a total of 35 degrees until 1pm, when the highest temperature of the day occurred. Find the lowest temperature during the night and the warmest temperature of the day.

The lowest temperature during the night was -27° and the warmest temperature of the day was 8°. Since the temperature falls 10° from -17°, subtract 10 from -17: -17 - 10 = -27, and the lowest temperature was -27°. From this lowest temperature it rises a total 35° which brings the thermometer up to 8° because -27 + 35 = 8. This can be thought of in two ways: first, because of the commutative property, -27 + 35 = 35 + -27, which is the same as 35 – 27, which equals 8. The other way is to recognize that the temperature must rise 27 degrees from -27° to get to 0°, but we know it rises another 8°, because the difference between 35 and 27 is 8.

Variables, Numbers, and Operation Symbols

Examples

Use variables, numbers, and operation symbols to express the following:

*3 less than a number **n***

*The quotient of 4 and a number **x***

*The difference between 10 and **y***

*The product of 12 and **m***

*The sum of **x** and 4*

*6 more than a number **r***

"3 less than a number n" means taking 3 away from the value of n, so this is expressed as $n - 3$.

"The quotient of 4 and a number x" means dividing 4 by x, so we write $\frac{4}{x}$.

"The difference between 10 and y" means subtracting y from 10, so we write $10 - y$.

"The product of 12 and m" means multiplying 12 and m, so we write $12 \times m$, or simply $12m$.

"The sum of x and 4" means adding x and 4, so we write x +_4.

"6 more than a number r" means adding 6 to r, so we write $r + 6$.

Addition and Subtraction with Positives and Negatives

Example Problem 1

On Monday of last week, Molly's credit card had a balance of $50 owing on it. Throughout the week Molly made new charges on her credit card when she spent $75 at the grocery store on Tuesday, $30 on a haircut on Wednesday, and $15 at the movies on Friday. On Saturday she made a payment of $200 to her credit card and then on Sunday made another charge of $40 to buy new shoes. Determine whether Molly's credit card has a balance on Sunday night, and if so, how much it is.

Molly's credit card has a balance of $10 on Sunday night. This can be found by subtracting Molly's charges and adding her payment to her balance. A charge on a credit card, or balance, is a negative number because it is owed to the credit card company. A payment on the card gives the company money they are owed, so it is a positive number added to the balance to make that balance *less* negative. In Molly's case, she starts the week with a $50 balance, which is like starting with -50. The three charges on Tuesday, Wednesday, and Friday need to be subtracted from this, to get $-50 - 75 - 30 - 15 = -170$. When Molly makes a payment of $200, then, she only owed $170 on her credit card, so that -170 + 200 = positive 30. (Positive balances are money the company owes to Molly!) After that she makes another charge of $40, which is subtracted from 30 to get a final amount of -10. This means that at the end of the week Molly owes her credit card company $10, and we say her credit card has a balance of $10.

Example Problem 2

A helicopter is flying directly above a submarine. The submarine travels to 600 feet below sea level, while the helicopter reaches its flying height of 1050 feet. Find how far away the submarine and helicopter are from each other.

The helicopter and submarine are 1650 feet apart. This is found by adding their distances to sea level, because we can think of sea level as a value of zero in this situation. The helicopter is 1050 feet above sea level, which is like +1050, and its distance to sea level, 0, is 1050 feet. The submarine is 600 feet below sea level, which is like -600, and the distance from the submarine to sea level is 600 feet. The total distance between the helicopter and submarine, then, is 1050 + 600 = 1650 feet.

Properties

Example Problem 1

State which property is being used in each number sentence:

$$2x + y = y + 2x$$
$$5 \times (x + 1) = (5 \times x) + (5 \times 1)$$
$$3 \times 1 = 3$$
$$6 \times m \times n = m \times n \times 6$$
$$4 \times (5a) = (4a) \times 5$$
$$s + 0 = s$$
$$10 + (6 + 1) = (10 + 6) + 1$$

The Commutative Property of Addition is shown here, which states that you can add terms in any order.

The Distributive Property is shown here, which states that a number multiplied to an expression in parentheses must be multiplied to every term in the parentheses.

The Identity Property of Multiplication is shown here, which states that multiplying a number or term by 1 does not change its value.

The Commutative Property of Multiplication is shown here, which states that you can multiply terms in any order.

The Associative Property of Multiplication is shown here, which states that any group of numbers and/or variables can be grouped together in parentheses to be multiplied first before multiplying by the remaining numbers and/or variables.

"$s + 0 = s$" – The Identity Property of Addition is shown here, which states that adding 0 to any number or term does not change the value of that number or term.

The Associative Property of Addition is shown here, which states that any group of numbers and/or variables can be grouped together in parentheses to be added first before adding the remaining numbers and/or variables.

EXAMPLE PROBLEM 2

SIMPLIFY THE FOLLOWING EXPRESSIONS AND STATE WHAT PROPERTY, OR PROPERTIES, YOU USED:

A. $3(2x - 1)$
B. $4x + y + 2x - 3y$
C. $2(5 + m) - 2m$
D. $7(2x)$

A. This simplifies to "$6x - 3$". The multiplication by 3 has to be distributed to both terms in the parentheses, which is the Distributive Property.
B. This simplifies to "$6x - 2y$", since combining like terms by adding them first ($4x + 2x = 6x$) and then adding those sums uses the Commutative Property of Addition.
C. This simplifies to 10. This is done using the Distributive Property to first multiply the 2 to each term in the parentheses to get "$10 + 2m - 2m$" and then combining like terms, using the Commutative Property of Addition. Since the like terms in this case are a positive $2m$ and a negative $2m$, they add to zero and therefore the answer is simply 10.
D. This simplifies to "$14x$" using the Associative Property of Multiplication.

EXAMPLE PROBLEM 3

USE THE DISTRIBUTIVE PROPERTY TO MATCH ONE EXPRESSION IN COLUMN I WITH AN EQUIVALENT EXPRESSION IN COLUMN II.

Column I	Column II
A. 4(3x-1)	U. 10x+25y
B. 8(9+2x)	V. 12x-4
C. 36-2x	W. 3(4x-8y)
D. 4(4a+5)	X. 72+16x
E. 12x-24y	Y. 2(18-x)
F. 5(2x+5y)	Z. 16a+20

A is equivalent to V, by distributing the '4' into the parentheses.

B is equivalent to X by distributing the '8' into the parentheses.

C is equivalent to Y by distributing the '2' in Y back into the parentheses, or by factoring 2 from both the '36' and the '$2x$'.

D is equivalent to Z by distributing the '4' into the parentheses.

E is equivalent to W by distributing the '3' in W back into the parentheses, or by factoring '3' from both the '12x' and '24y'.

F is equivalent to U by distributing the '5' into the parentheses.

PROPORTIONS

EXAMPLE PROBLEM 1

USING THE TABLE BELOW, FIND THE VALUES OF A AND B.

Gallons of Gas	Price in Dollars
2	a
5	20
b	32
9	36

The value of a is 8 and the value of b is also 8. They can both be found by setting up proportions. To find the value of a, a proportion can be set up comparing 2 and a with the values in the second row, 5 and 20: $\frac{2}{a} = \frac{5}{20}$. Cross multiplying yields $40 = 5a$, and division by 5 shows that $a = 8$.

To find the value of b, another proportion can be set up, comparing b and 32 with any other pair of data in the table. Using 9 and 36 yields the proportion $\frac{b}{32} = \frac{9}{36}$, and cross multiplying yields $36b = 288$. Division by 36 shows that $b = 8$.

EXAMPLE PROBLEM 2

USING THE TABLES COMPARING JANAYA'S AND TIM'S RUNNING SPEEDS, DECIDE WHO WILL WIN A RACE THAT IS 100 METERS LONG.

Janaya

Distance	Time
10m	1.4 seconds
45m	6.3 seconds
85m	11.9 seconds

Tim

Distance	Time
12m	1.8 seconds
50m	7.5 seconds
85m	11.25 seconds

Janaya will win a 100m race against Tim, because Janaya will run 100m in 14 seconds, and Tim will run 100m in 15 seconds. Set up proportions to solve for what each runner's time will be for a 100m distance. To solve for Janaya's time, we can compare 100m with the unknown time, x, to any other pair of data in her table. If we use 10m and 1.4 seconds, the proportion $\frac{10}{1.4} = \frac{100}{x}$ yields $10x = 140$ after cross-multiplication and division by 10 yields $x = 14$. To solve for Tim's time, we can compare 100m with his unknown time, y, to any other pair of data in his table. If we use 50m and 7.5 seconds, the proportion $\frac{50}{7.5} = \frac{100}{y}$ will give $50y = 750$ and division by 50 will give $y = 15$. Since it will take Tim 1 second longer, Janaya will win.

COORDINATE PLANE

Four quadrants and the range of x and y-values

The four quadrants in a coordinate plane are called Quadrant I, Quadrant II, Quadrant III, and Quadrant IV. Quadrant I is the upper right quadrant of the plane and contains ordered pairs where $x > 0$ and $y > 0$. Quadrant II is the upper left quadrant of the plane and contains ordered pairs where $x < 0$ and $y > 0$. Quadrant III is the lower left quadrant of the plane and contains ordered pairs where $x < 0$ and $y < 0$. Quadrant IV is the lower right quadrant of the plane and contains ordered pairs where $x > 0$ and $y < 0$. The coordinate plane below shows the four quadrants:

EXAMPLE PROBLEM 1

Plot the data in the table below on a coordinate plane and find the value of y when $x = 1$.

X	Y
-4	-1
-2	1
0	3
2	5

Pairs of values (x, y) in the table are plotted on the coordinate plane below:

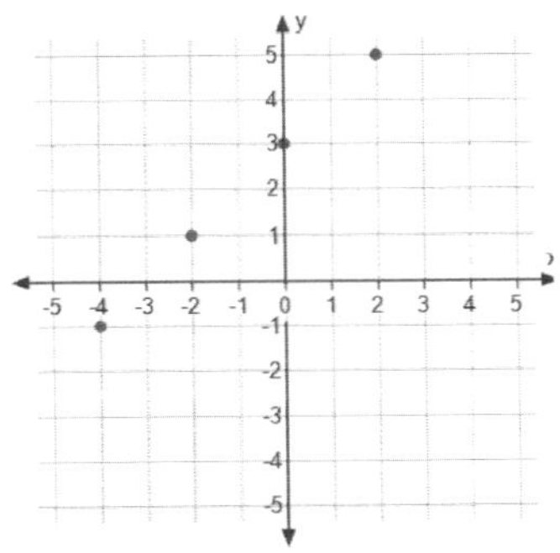

The value of y is 4 when $x = 1$. This can be found by looking at the graph or the table to determine what the pattern of the data is and where the point would lie when $x = 1$. The pattern in the graph and table is that y increases at a rate of 1 vertically for every 1 horizontally; in other words, for every time $x$increases by 1, y increases by 1 also. It can then be determined that since the y-value was 3 when the x-value was 0, the y-value will be 4 when the x-value is 1.

EXAMPLE PROBLEM 2

PLOT THE FOLLOWING POINTS IN A COORDINATE PLANE AND DESCRIBE EACH POINT'S LOCATION:

Point A: (5, 0)
Point B: (-2, 2)
Point C: (-3, -1)
Point D: (3, 1)
Point E: (0, 0)
Point F: (0, -4)
Point G: (2, -3)

The graph below shows the location of the points:

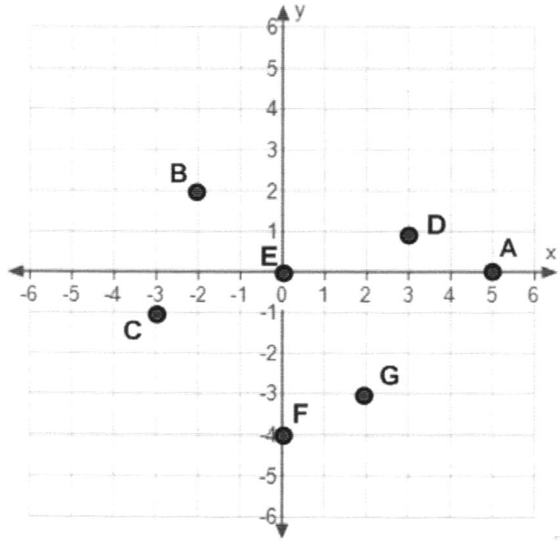

Point A is located on the $x - axis$, 5 units to the right of the origin. Point B is located in Quadrant II, 2 units to the left of the origin and 2 units up. Point C is located in Quadrant III, 3 units to the left of the origin and 1 unit down. Point D is located in Quadrant I, 3 units to the right of the origin and 1 unit up. Point E is located at the origin. Point F is located on the $y - axis$, 4 units down from the origin. Point G is located in Quadrant IV, 2 units to the right of the origin and 3 units down.

EXAMPLE PROBLEM 3

FIND THE PERIMETER OF THE RECTANGLE IN THE COORDINATE PLANE BELOW USING THE VALUES OF THE COORDINATES OF THE VERTICES:

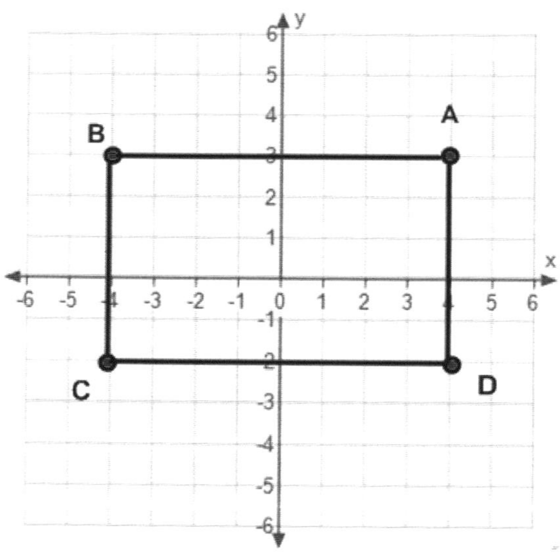

The perimeter of the rectangle is 26 units. This can be found by first finding the ordered pairs of each vertex of the rectangle, which are A= (4, 3), B= (-4, 3), C= (-4, -2), and D= (4, -2), and then using these to find the lengths of the four sides of the rectangle. Since each consecutive pair of vertices share either the same $x-$ coordinate or $y-$ coordinate, it is only necessary to consider the coordinates that are different in value. The distances from A to B and from C to D are each 8, which can be found by finding the distance between their $x-$ coordinates. The distance between 4 and -4 is 8, because 4 is 4 units away from zero and -4 is also 4 units away from zero which gives a total length of $4+4=8$. The distance from B to C and from D to A are each 5, which can be found by finding the distance between their $y-$ coordinates. The distance between 3 and -2 is 5, because 3 is 3 units away from zero and -2 is 2 units away from zero which gives a total length of $3+2=5$. Therefore the total perimeter of the rectangle is $8+8+5+5=26$ units.

Example Problem 4

FIND THE REMAINING ORDERED PAIRS OF THE VERTICES OF A SQUARE IN THE COORDINATE PLANE BELOW IF ONE SIDE LENGTH OF THE SQUARE IS 5 UNITS AND IT HAS A VERTEX IN EACH QUADRANT.

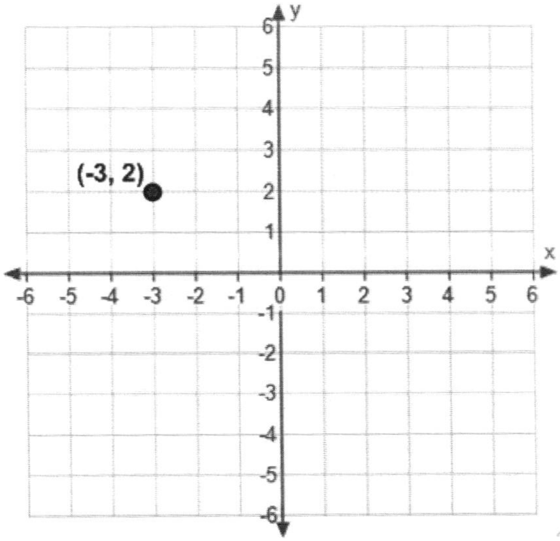

The remaining vertices have the ordered pairs of (-3, -3), (2, -3), and (2, 2). This is found by first figuring out what point in Quadrant III is 5 units away from the given point. It will have the same $x-$coordinate, so the value of y needs to be 5 units away from 2. Going 2 units away from 2 gets to 0, and then 3 more units must be traveled, getting to the point (-3, -3). Then figure out what point in Quadrant IV is 5 units away from (-3, -3). It will have the same $y-$coordinate, so the value of x needs to be 5 units away from -3. Going 3 units to the right of -3 gets to 0, and then 2 more units must be traveled, getting to the point (2, -3). Finally figure out what point in Quadrant I is 5 units away from (2, -3). It will have the same $x-$coordinate as the point in Quadrant IV, and the same y-coordinate as the point in Quadrant II, so the point must be (2, 2). This can be verified: the value of y needs to be 5 units away from -3. Going 3 units away from -3 gets to 0, and then 2 more units must be traveled, getting to the point (2, 2).

COORDINATE GRID

EXAMPLE PROBLEM 1

YOUR NEIGHBORHOOD CAN BE REPRESENTED BY A COORDINATE GRID, WITH EACH UNIT REPRESENTING 1 BLOCK. YOUR HOUSE IS LOCATED AT (1,5), THE PARK IS LOCATED AT (5,5), THE DRUG STORE IS LOCATED AT (5,0), AND THE GAS STATION IS LOCATED AT (1,0). EACH MORNING YOU GO FOR A RUN FROM YOUR HOUSE ALONG A ROUTE TO THE PARK, THEN THE DRUG STORE, THE GAS STATION, AND THEN BACK HOME. PLOT THIS ROUTE ON A COORDINATE GRID AND DETERMINE HOW MANY BLOCKS YOU RUN.

You run 18 blocks on this route:

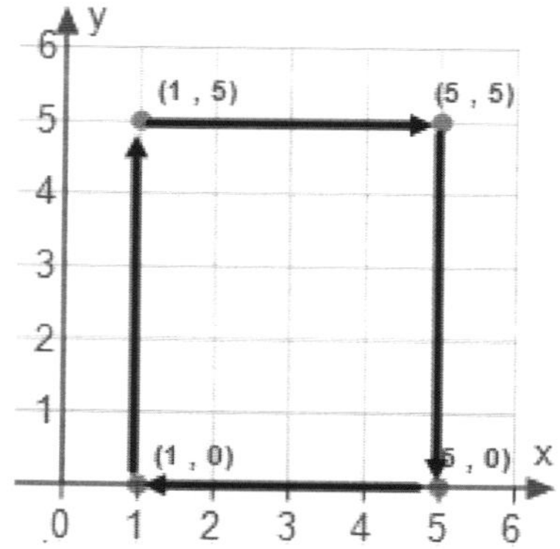

With each dot representing a location in your neighborhood, the route forms a rectangle. The first part of the route is 4 blocks to get from your house to the park, then 5 blocks to get from the park to the drug store, 4 more blocks to get from the drug store to the gas station, and finally 5 blocks to get from the gas station back to your house. Adding all these together gives you $4 + 5 + 4 + 5 = 18$ blocks. These distances can be found by either counting the number of squares on the grid between each location, or by finding the distance between the x or y coordinates (depending whether you're moving horizontally or vertically on the graph, respectively) of two points. For example, the distance between your house at (1,5) and the park at (5,5) is $5 - 1 = 4$ blocks, because you need to go 4 blocks over to get from the x -coordinate of 1 to the x-coordinate of 5, while not moving y-coordinates at all.

EXAMPLE PROBLEM 2

PLATT MIDDLE SCHOOL WAS DESIGNED USING A COORDINATE GRID WITH EACH UNIT OF MEASURE REPRESENTING 1 BLOCK. IN THE SCHOOL, THE LIBRARY IS LOCATED AT (1, 4), THE CAFETERIA IS LOCATED AT (-3, 4) AND THE GYM IS LOCATED AT (1, -2). PLOT THESE POINTS ON A COORDINATE GRID AND FIND THE SHORTEST DISTANCE A STUDENT NEEDS TO WALK TO GET FROM GYM CLASS TO THE LIBRARY AND THEN TO LUNCH.

The student will need to walk 10 blocks. This can be found by first finding the distance from the gym at (1, -2) to the library at (1, 4), and then the library to the cafeteria at (-3, 4). To get from the gym to the library the student will need to walk along a straight path along the x-coordinate of 1, from y-coordinates -2 to 4. The distance -2 is from 0 is 2, and the distance 4 is from 0 is 4. Therefore, the student must walk $2 + 4 = 6$ blocks from the gym to the library. Then the student will walk in a straight path along the y-coordinate of 4 from x-coordinates 1 to -3. The distance 1 is from 0 is 1, and the distance -3 is from 0 is 3. Therefore, the student must walk $1 + 3 = 4$ blocks from the library to lunch in the cafeteria. Thus, the student must walk a total of $6 + 4 = 10$ blocks to get from the gym to the library and then to lunch. The graph below shows the location of the places in the school and the student's path:

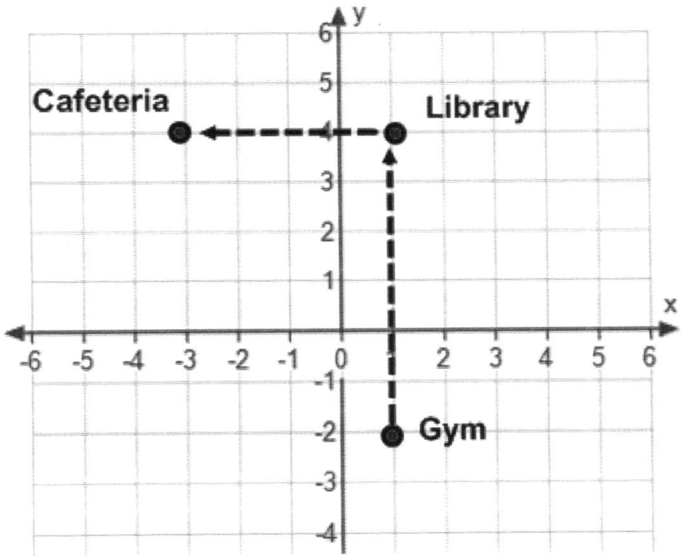

EXAMPLE PROBLEM 3

THE DOWNTOWN AREA OF CANNONVILLE HAS STREETS THAT FOLLOW A COORDINATE GRID. THE MAYOR IS PLANNING A PARADE THROUGH DOWNTOWN AND THE CITY COUNCIL HAS LIMITED THE LENGTH OF THE PARADE TO 16 BLOCKS. THE MAYOR WANTS THE PARADE TO TRAVEL FROM THE ZOO AT (-5, -4) TO THE PARK AT (-3, -4), TO THE BAKERY AT (-3, 1), TO THE LIBRARY AT (-1, 1), TO THE POST OFFICE AT (-1, -1), TO CITY HALL AT (2, -1), AND ENDING AT THE TOWN SQUARE AT (2, 2). PLOT THIS PROPOSED ROUTE OF THE PARADE ON A COORDINATE PLANE AND DETERMINE IF IT WILL FIT THE REQUIREMENT OF THE CITY COUNCIL.

The distance of the proposed parade is 17 blocks so it will not make the 16 block requirement from the city council. This distance can be found by determining the distance between each pair of consecutive parade locations. Since each pair of consecutive locations share either an x or y —coordinate, the distance is found by calculating the distance between the different coordinates. When finding the distance between coordinates of opposite signs, first find the absolute value of each, which gives the distance of each from 0, and add them together. The distances are: **1.** Zoo to Park is 2 blocks, which is the distance between x −coordinates -5 and -3. **2.** Park to Bakery is 5 blocks, which is the distance between y-coordinates -4 and 1 because $|-4| + |1| = 5$. **3.** Bakery to the Library is 2 blocks, which is the distance between x −coordinates -3 and -1. **4.** Library to Post Office is 2 blocks, which is the distance between y-coordinates 1 and -1 because $|-1| + |1| = 2$. **5.** Post Office to City Hall is 3 blocks, which is the distance between$x$-coordinates -1 and 2 because $|-1| + |2| = 3$. **6.** City Hall to Town Square is 3 blocks, which is the distance between y-coordinates -1 and 2 because $|-1| + |2| = 3$. **7.** The total distance is then $2 + 5 + 2 + 2 + 3 + 3 = 17$.

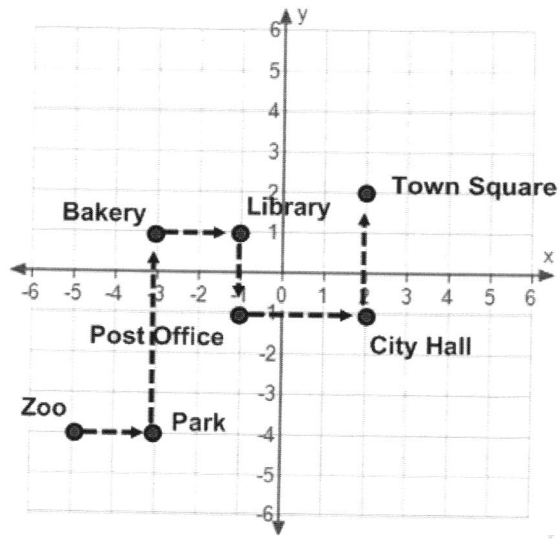

Reflections

Example Problem 1

LABEL THE FOLLOWING POINTS AND THEIR INDICATED REFLECTIONS IN A COORDINATE PLANE AND GIVE THE COORDINATES OF THE REFLECTIONS:

Point A: (4, 3) reflected across the x − axis

Point B: (1, 2) reflected across the y − axis

Point C: (-2, -5) reflected across the y − axis

Point D: (3, 1) reflected across the x − axis and then the y − axis

The graph below shows the points and their reflections:

The reflection of Point A is labeled as A' and has coordinates (4, -3). Because it is reflected across the $x - axis$, the $y - value$ changes in sign.

The reflection of Point B is labeled as B' and has coordinates (-1, 2). Because it is reflected across the $y - axis$, the $x - value$ changes in sign.

The reflection of Point C is labeled as C' and has coordinates (2, -5). Because it is reflected across the $y - axis$, the $x - value$ changes in sign.

The reflection of Point D is labeled as D' and has coordinates (-3, -1). Because it is reflected across both the x and $y - axes$, both the x and $y - values$ change in sign.

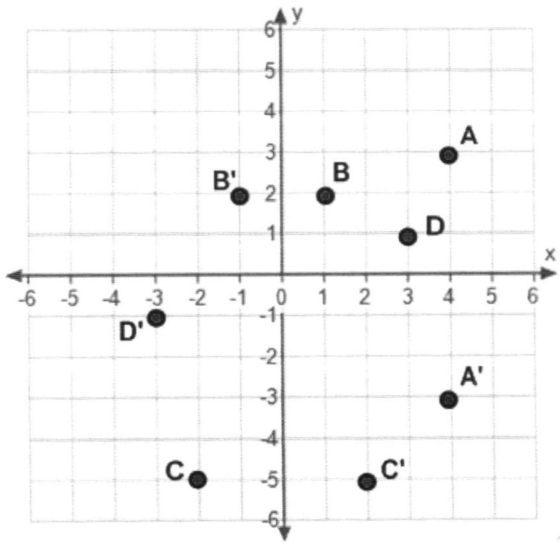

Example Problem 2

<u>Identify the reflections that produce the second of each pair from the first of each pair:</u>

(2, 6) and (-2, 6)
(-4, 0) and (4, 0)
(-1, -1) and (-1, 1)
(5, -7) and (-5, 7)

The reflection from (2, 6) to (-2, 6) is a reflection across the $y - axis$. This is because the $x - value$ has changed in sign.

The reflection from (-4, 0) to (4, 0) is a reflection across the $y - axis$. This is because the $x - value$ has changed in sign.

The reflection from (-1, -1) to (-1, 1) is a reflection across the $x - axis$. This is because the $y - value$ has changed in sign.

The reflection from (5, -7) to (-5, 7) is a reflection across both the x and $y - axis$. This is because both the x and $y - values$ have changed in sign.

Fractions

Example Problem 1

You and your best friend plan to split the remaining amount of a large pizza. If there is $\frac{3}{4}$ of the pizza left, find what fraction of the original pizza each of you will get and represent the solution with a diagram.

You each get $\frac{3}{8}$ of the original pizza. This is found by dividing $\frac{3}{4}$ by 2. When dividing with fractions, dividing by a number is the same as multiplying by the reciprocal of that number, so that $\frac{3}{4} \div 2 = \frac{3}{4} \times \frac{1}{2}$.

Multiply the numerators together to obtain the numerator of the product, and multiply the denominators to get the denominator of the product: $\frac{3}{4} \times \frac{1}{2} = \frac{3}{8}$. This division problem can be represented by the diagram shown.

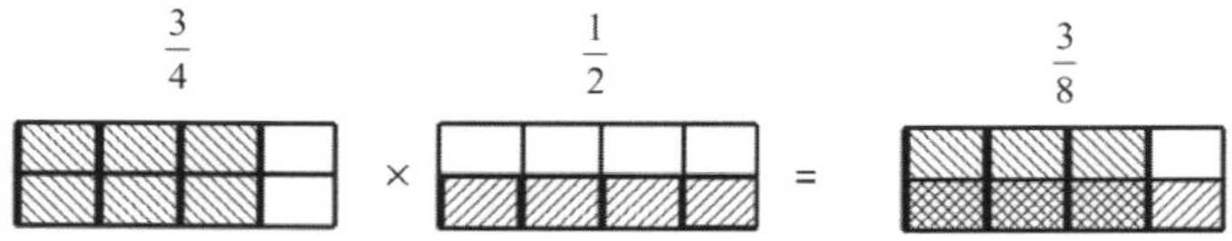

In the first part of the diagram, $\frac{3}{4}$ of the squares are shaded. In the second diagram, $\frac{1}{2}$ of the squares are shaded. Any squares that are shaded in both diagrams will be the answer. The overlap of the two diagrams shows that 3 of the 8 squares overlap, or $\frac{3}{8}$ of the whole. Or, consider dividing the first diagram, which has 6 out of the 8 squares shaded, by two. This would mean taking away half of the shaded squares, which would also result in 3 of the 8 squares shaded, or an answer of $\frac{3}{8}$.

Example Problem 2

Ms. Redding is going to frame two new rectangular posters she bought while on vacation. Before placing the order for the frames she needs to know the dimensions of each poster. When she bought the posters she was told that the area of each is $^2/_3$ square yards, the width of one is $^3/_4$ yards and the width of the other is $^1/_2$ yard. Find the length of each poster.

The lengths of the two posters are $^8/_9$ yards and $1\,^1/_3$ yards, respectively. Because $Area = length \times width$ for any rectangle, then $l = \frac{A}{w}$. To solve for the length of each rectangle, divide the area ($^2/_3$ square yards) by each width. When dividing by a fraction you must multiply by the reciprocal of that fraction.

For the first poster, $l = \frac{2}{3} \div \frac{3}{4} = \frac{2}{3} \times \frac{4}{3} = \frac{8}{9}$, and the length of the first poster is $^8/_9$ yards. For the second poster, $l = \frac{2}{3} \div \frac{1}{2} = \frac{2}{3} \times \frac{2}{1} = \frac{4}{3} = 1\,^1/_3$, and the length of the second poster is $1\,^1/_3$ yards.

Expressions

Example Problem 1

Simplify the following expressions:

$$(x + 2) \times (x + 2) \times (x + 2)$$

$$(3 - y) \times (3 - y) \times (4x) \times (4x) \times (4x)$$

$$(5 - m) \times (5 - m)^2 \times (6 - m)$$

$(x + 2) \times (x + 2) \times (x + 2) = (x + 2)^3$ This is because there are three instances of $(x + 2)$ being multiplied together, which is the same as raising the quantity $(x + 2)$ to the third power.

$(3 - y) \times (3 - y) \times (4x) \times (4x) \times (4x) = (3 - y)^2 \times (4x)^3$ This is because there are two instances of $(3 - y)$ being multiplied together, which is the same as raising the entity $(3 - y)$ to the second power. That is then being multiplied by three instances of $(4x)$, which is the same as multiplying by $(4x)$ raised to the third power.

$(5 - m) \times (5 - m)^2 \times (6 - m) = (5 - m)^3 \times (6 - m)$ This is because there are three instances of $(5 - m)$ being multiplied together, because $(5 - m)^2 = (5 - m) \times (5 - m)$.

EXAMPLE PROBLEM 2

EVALUATE THE FOLLOWING:

$$(3 - 1) + 4^2 \times 2$$

$$3^3 + (3 \times 3)$$

$$5^2 - (6 - 2)^2$$

Evaluate these expressions following the order of operations: parentheses, exponents, multiplication/division, and addition/subtraction.

$(3 - 1) + 4^2 \times 2$ is equivalent to 34: $(3 - 1) + 4^2 \times 2 = (2) + 4^2 \times 2 = (2) + 16 \times 2 = (2) + 32 = 34$

$3^3 + (3 \times 3)$ is equivalent to 36: $3^3 + (3 \times 3) = 3^3 + 9 = 27 + 9 = 36$

$5^2 - (6 - 2)^2$ is equivalent to 9: $5^2 - (6 - 2)^2 = 5^2 - (4)^2 = 25 - 16 = 9$

EXAMPLE PROBLEM 3

SIMPLIFY THE FOLLOWING EXPRESSIONS AND IDENTIFY THE TERMS, PRODUCTS, FACTORS, SUMS, QUOTIENTS, AND/OR COEFFICIENTS IN EACH:

A. $4x + 3x - 2y$
B. $10(3 + 1)$
C. $\frac{10+5+1}{2}$

There are three terms in the original expression, $4x$, $3x$, and $-2y$. There are also three coefficients in the expression, 4, 3, and -2, respectively. Since $7x$ is the sum of $4x$ and $3x$, the expression simplifies to $7x - 2y$.

There are two terms in the original expression, 3 and 1, and one coefficient, 10, multiplying the sum of the two terms. The sum of 3 and 1 is 4, and the product of 10 and 4 is 40. Therefore, 10 and 4 are factors of 40.

Since we can write this as $(10 + 5 + 1) \div 2$, there are four terms in the original expression, 10, 5, 1 and 2. The sum of 10, 5, and 1 is 16, and the quotient of 16 and 2 is 8. Therefore, 2 and 8 are factors of 16.

Example Problem 4

Write expressions to represent the following situations:

Turner has saved $75 toward the purchase of an iPod. How much more money does he need to save?

This week Marcus mowed twice the amount of lawns he mowed last week. How many lawns did Marcus mow this week?

Jenny earns $4 for every room she cleans in her house. How much money will she earn cleaning her whole house?

Turner has saved $75 toward the purchase of an iPod. The amount of money he still needs to save can be expressed by $C - 75$, representing the difference between total cost, C, of the iPod and what he already has.

This week Marcus mowed twice the amount of lawns he mowed last week. The number of lawns he mowed this week can be expressed as $2l$, representing two times the number of lawns mowed last week, l.

Jenny earns $4 for every room she cleans in her house. The amount of money she will earn cleaning her whole house can be expressed by $4r$, representing 4 times the number of rooms, r, in her whole house.

Example Problem 5

Write expressions to represent the following situations and then solve them:

Caroline has 3 more hours of homework tonight than last night. How much homework does Caroline have tonight if she had one hour of homework last night?

This month Fred will only work one-third of the hours he worked last month. How many hours will Fred work this month if he worked 150 hours last month?

The first part of this situation can be expressed by $h + 3$, representing the number of hours of homework Caroline has tonight in terms of 3 more than she had last night, h. If she had one hour of homework last night, then she has 4 hours of homework tonight, because $1 + 3 = 4$.

This can be expressed by $\frac{w}{3}$, representing the number of hours Fred will work this month in terms of one third of the number he worked last month, w. If he worked 150 hours last month, then he will work 50 hours this month, because $\frac{150}{3} = 50$.

Writing Equations

Example Problem 1

Write and solve equations that represent the following situations:

You are 16 years old and twice as old as your sister. How old is your sister?

Your mother is 5 times as old as your sister. How old is your mother?

Your cousin's age is the sum of your age and your sister's age. How old is your cousin?

This situation is represented by the equation $2x = 16$, where x represents your sister's age. Solve this equation by dividing both sides by 2, resulting in $x = 8$. Therefore, your sister is 8 years old.

Before we knew your sister's age, this was represented by $m = 5x$, where m is your mother's age and x is your sister's. Since it is now known that your sister is 8 years old, this situation is represented by the equation $5 \times 8 = m$. Solving this equation gives an answer of $5 \times 8 = 40$, so your mother is 40 years old.

Until we knew your sister's age, this was represented by $c = 16 + x$. Since your sister is 8 years, this situation can be represented by the equation $16 + 8 = c$, where c represents your cousin's age. Solving this equation gives an answer of $16 + 8 = 24$, so your cousin is 24 years old.

Example Problem 2

Determine the equation that represents the cost, C, for any number of shirts, x, using the table of information below, and find how much it will cost to buy 12 shirts:

Number of Shirts	Cost (in dollars)
1	5
2	10
3	15
4	20

The equation that represents the situation is $C = 5x$. This is found by determining the relationship between the independent variable, which is the number of t-shirts, and the dependent variable, which is the cost. In the table it can be seen that for each shirt bought, the cost goes up by 5 dollars. It is then also seen that multiplying the number of shirts by 5 gives the cost, because $1 \times 5 = 5, 2 \times 5 = 10, 3 \times 5 = 15$, and $4 \times 5 = 20$. Therefore, for any x number of shirts, that number can just be multiplied by 5 to get the cost, which is represented by $C = 5x$.

It will cost $60 to buy 12 shirts. This is found by using the equation that represents the data, substituting12 for x, the number of shirts: $C = 5 \times 12 = 60$.

Example Problem 3

<u>Write the equation to represent the following table of values and graph them. Using the graph, predict the cost of mailing a 6 pound package.</u>

The cost of mailing a package at the post office.	
Weight (in lbs)	**Cost (in dollars)**
1	1.5
2	3
3	4.5
4	6

The equation that represents the cost, C, in terms of the weight, w, of a package is $C = 1.5w$, because for each additional pound, the cost increases by $1.50 per pound. These values are graphed in the graph below:

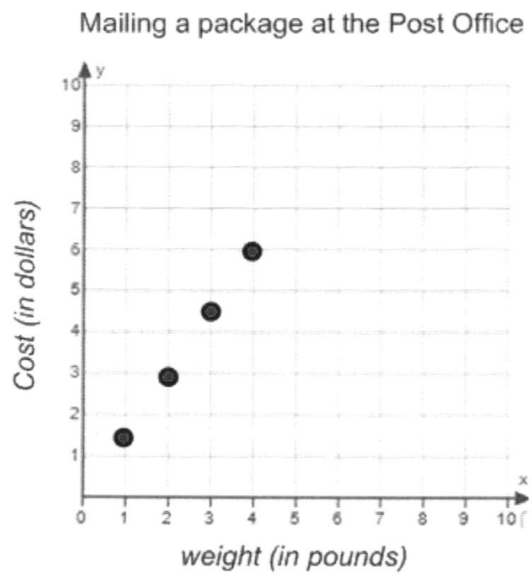

Looking at the graph, the points are going up at a constant rate of $1.50 for each pound. The next point would be at (5, 7.5), and then the next point would be at (6, 9). This means that the cost of mailing a 6 pound package would be $9.

CHECKING EQUATIONS

EXAMPLE PROBLEM 1

Match each expression in Column I with its equivalent expression in Column II. Verify that the expressions are equivalent by substituting any non-zero value for x.

Column I	Column II
A. $4x$	X. $x + 2x + x$
B. $10x + 12$	Y. $3x - x - x$
C. x	Z. $3x + 5 + 7x + 7$

A is equivalent to X. If $x = 3$, we see that $4x = 4 \times 3 = 12$, and $x + 2x + x = 3 + 2 \times 3 + 3 = 3 + 6 + 3 = 12$. Since the expressions have the same value when $x = 3$, the expressions are equivalent.

B is equivalent to Z. If $x = 2$, we see that $B = 10x + 12 = 10 \times 2 + 12 = 20 + 12 = 32$, and $Z = 3x + 5 + 7x + 7 = 3 \times 2 + 5 + 7 \times 2 + 7 = 6 + 5 + 14 + 7 = 32$. Since the expressions have the same value when $x = 2$, the expressions are equivalent.

C is equivalent to Y. If $x = 5$, we see that $x = 5$, and $3x - x - x = 3 \times 5 - 5 - 5 = 15 - 5 - 5 = 10 - 5 = 5$. Since the expressions have the same value when $x = 5$, the expressions are equivalent.

EXAMPLE PROBLEM 2

The equation $y = 2x + 5$ represents the line that contains all points (x, y) that satisfy the equation. Decide which, if any, of the following points lie on the line.

(1,8) (0,5) (2,9) (2,5)

The points (0,5) *and* (2,9) lie on the line. Any points that lie on the line have x and y values that make the equation true. Plug in the first value of each pair for x and the second value of each pair for y, and see whether the equation is true. For the point (0,5): $5 = 2 \times 0 + 5 = 0 + 5 = 5$, and the equation is still true. For the point (2,9): $9 = 2 \times 2 + 5 = 4 + 5 = 9$, and the equation is still true. These points make the equation true and lie on the line. The other two points do not work in the equation. For (1,8): $8 = 2 \times 1 + 5 = 2 + 5 \neq 7$. For (2,5): $5 = 2 \times 2 + 5 = 4 + 5 \neq 9$. (This could also be discovered by referring back to the point (2,9) that is on the line. Since y equals 9 when x is 2, the point (2,5) could be eliminated without testing it in the equation.)

Example Problem 3

Solve the inequality for a and check the answer by plugging in a possible value:

$$2a + 6 > 30$$

The solution is $a > 12$. This means that a can be any value greater than 12. This is solved the same way an equation is solved, doing whatever is done to one side of the inequality to the other:

$2a + 6 > 30$ (first subtract 6 from both sides)

$2a > 24$ (divide both sides by 2)

$a > 12$

To check the solution, any value that is greater than 12 can be chosen for a. If 20 is chosen, check to see that the left side of the inequality will have a greater value than 30:

$$2 \times 20 + 6 > 30$$

$$40 + 6 > 30$$

$$46 > 30$$

Because it is true that 46 is greater than 30, the inequality was solved correctly.

Example Problem 4

Find the solution to the following equation and check the solution by plugging it back into the equation:

$$2p - 11 = 19$$

The solution is $p = 15$. This is found by manipulating the equation to get p by itself on one side of the equal sign. This can be done best by getting rid of the numbers in the reverse order of the normal order of operations. Surrounding the p there is a 2 being multiplied to it and an 11 being subtracted from it. In order of operations, multiplication would be done first and subtraction after, so to undo this expression the subtraction must be handled first, then the multiplication:

$2p - 11 = 19$ (first add 11 to both sides to undo the subtraction by 11)

$2p = 30$ (then divide both sides by 2 to undo the multiplication by 2)

$p = 15$

By plugging the solution back into the original equation it can be verified: $2 \times 15 - 11 = 30 - 11 = 19 = 19$. Since both sides of the equation have a value of 19, the solution is correct.

TABLE REPRESENTING AN EQUATION

EXAMPLE

The equation $T = 1l$, represents T, the total time in minutes a racecar driver drives for l number of laps. Determine what the 1 in the equation means, and make a table of values that represents this equation and graph them.

The 1 in the equation represents the time the driver takes to complete one lap. This means that every lap takes the driver 1 minute. The table and graph below show this data:

Number of laps	Time (in minutes)
1	1
2	2
3	3
4	4

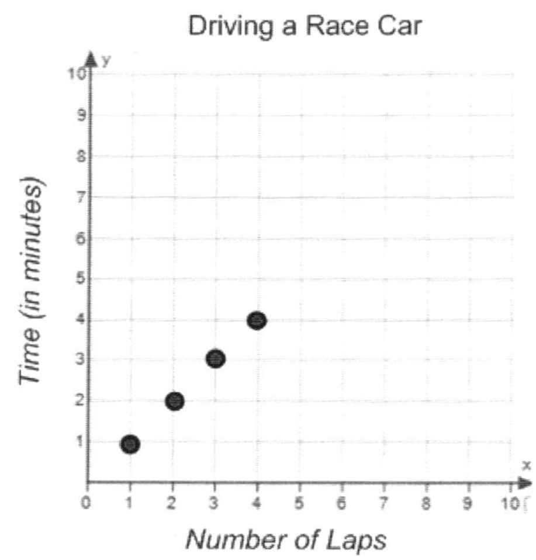

SURFACE AREA AND VOLUME

EXAMPLE PROBLEM 1

FIND THE SURFACE AREA AND VOLUME OF A CUBE WITH SIDE OF LENGTH 3CM GIVEN THE FOLLOWING FORMULAS:

$$SA = 6s^2 \text{ and } V = s^3$$

The Surface Area of the cube is 54 square cm and the Volume of the cube is 27 cubic cm. In a cube, the length, width, and height are all the same measurement, which is why the formulas only have one variable, s, which refers to the length of each side. The answers are found by substituting 3 for s in each formula. Surface Area: $SA = 6 \times 3^2 = 6 \times 9 = 54cm^2$. Volume: $V = 3^3 = 27cm^3$.

EXAMPLE PROBLEM 2

FIND THE SURFACE AREA AND VOLUME OF A CYLINDER WITH A HEIGHT OF 4CM AND RADIUS OF 6CM, GIVEN THE FORMULAS BELOW.

$$SA = 2\pi r^2 + 2\pi rh \text{ and } V = \pi r^2 h$$

The Surface Area of the cylinder is 120π square cm and the Volume of the cylinder is 144π cubic cm. Substitute 4 for h in each formula, since h represents the height, and 6 for r in each formula, since r represents the radius. Surface Area:

$$SA = 2\pi \times 6^2 + 2\pi \times 6 \times 4 = 2\pi \times 36 + 2\pi \times 24 = 72\pi + 48\pi = 120\pi\ cm^2.$$

Volume: $V = \pi \times 6^2 \times 4 = \pi \times 36 \times 4 = 144\pi\ cm^3$.

AREA

EXAMPLE PROBLEM 1

FIND THE AREA OF THE FOLLOWING ISOSCELES TRAPEZOID:

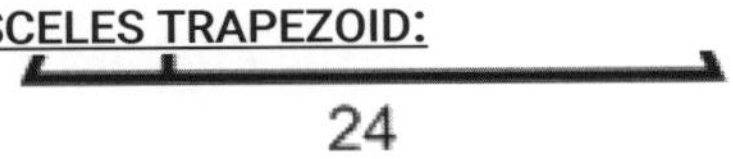

The area of the trapezoid is 144 square units and can be found by breaking the shape into two triangles and one rectangle, like so:

- Since the top base of the trapezoid has a length of 12 and is also the top of the rectangle, then the bottom of the rectangle also has a length of 12. Because the whole base had a length of 24, this leaves 12 for the two bases of the triangles. Dividing this remaining portion in half (because we are told the trapezoid is isosceles) gives each triangle a base of 6. The area of the rectangle is $12 \times 8 = 96$, and the area of each triangle is $\frac{6\times 8}{2} = \frac{48}{2} = 24$. The total area is then $96 + 24 + 24 = 144$ square units.

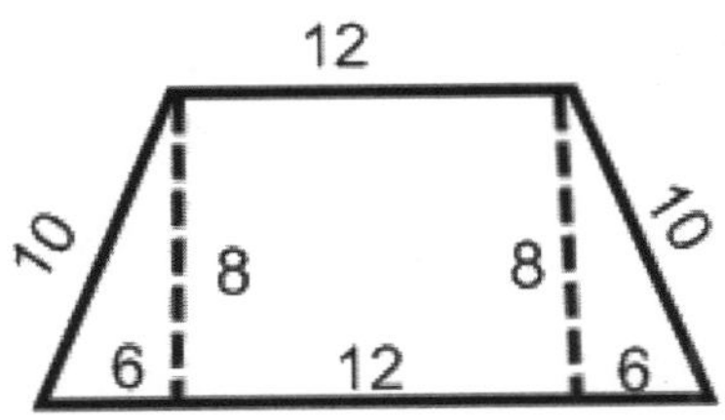

Example Problem 2

Mr. Byron is going to buy a new plot of land to build a cabin. The two plots of land are each triangles, but one is a right triangle and the other is an isosceles triangle. Decide which plot will give Mr. Byron the most land to build his cabin using the dimensions given below in feet:

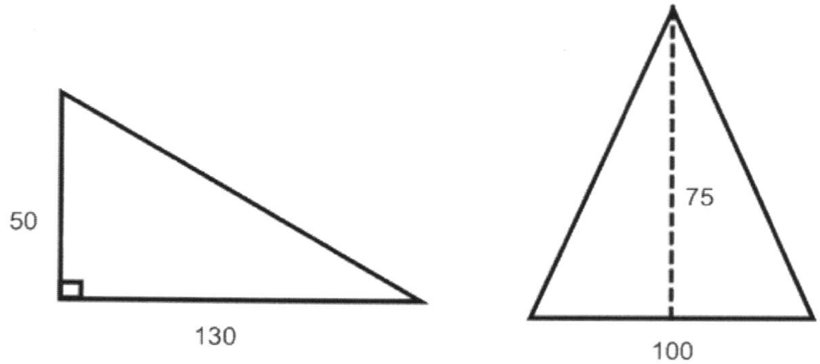

The isosceles triangle will give Mr. Byron the most land, because it has an area of 3750 square feet, while the right triangle only has an area of 3250 square feet. This is found by using the formula for the area of a triangle, $A = \frac{b\times h}{2}$. For the isosceles triangle, $A = \frac{100\times 75}{2} = \frac{7500}{2} = 3750$ square feet, and for the right triangle, $A = \frac{130\times 50}{2} = \frac{6500}{2} = 3250$ square feet. Therefore, the plot of land that is an isosceles triangle has an area that is 500 square feet larger than the right triangle, so Mr. Byron will want to purchase that plot.

Example Problem 3

Jeremy is staining the cement floor in his basement. He wants to stain the shape of a hexagon in the middle of the floor. He outlines a regular hexagon that has a side of length 6 feet on all sides and a height of 10.4 feet. Find the area Jeremy needs enough stain to cover.

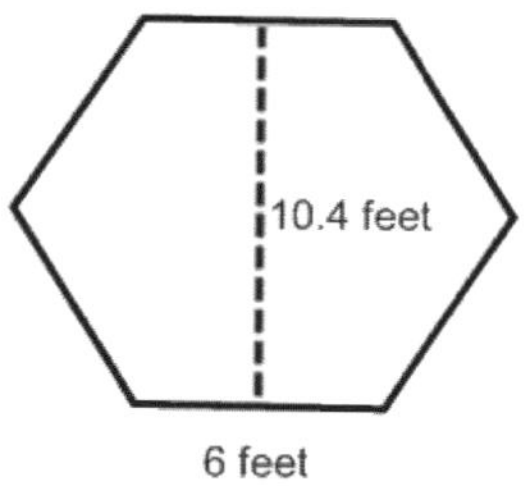

Jeremy will need enough stain to cover 93.6 square feet. This area of the hexagon is found by breaking the hexagon into 6 triangles. Because it is a regular hexagon, each side length is 6 and the height of one triangle is half the height of the whole hexagon, or $\frac{10.4}{2} = 5.2$. Therefore all the triangles are congruent as seen in the diagram below:

Using the formula for area of a triangle, $A = \frac{b \times h}{2}$, each triangle has an area of $\frac{6 \times 5.2}{2} = \frac{31.2}{2} = 15.6$ square feet. Since each of the 6 triangles has the same area, the total area of the hexagon is then $15.6 \times 6 = 93.6$ square feet.

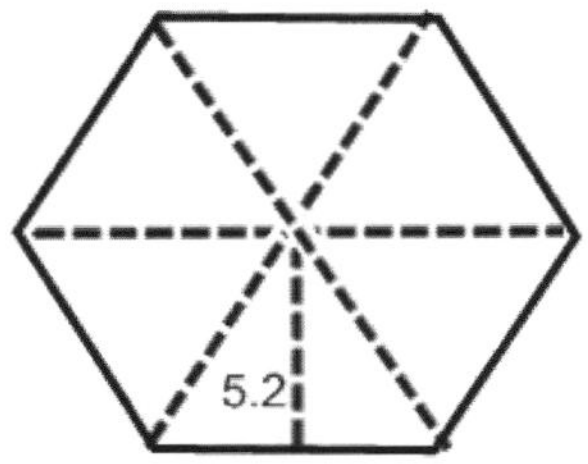

Example Problem 4

<u>**Find the area of the right triangle that has its longest side connecting points A (3, 8) and B (9, 4), and has one horizontal leg and one vertical leg.**</u>

The area of this triangle is 12 square units.

To solve for the area, it may be helpful to draw a diagram. Since we are told one leg is horizontal and the other vertical, the legs of the right triangle meet at the ordered pair (3, 4) (or at (9, 8) which would give the same area). The height of the triangle is the distance from (3, 4) to point A at (3, 8) which is 4 units. The base of the triangle is the distance from (3, 4) to point B at (9, 4) which is 6 units. The area of a triangle is found by the formula $A = \frac{b \times h}{2}$ and for this triangle the area is $A = \frac{6 \times 4}{2} = \frac{24}{2} = 12 \text{ units}^2$.

Volume

Example Problem 1

Ryland Raisin Company is creating new mini-boxes of raisins to sell at school lunches. They have decided to package them in a box that is a cube with dimensions of

$\frac{4}{3}in \times \frac{4}{3}in \times \frac{4}{3}in$. Find how many mini-boxes with side lengths of $\frac{1}{3}$ in can fit into a raisin box package and what volume the larger box can hold.

There are 64 cubes with side lengths of $\frac{1}{3}$ in that can fit into this new raisin box. The volume of the box is $\frac{64}{27}\text{in}^3 = 2\frac{10}{27}\text{in}^3$.

The number of $\frac{1}{3}$ in sided cubes that fit into the box can be found by creating a diagram of the box with its dimensions broken down into $\frac{1}{3}in$ portions as seen below:

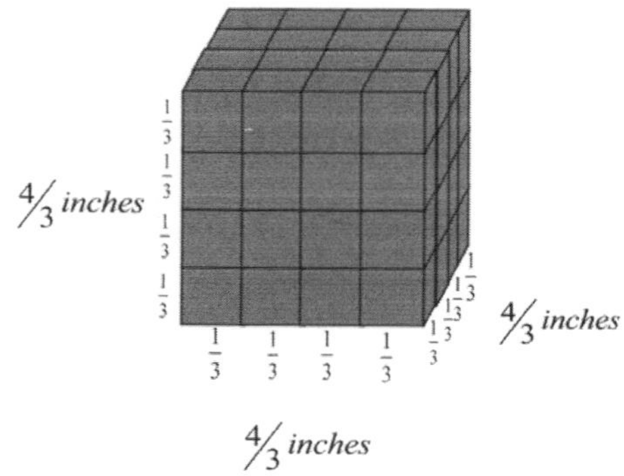

The top row of the box shows there are 16 cubes with sides of $\frac{1}{3}in$. There are 4 of these rows, which makes a total of $16 \times 4 = 64$ cubes. Since the volume of each little cube is $\frac{1}{3} \times \frac{1}{3} \times \frac{1}{3} = \frac{1}{27}in^3$, then the total volume is $64 \times \frac{1}{27} = \frac{64}{27} = 2\frac{10}{27}in^3$. This total volume can also be found by multiplying the dimensions of the raisin box package directly: $\frac{4}{3} \times \frac{4}{3} \times \frac{4}{3} = \frac{64}{27} = 2\frac{10}{27}in^3$.

EXAMPLE PROBLEM 2

At the grocery store you see two different kinds of cereal on sale for the same price. Box A has dimensions $\frac{3}{4}ft \times \frac{1}{2}ft \times \frac{2}{3}ft$ and Box B has dimensions $\frac{9}{10}ft \times \frac{1}{3}ft \times \frac{4}{5}ft$. Decide which box will give you the most cereal for your money.

Box A will give you more cereal for your money because the box can hold more volume than Box B. Find the volume of each box using the formula $V = l \times w \times h$. The volume of Box A is $\frac{3}{4} \times \frac{1}{2} \times \frac{2}{3} = \frac{6}{24} = \frac{1}{4}\text{ft}^3$, and the volume of Box B is $\frac{9}{10} \times \frac{1}{3} \times \frac{4}{5} = \frac{36}{150} = \frac{6}{25}\text{ft}^3$. Because $\frac{1}{4} = .25$ and $\frac{6}{25} = .24$, the volume of Box A is slightly larger than the volume of Box B and therefore a better deal because it will hold more cereal.

MEAN, MEDIAN, AND MODE

EXAMPLE PROBLEM 1

DEFINE THE FOLLOWING TERMS AND FIND EACH FOR THE DATA LISTED BELOW:

- Mean
- Median
- Mode

22, 17, 14, 15, 11, 20, 16, 15, 12, 14, 14

The *Mean* is the average of a set of data. This is found by dividing the sum of the data values by the number of values there are. The mean of the given data is 15.455, which is found by dividing the sum of the data by 11 because there are 11 terms in the data: $\frac{22+17+14+15+11+20+16+15+12+14+14}{11} = 15.455$.

The *Median* is the middle number in a set of data, and can be found by listing the data in order from least to greatest and crossing one off on either end until the middle is reached. If there are two middle terms the average of them is the median of the data. The median of the given data is 15:
$11, 12, 14, 14, 14, 15, 15, 16, 17, 20, 22$.

The *mode* is the value in a set of data that occurs the most often. In the given data the mode is 14, because that value occurs 3 times while all other values are only in the list 1 or 2 times.

Example Problem 2

The following are the test scores Michaela earned in math class. Her teacher is deciding whether the mean or the median score would best represent Michaela's final grade in math. Based on the data, determine if the teacher should use the mean or the median.

Michaela's Test Scores

50, 55, 58, 58, 90, 92, 99

Michaela's teacher should use the mean test score. The mean test score is found by dividing the sum of the data values by how many there are. The mean of Michaela's test scores is $\frac{50+55+58+58+90+92+99}{7} = \frac{502}{7} = 71.7$. The median of Michaela's test scores is the number in the middle, which is 58: $50, 55, 58, 58, 90, 92, 99$. Since Michaela appears to have improved, it is more reasonable for her to have a passing grade of 71.7% than a failing grade at 58%. Therefore the mean better represents this data.

Example Problem 3

You want to go to the ballpark to buy tickets to a baseball game. To ensure that you are able to get tickets you will need to get in the line that has the least waiting time. At the ballpark there are two lines: Red and Blue. You surveyed your friends who have bought tickets in the past to find their wait times. Analyze the data you collected below, decide which line you should wait in to purchase tickets. Time (in minutes):

Red Line: 5, 12, 7, 15, 11, 12, 6, 10, 9 Blue Line: 9, 9, 26, 6, 10, 8, 11, 10, 8

You should wait in the Blue Line. This is because the Red Line has a median wait time of 10 minutes while the Blue Line has a median wait time of 9 minutes. This is found by first listing the data points in order from least to greatest and finding the middle number, which is the median of the data. Crossing off the numbers on the left and right side until reaching the middle will find the middle number: Red Line: 5, 6, 7, 9, 10, 11, 12, 12, 15 and Blue Line: 6, 8, 8, 9, 9, 10, 10, 11, 26.

EXAMPLE PROBLEM 4

YOU HAVE GATHERED DATA ON THE WAIT TIMES FOR TWO DIFFERENT LINES AT THE BALLPARK. YOU DECIDE TO WAIT IN THE BLUE LINE BECAUSE IT HAS THE LOWER MEDIAN WAIT TIME. YOUR FRIEND TELLS YOU, HOWEVER, THAT YOU SHOULD WAIT IN THE RED LINE BECAUSE IT HAS THE SHORTEST WAIT TIME RECORDED. CONSIDER THE DATA BELOW, DECIDE IF YOU SHOULD CHANGE YOUR MIND AND TAKE YOUR FRIEND'S ADVICE.

TIME (IN MINUTES):

RED LINE: 5, 12, 7, 15, 11, 12, 6, 10, 9 BLUE LINE: 9, 9, 26, 6, 10, 8, 11, 10, 8

You should not take your friend's advice. You should still choose the Blue Line because the Blue Line's median is 9 minutes, while the Red Line's median is 10 minutes. The data point of 26 in the Blue Line is considered an outlier because it varies greatly from the median compared to the other data points in the set. If you ignore that outlier, the median is still 9! Even ignoring the highest wait time for each line, the mean wait time is higher for the red line, so although the Red Line had the shortest wait time and Blue Line had the longest wait time that is not the best judge of predicting wait time.

EXAMPLE PROBLEM 5

PREDICT WHAT THE MEDIAN OF THE DATA IS BY ANALYZING THE DOT PLOT BELOW. CALCULATE THE MEDIAN TO CHECK THE PREDICTION.

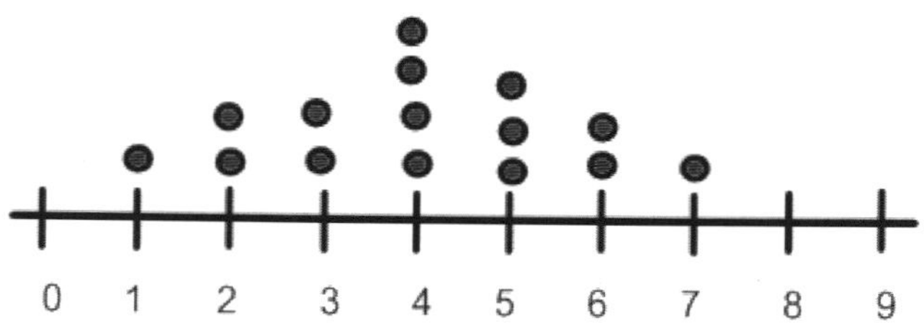

It appears that the median of the data is 4, as its values fall in the middle of all of the dots on the dot plot. Calculating the median is done by first listing the data in order from least to greatest. Each dot on the dot plot represents the number it is above, so therefore the data values are 1, 2, 2, 3, 3, 4, 4, 4, 4, 5, 5, 5, 6, 6, 7. To find the median the values must be crossed off until the middle number is reached:

1, 2, 2, 3, 3, 4, 4, 4, 4, 5, 5, 5, 6, 6, 7. The appearance of the median in the dot plot is accurate, as the median is 4.

STATISTICAL QUESTIONS AND VARIABILITY

DETERMINE WHETHER THE FOLLOWING QUESTIONS ARE CONSIDERED STATISTICAL QUESTIONS AND EXPLAIN WHY OR WHY NOT:

'HOW MANY PETS DO THE FAMILIES IN MY NEIGHBORHOOD HAVE?'

'WHAT SIZE ARE MY SHOES?'

'HOW MANY PAGES DID I READ IN THE LAST HOUR?'

'HOW LONG DID IT TAKE THE STUDENTS IN MY CLASS TO GET TO SCHOOL TODAY?'

Yes, this is a statistical question because it will have variability. The families in your neighborhood will not each have the same number of pets, but there will be a variation in the data collected and conclusions can be drawn from this.

No, this is not a statistical question. There will be no variation because there is one answer.

No, this is not a statistical question. There will be no variation because there is one answer.

Yes, this is a statistical question because it has variability. There will be many different answers to this question and conclusions can be drawn from the data.

DATA REPRESENTATION AND ANALYSIS

EXAMPLE PROBLEM 1

REPRESENT THE FOLLOWING DATA IN A DOT PLOT AND FIND THE MODE OF THE DATA:

THE AMOUNT OF MONEY YOUR FRIENDS MAKE BABYSITTING PER HOUR

5, 2, 7, 9, 4, 5, 6, 7, 9, 7

THE DATA IS REPRESENTED IN A DOT PLOT BELOW:

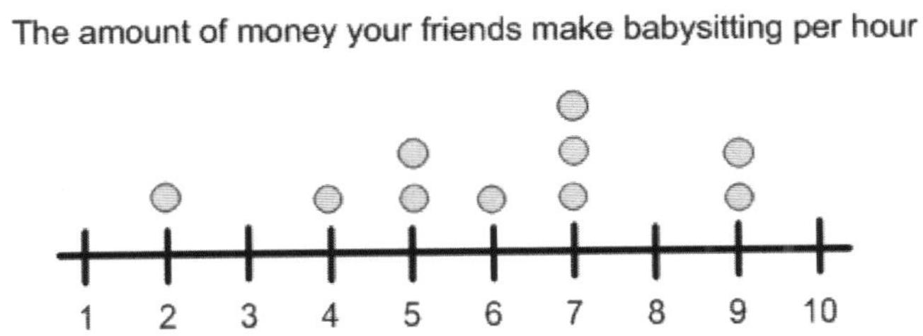

This is made by creating a number line that can display the range of data and then placing one dot above each number for each data value equal to that number. The mode of this data is 7, which is the number that occurs in the data most. The mode is easy to see in a dot plot because it is the number that has the most dots. In this data, three people get $7/hour babysitting while only one or two people get paid the other amounts in the list.

EXAMPLE PROBLEM 2

REPRESENT THE FOLLOWING DATA IN A BOX PLOT:
MICHAEL'S MATH TEST GRADES LAST SEMESTER
88, 90, 95, 82, 98, 90, 77, 89, 91

The data is represented in the box plot below:

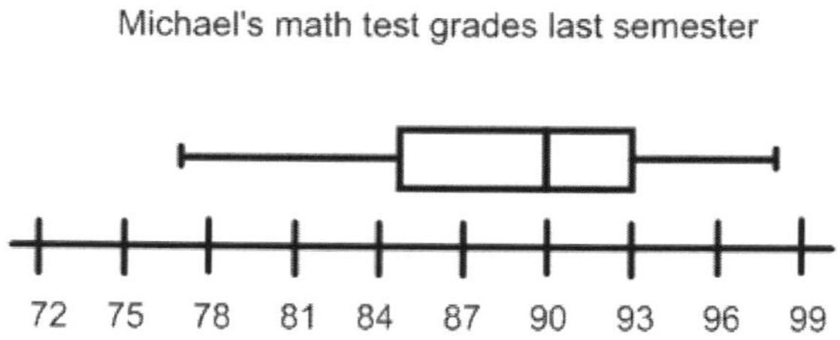

This is made by creating a number line that will fit the distribution of the data and then determining the five points that are needed to create the box plot, which are: the minimum, the maximum, the median, the lower quartile, and the upper quartile. The minimum is the number in the list with the least value, 77, and the maximum is the number with the greatest value, 98. A small tick mark is placed above those two values on the number line. The median of the data is 90, which is found by listing the data in order from least to greatest and finding the number in the middle: $77, 82, 88, 89, 90, 90, 91, 95, 98$. The lower quartile is the median of the lower half of the data, which is 85 because the middle of the lower half of the data is between the two middle numbers 82 and 88, and is therefore found by finding their average: $\frac{82+88}{2} = 85$. The upper quartile is the median of the upper half of the data, which is 93 because it is between 91 and 95, and their average is $\frac{91+95}{2} = 93$. A tick mark is placed above the median and upper and lower quartile values on the number line and a box is created around those three marks. A line is then extended from the ends of the box to the minimum and maximum.

EXAMPLE PROBLEM 3

REPRESENT THE DATA BELOW IN A HISTOGRAM:
THE AMOUNT OF HOMEWORK YOUR FRIENDS DID LAST NIGHT, IN MINUTES
45, 25, 33, 65, 37, 55, 45, 42, 31, 49, 48, 22

The histogram below represents the data:

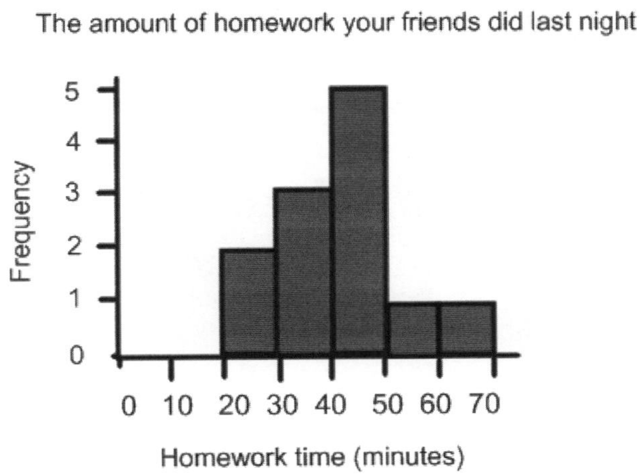

This is made by creating a graph and labeling the x-axis with homework time, the y-axis with frequency, and creating appropriate intervals for each. (Generally, divide the range of the data into 5 – 7 intervals.) The data values in each interval, which are 10 minute intervals in this histogram, are counted to determine the frequency of data values in those intervals. Adjacent rectangles are created to show the distribution of data. There are 2 pieces of data that fall between 20 and 30 minutes, so that interval has a frequency of 2. There are 3 pieces of data that fall between 30 and 40 minutes, so that interval has a frequency of 3. There are 5 pieces of data that fall between 40 and 50 minutes, so that interval has a frequency of 5. And there is 1 piece of data each that falls between 50 and 60 minutes and 60 and 70 minutes, so those each have a frequency of one.

EXAMPLE PROBLEM 4

MR. SMITH WAS DECIDING WHICH OF TWO INTERSECTIONS TO POST SIGNS AT FOR HIS GARAGE SALE. HE SAT AT ONE INTERSECTION EACH DAY FOR 30 MINUTE TIME INTERVALS FOR TWO CONSECUTIVE DAYS. SUMMARIZE THE MEANING OF HIS DATA RECORDED BELOW AND PREDICT WHAT CONCLUSIONS HE MAY DRAW.
NUMBER OF CARS THAT DROVE BY

Time	Intersection 1	Intersection 2
7am-7:30	8	1
9am-9:30	10	6
11am-11:30	11	10
1pm-1:30	0	9
3pm-3:30	5	10
5pm-5:30	2	4

Mr. Smith will most likely want to place signs for his garage sale at Intersection 2. This is because over the course of the day that Mr. Smith observed Intersection 2, 40 cars drove by, whereas over the course of the day that he observed Intersection 1, only 36 cars drove by. However, Mr. Smith's data shows observations that might make him choose Intersection 1. For example, Mr. Smith might know that morning hours are usually the busiest for garage sales and thus he might want to put his signs at Intersection 1 because more cars drive through that intersection in the morning hours. But, it seems as though the traffic at Intersection 1 tapers off greatly in the afternoon and Mr. Smith might be more concerned with having the possibility of a steady flow of customers at his garage sale all day.

Example Problem 5

THE LOCAL HOSPITAL RECORDED THE LENGTHS OF THE BABIES BORN YESTERDAY, GIVEN BELOW. ANALYZE THE DATA AND DETERMINE WHAT UNITS WERE BEING USED IN THE MEASUREMENTS. WITH THE CONCLUSION JUSTIFY ANY CHANGES YOU WOULD RECOMMEND FOR THE COLLECTION OF THE DATA.

LENGTHS OF BABIES

1.5, 1.75, 2, 16, 17.5, 17.5, 18.5, 19, 20, 20, 21, 22

It is clear that there are two different units of measurement being used to measure the lengths of babies. All of the data points between 16 and 22 are reasonable if measured in inches. The data points of 1.5, 1.75, and 2 cannot have been measured in inches and were most likely measured in feet. The data points of 1.5, 1.75, and 2 are reasonable if measured in feet, however all the other pieces of data are not reasonable to have been measured in feet. Therefore, the hospital will need to choose one unit of measure when collecting the data on the lengths of the babies born there. One suggestion would be to measure all babies in inches, and thus change the values of 1.5, 1,75, and 2 in the data to 18, 21, and 24.

Example Problem 6

Mr. Gordon is Principal at Detroit's largest Middle School and decided to allow students to choose what time they would eat lunch on a given day. To do this he surveyed a group of students and the data is represented in the histogram below. Principal Gordon concluded that he would allow students to eat at their desired lunch time, 11:00-11:30, because the most students wanted to eat during that time. Explain whether or not Principal Gordon's conclusion was justified based on the data in the histogram.

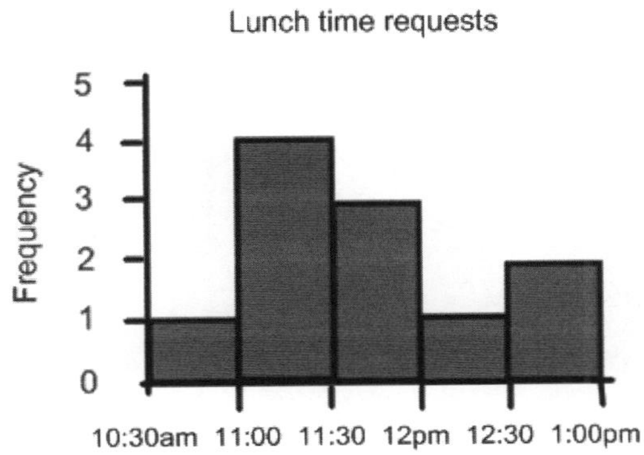

No, Mr. Gordon's conclusion is not justified based on the data given in the histogram. Although the majority of the students he surveyed do want to eat lunch between 11 and 11:30, he only surveyed 11 students. This can be found by adding the frequency of each lunch time period. Surveying a group of 11 students might be a reasonable choice for a very small school, but since Mr. Gordon is the Principal at the largest middle school in Detroit, a sample size of 11 students is not enough to draw justifiable conclusions from. It is possible that the majority of all students will want to each lunch between 11 and 11:30, but Mr. Gordon will need a larger sample size to be able to justify the conclusion that it represents the majority of students' preferences.

Net Figure

Example Problem 1

Sheila is going to make her own canvas tent for camping. She wants to make a tent that is the shape of a triangular prism. Given the dimensions below, create a net figure of the tent and determine how much canvas Sheila will need to make it.

6 feet

Sheila will need 152 square feet of canvas. This is found by determining the surface area of the triangular prism. In the net figure below, it is clear to see that the sum of the areas of two triangles and three rectangles will give the full surface area.

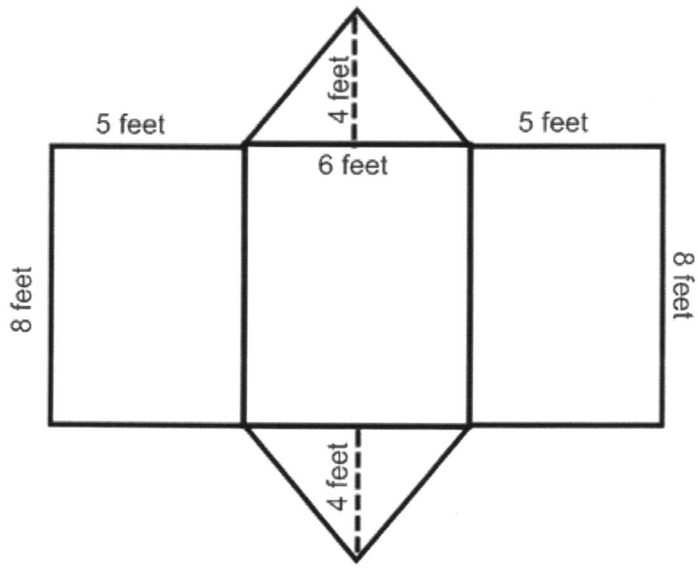

Each triangle has a base of 6 feet and height of 4 feet, so the area of each triangle is $\frac{6\times4}{2} = \frac{24}{2} = 12\text{ft}^2$. Each outer rectangle in the net figure has a length of 8 feet and a width of 5 feet, so the area of each of those rectangles is $5 \times 8 = 40\text{ft}^2$. The other rectangle has a length of 8 and a width of 6, so has an area of $6 \times 8 = 48\text{ft}^2$. The total surface area is found by adding the area of all 5 of the separate shapes together: $12 + 12 + 40 + 40 + 48 = 152\text{ft}^2$.

Example Problem 2

DRAW A NET FIGURE OF THE PRESENT BELOW AND DETERMINE HOW MUCH WRAPPING PAPER WILL BE NEEDED TO WRAP IT.

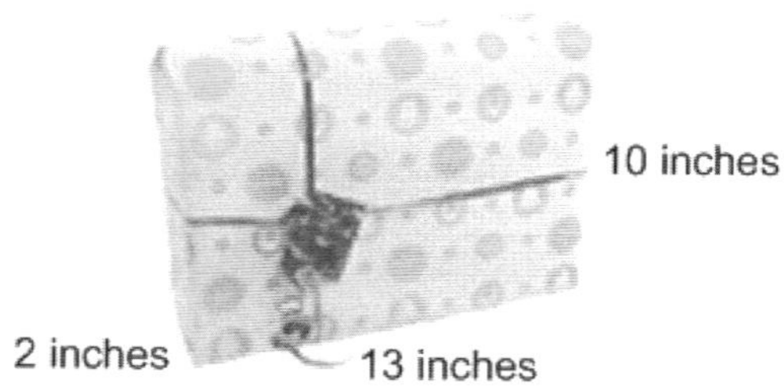

352 square inches of wrapping paper will be needed to wrap the present, which is the surface area of the box. In the net figure below, it is seen that there are two rectangles with dimensions $13\text{in} \times 2\text{in}$ which each have an area of $13 \times 2 = 26\text{in}^2$, two rectangles with dimensions $10\text{in} \times 2\text{in}$ which each have an area of $10 \times 2 = 20\text{in}^2$, and two rectangles with dimensions $13\text{in} \times 10\text{in}$ which each have an area of

$13 \times 10 = 130\text{in}^2$. The total surface area is found by adding together the areas of the 6 rectangles: $26 + 26 + 20 + 20 + 130 + 130 = 352\text{in}^2$.

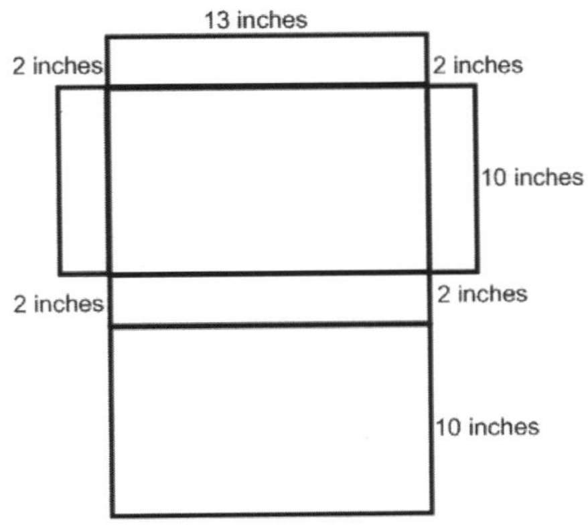

Inequalities

Example Problem 1

Write inequalities to represent the following situations, and graph them on number lines:

The speed limit on the highway is 65mph.

Your teacher is older than 30 years old.

A. This is represented by the inequality $x \leq 65$, because a person can drive at any speed less than or equal to 65mph. This is graphed on the number line below, showing a closed circle on the 65 and an arrow shading to the left, because the safe speeds include 65 and anything less than it:

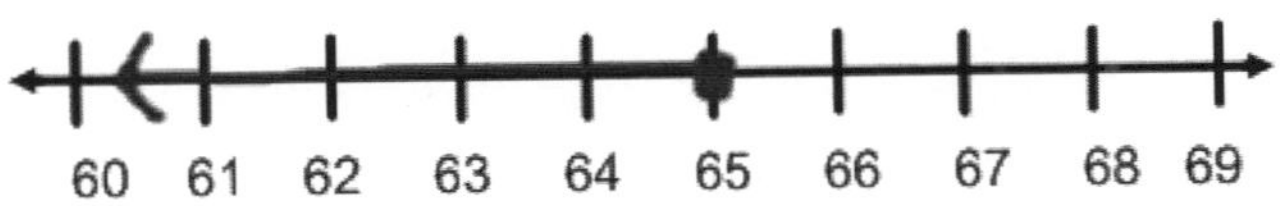

B. This is represented by the inequality $x > 30$, because your teacher is any age greater than 30 years old, but not equal to 30. This is graphed on the number line below, showing an open circle at 30 and an arrow shading to the right, which means that 30 is not included in the possible ages for your teacher but any number greater is:

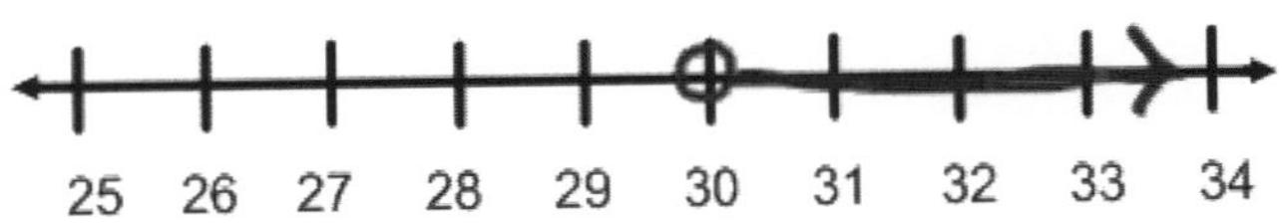

Example Problem 2

Write inequalities to represent the following situations, and give one possible solution for each:

You will not go to school for more than 5 days this week.

Your dad makes at least $100 a day at work.

The bowling alley requires a birthday party size of less than 20 kids.

This is represented by the inequality $x \leq 5$, because you might go to school 5 days or you might go to school any amount less than that. One solution could be 4, because you might get sick one day this week and only go to school 4 days.

This is represented by the inequality $x \geq 100$, because your dad will make $100 or more at work each day. One solution could be $125.

This is represented by the inequality $x < 20$, because there cannot be 20 kids in the party but there can be any amount less than that. One solution could be 15 kids at the birthday party.

Example Problem 3

Write an inequality to represent each of the following situations and explain the meaning:

Jim's golf score was 8 under par while Tom's golf score was 2 under par.

Water boils at 212°F and freezes at 32°F.

Yesterday the temperature was −17°F and today the temperature is −21°F.

If we assume 'par' is like zero on the number line, this can be represented by $-8 < -2$, which means that it took Tom a greater number of strokes to finish his golf game, because -2 is greater than -8.

This can be represented by $32° < 212°$, which means that the boiling point of water is warmer than the freezing point of water, because 212° is greater than 32°.

This can be represented by $-21° < -17°$, which means that it was warmer out yesterday because −17° is greater than −21°.

Example Problem 4

Describe scenarios that might correspond to the following inequalities:

$$-20°F < -5°F$$

$$-\$50 < -\$40$$

$$-6 < -2$$

This represents two different temperatures. One scenario could be that one day it was $-20°F$ in Alaska while the next day it was $-5°F$ there. Since $-5°F$ is greater than $-20°F$, it was warmer the second day.

This represents two amounts of money. One scenario could be that Jenny owes the bank $50 while her friend Susan owes the bank $40. Jenny has a greater debt so therefore a more negative balance, and less money than Susan.

This simply compares two negative integers. One scenario could be that they represent the scores of two golfers. If Max got a golf score of -6 ("six under par") and his friend got a golf score of -2 ("two under par"), then that means it took Max fewer swings to finish the game than it took his friend.

EXAMPLE PROBLEM 5

REPRESENT EACH SCENARIO BELOW WITH AN ABSOLUTE VALUE INEQUALITY AND GIVE ONE POSSIBLE SOLUTION:

A. *Last week Mr. Anderson lost 6 of his cattle to Mad Cow Disease and this week he lost even more.*

B. *Yesterday Andrus took an elevator from his city street underground 4 stories to the subway. Today Andrus took the same elevator down a fewer number of stories.*

C. *On Monday Sally withdrew $50 from her bank account and on Tuesday she made a larger withdrawal.*

The inequality $|-6| < |x|$ represents the number of cattle Mr. Anderson lost this week, x, compared to the number he lost last week. One possible solution would be $x = -10$, or losing 10 cattle, because $|-6| < |-10|$.

The inequality $|x| < |-4|$ represents how far below ground level Andrus traveled today, x, compared to yesterday. One possible solution would be $x = -1$, or traveling 1 story below ground level, because $|-1| < |-4|$.

The inequality $|-50| < |x|$ represents the amount of Sally's withdrawal on Tuesday, x, compared to her withdrawal Monday. One possible solution would be $x = -100$, or withdrawing $100, because $|-50| < |-100|$.

EXAMPLE PROBLEM 6

DESCRIBE A SCENARIO THAT THE FOLLOWING ABSOLUTE VALUE INEQUALITIES COULD REPRESENT:

A. $|-10\ feet| > |-3\ feet|$

B. $|-300\ points| > |-50\ points|$

This inequality could represent the depth of two fish swimming in the ocean. One fish is 10 feet below sea level, or -10 feet, while the other fish is 3 feet below sea level, or -3 feet. The absolute value of -10 is greater than the absolute value of -3, which illustrates the fact the fish swimming 10 feet below sea level is a greater distance from sea level.

This inequality could represent changes in the value of the stock market on two different days. On one day the stock market fell 300 points and the next day the stock market fell 50 points. The absolute value of -300 is greater than the absolute value of -50, illustrating that 300 points is a greater fall than 50 points.

EXAMPLE PROBLEM 7

WRITE INEQUALITIES TO REPRESENT THE FOLLOWING SITUATIONS, AND GRAPH THEM ON NUMBER LINES:

THE MINIMUM COST OF A SCHOOL PHOTO PACKAGE IS $10.

A PERSON HAS TO BE LESS THAN 48 INCHES TALL TO RIDE THE KIDDIE RIDES AT THE AMUSEMENT PARK.

This statement is represented by the inequality $x \geq 10$, because you can spend $10 or more on photos. This is graphed on the number line below, showing a closed circle on the 10 and an arrow shading to the right, because the amount you can spend includes 10 dollars or any number greater than that.

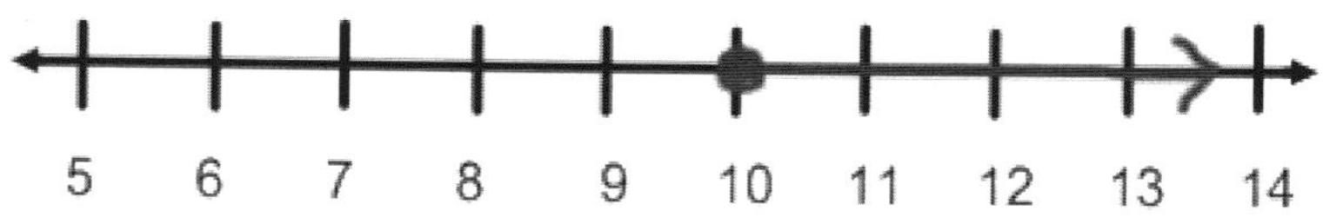

This statement is represented by the inequality $x < 48$ because the acceptable heights are all those less than 48 inches. This is graphed on the number line below, showing an open circle on the 48 and an arrow shading to the left, because 48 is not included in the acceptable heights, but anything less than it is:

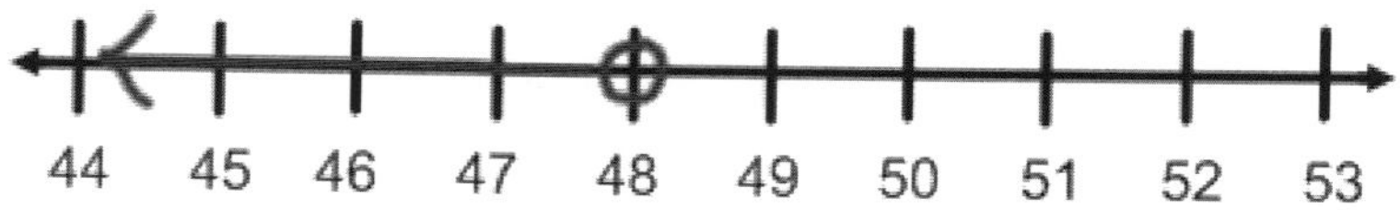

INDEPENDENT VARIABLE AND DEPENDENT VARIABLE

The independent variable is that quantity in a situation that affects the value of the other when changed.

The dependent variable is that quantity in a situation that depends on the value of another variable.

FOR THE FOLLOWING EXAMPLES:

THE TOTAL AMOUNT OF MONEY M YOU EARN FOR MOWING N LAWNS.

THE PRICE P YOU PAY FOR RENTING X VIDEOS.

THE DISTANCE D YOU TRAVEL ON A BUS OVER TIME T.

The number of lawns you mow, *n*, is the independent variable, while the amount of money you earn, *m*, will depend on how many lawns you mow and thus is the dependent variable.

The number of videos, *x*, you rent is the independent variable, and the price, *p*, you pay is the dependent variable because it depends on how many videos you rent.

The time, *t*, is the independent variable, and the distance, *d*, is the dependent variable because the distance you travel will depend on how long you travel for.

Opposite

The 'opposite' of a number is the number that is the same distance away from zero as the given number but on the other side of zero on a number line. The 'opposite' of a number always has a sign opposite the given number.

The opposite of -4 is 4.

The opposite of 7 is -7.

The opposite of 21 is -21.

The opposite of -10 is 10.

The opposite of 0 is 0. This is because the only number that is the same distance zero is from zero is zero. Zero is neither positive nor negative, so it will not change signs.

The opposite of 13 is -13.

The opposite of -13 is 13.

Number Line

Example Problem 1

Label a number line with the following values:

Point A: 2
Point B: The opposite of 3
Point C: 0
Point D: -2
Point E: The opposite of -5
Point F: The opposite of -1

The number line below shows the points:

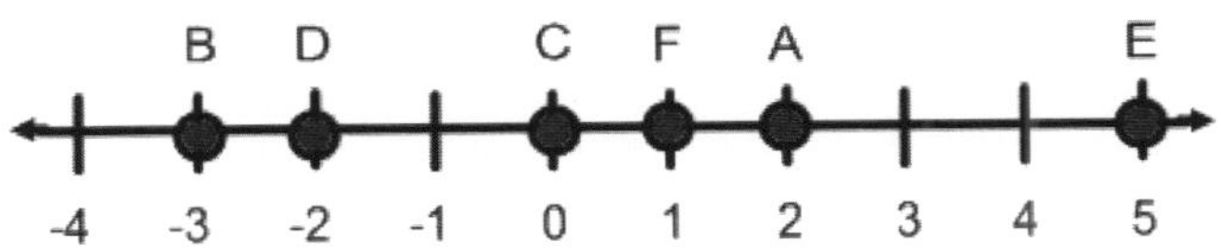

Point A is located at 2 on the number line. Point B is located at -3, which is the opposite of 3. Point C is located at 0. Point D is located at -2. Point E is located at 5, which is the opposite of -5. And Point F is located at 1, which is the opposite of -1.

EXAMPLE PROBLEM 2

DETERMINE THE FOLLOWING VALUES, THEN PLOT THE POINTS ON A NUMBER LINE AND WRITE AN INEQUALITY THAT REPRESENTS EACH RELATION BETWEEN THE POINTS:

5 UNITS TO THE RIGHT OF -2

3 UNITS TO THE LEFT OF 1

The number that is 5 units to the right of -2 is 3. The number line below shows these values and it is seen that $3 > -2$ because 3 is located to the right of -2.

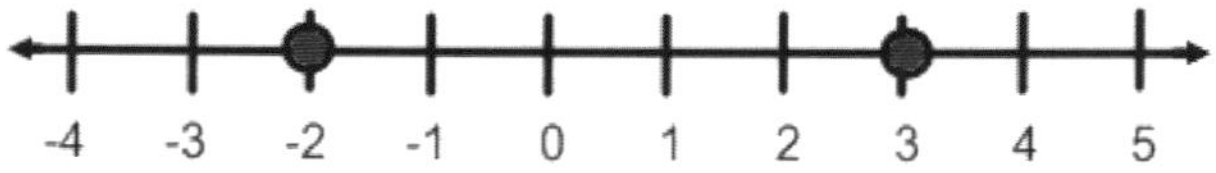

The number that is 3 units to the left of 1 is -2. The number line below shows these values and it is seen that $-2 < 1$ because -2 is located to the left of 1.

EXAMPLE PROBLEM 3

DETERMINE THE FOLLOWING VALUES, THEN PLOT THE POINTS ON A NUMBER LINE AND WRITE AN INEQUALITY THAT REPRESENTS EACH RELATION BETWEEN THE POINTS:

1 UNIT TO THE LEFT OF 1

2 UNITS TO THE LEFT OF -2

A. The number that is 1 unit to the left of 1 is 0. The number line below shows these values and it is seen that $0 < 1$ because 0 is located to the left of 1.

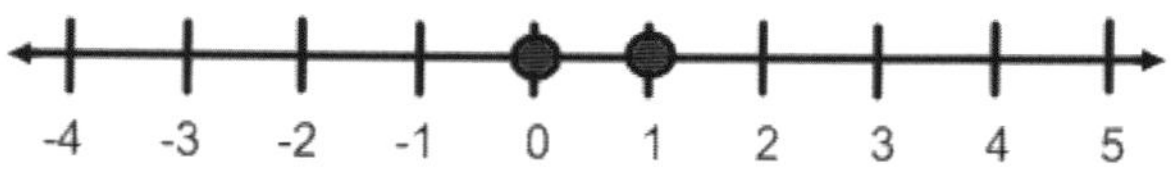

B. The number that is 2 units to the left of -2 is -4. The number line below shows these values and it is seen that $-4 < -2$ because -4 is located to the left of -2.

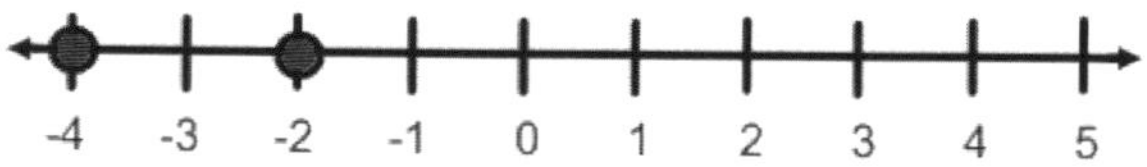

ABSOLUTE VALUE

Absolute Value is how far away a number is from zero on a number line, or the distance between zero and that number. The absolute value of a number is always positive, because distance is positive.

The absolute value of 40 is 40, because it is 40 units away from zero.

The absolute value of -12 is 12 because it is 12 units away from zero.

The absolute value of -25 is 25 because it is 25 units away from zero.

The absolute value of 18 is 18 because it is 18 units away from zero.

The absolute value of -100 is 100 because it is 100 units away from zero.

Example Problem 1

Write an absolute value equation to express the following situations:
After the first day of a bike race, Peter is 45 seconds behind the lead racer.
Marla owes her mom $10.
The scuba diver is 20 feet below sea level.

This situation can be represented by $|-45| = 45$. When we say a racer is behind, it actually means that racer's time is longer than the leader's. To catch the leader, then, Peter needs to subtract 45 seconds from his time, and this equation shows that the difference between the times is 45 seconds.

This situation can be represented by $|-10| = 10$. This shows that Marla is in debt $10 to her mom, but Marla does not actually have a negative amount of money so it is expressed as absolute value, which shows that Marla needs to pay $10 to her mom.

This situation can be represented by $|-20| = 20$. This shows that the scuba diver is 20 feet under the measurement we mark as '0' on the earth, sea level. However, the scuba diver is not actually a negative distance from sea level so it is expressed in absolute value, showing the scuba diver is a distance of 20 feet away from sea level.

Range

The range helps to quantify the amount of variation in a set of data. It is the difference between the maximum value and the minimum value and can be found by subtracting the minimum value in a set from the maximum value in a set.

Example Problem 1

Find the range of each situation below and describe its meaning:
The height of students in Mickey's class (in inches):
58, 62, 59, 61.5, 61, 58, 60, 59.5, 61, 58, 59, 61, 60.5, 58.5
The amount of money each friend spent at dinner (in dollars):
15, 7, 11.50, 21, 14, 17.50, 10, 9, 23.50, 14

For the height of students in Mickey's class the range is 4 inches. The maximum height is 62 inches and the minimum height is 58 inches, so therefore the range is $62 - 58 = 4$. This means that all students in Mickey's class are fairly close together in height as this is a small range to hold all of the data. If the whole class was lined up the difference in height from the tallest person to the shortest would be only 4 inches.

For the amount of money each friend spent at dinner, the range is $16.50. The maximum value is $23.50 and the minimum value is $7, so therefore the range is $23.50 - 7 = 16.50$. This means that the friends spent a wide range at dinner, meaning some friends bought much more expensive meals or more food than some of the others.

Example Problem 2

The following data shows the cost of used cars in the sales lot. Plot the data on a line plot and describe the meaning of the range of data.

Price of Used Cars For Sale (in dollars)

14,000 7,500 8,000 600

19,000 18,500 9,500 3,000

5,500 950 16,000 2,000

The data is displayed on the line plot below:

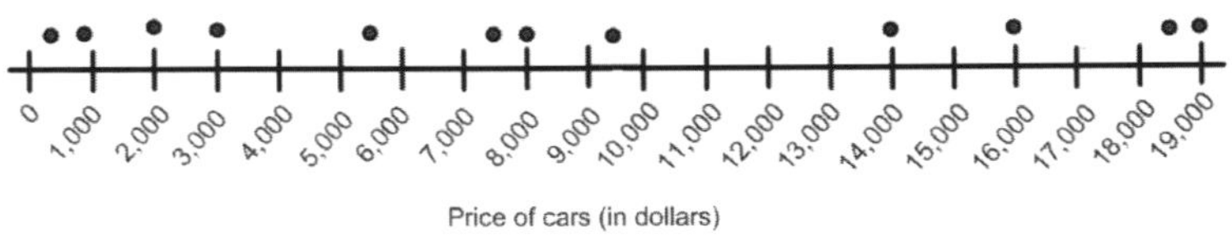

The range of the data is $18,400. This is found by subtracting the smallest value, $600, from the largest value, $19,000. This is a large range for the price of the cars in the lot. Looking at the line plot it is easy to see that the prices of cars are very spread out. This might mean that the lot has some fairly new used cars and also some very old cars for sale.

Example Problem 3

The following table shows the amount of television each student watched the night before the math test. Any student who watched television for a greater amount of time than the median earned a D on the test. Find the range of the data and determine who got a D on the test.

Student	Hours of TV watched	Student	Hours of TV watched
Billy	1	Brock	2
Paige	6	Colleen	3.5
Margaret	.5	Courtney	0
Skylar	2	Blair	3
James	0	Theresa	1
Fiona	0	Tyler	4.5
Kyle	3	Troy	1.5

The range of the data is 6 hours. This is found by subtracting the smallest value, 0, from the largest value, 6.

The median of the data must be found in order to determine who earned a D on the test. The median of the data is 1.75 hours. This is found by ordering the numbers from least to greatest and finding the middle number, like so: 0, 0, 0, .5, 1, 1, 1.5, 2, 2, 3, 3, 3.5, 4.5, 6. Since there are two numbers in the middle of the data, the average of those two must be found. Therefore, the median of the data is $\frac{1.5+2}{2} = \frac{3.5}{2} = 1.75$. Since any student who watched TV for more than 1.75 hours earned a D on the test, Paige, Skylar, Kyle, Brock, Colleen, Blair, and Tyler all earned D's on the test.

EXAMPLE PROBLEM 4

THE STUDENTS IN MARK'S CLASS FILLED IN THE TABLE TO REPRESENT HOW MANY SIBLINGS THEY EACH HAVE. USE THE TABLE TO FIND THE RANGE OF THE DATA AND DESCRIBE THE SHAPE MADE BY A LINE PLOT OF THE DATA.

Number of siblings	Number of students
0	𝍷𝍷
1	𝍷𝍷𝍷𝍷
2	𝍸𝍷𝍷
3	𝍷𝍷𝍷
4	𝍷𝍷
5	
6	𝍷

The range of the data is 6. This is found by subtracting the smallest number, 0, from the largest number, 6. The shape of the line plot of this data is similar to a bell curve, or that of a small hill. The majority of the dots are above the 2, which is the mode of the data because it occurs most frequently. It is also the median of the data, because it is the value in the middle. The dots on either side of 2 are similar-sized groups getting smaller the farther away from 2 the values get. This can be seen in the line plot below:

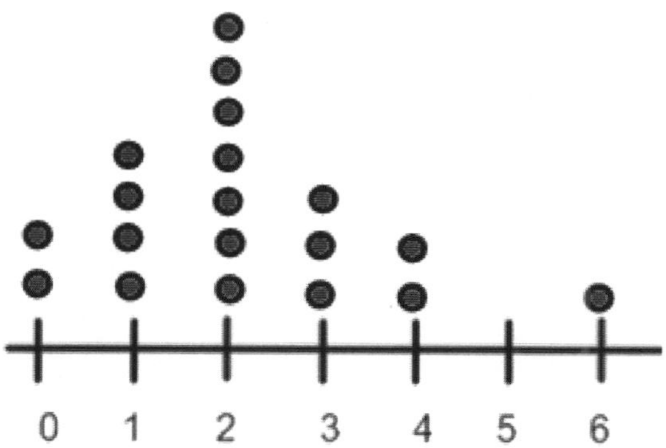

Example Problem 5

<u>Given the following graph of data of four students' speeds to walk to school, determine what units must have been used.</u>

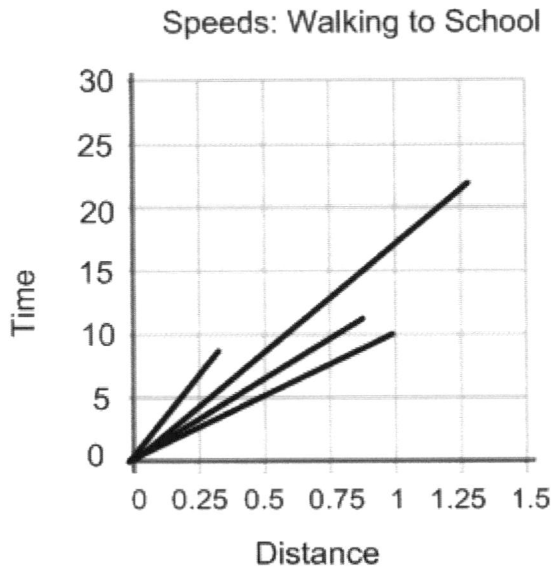

The units that must have been used are Distance in Miles and Time in Minutes. If the distance measurement is considered first, there is no other reasonable measurement other than miles. It would not make sense for the measurements to be in feet, as walking less than 1.5 feet to school would not be considered because everyone has to walk at least a few feet to get into the building, and no one can live 1.5 feet from the school. Similarly, meters or yards or anything less than those would also not be a reasonable measurement.

Considering that the distance is measured in miles, the most likely unit of time measurement is in minutes. Hours is very unreasonable as it would not take someone over 20 hours to walk 1.25 miles, and seconds is as equally unreasonable as it would not take someone just over 20 seconds to walk 1.25 miles.

The only other possible measurement would be distance in kilometers, but the times in minutes are maybe a little too slow to represent walking distances in kilometers.

Important Terms

- Sample size - Sample size is the number of people surveyed or the number of observations made in a statistical experiment. For example, if the mayor of a town surveyed 800 residents to determine the town's opinion on a new park, then the sample size is 800 and the mayor has hopefully judged that this will be a large enough sample to represent the whole population.
- Data set - Data set is a list, or set, of all the numbers or values that are the results from a statistical experiment. An example would be that the following data set represents the shoe sizes of Fred's friends: {6, 7.5, 8, 8, 8.5, 9.5, 10}. That list of numbers is the data set and each number represents the shoe size of Fred's friends.

- First quartile - The first quartile is the number that is the median of the lower half of a data set that is, the half between the minimum and the median. All pieces of data less than the first quartile are in the lowest 25% of the data. It can also be referred to as the 'lower quartile'.
- Second quartile - The second quartile is more commonly called the median, and is the middle number of a data set. It splits the data in half, so that 50% of the data is less than this number and 50% of the data is greater than this number.
- Third quartile - The third quartile is the number that is the median of the upper half of a data set, that is, the half between the median and the maximum. All pieces of data greater than it are in the top 25% of the data. It can also be referred to as the 'upper quartile'.
- Maximum - The maximum is the greatest value in a data set.
- Minimum - The minimum is the least value in a data set.
- Integer - An integer is any whole number, including 0 and all the negative whole numbers as well. The values $-100, -12, -1,\ 4,$ and 13 are all integers because they are all whole numbers, whether positive or negative. The values -2.65, $\frac{1}{3}$, and $\sqrt{6}$ are not integers because they are not whole numbers.
- Rational number - A rational number is any number that can be expressed as a fraction. Equivalently, a rational number is any number that can be expressed as a terminating or repeating decimal. Rational numbers can be both positive and negative. The values $-\frac{2}{5}$ and 3 are rational numbers because $-\frac{2}{5}$ is a fraction and 3 can be expressed as a fraction as $\frac{3}{1}$. Any integer can be expressed as a fraction as itself over 1, so all integers are also rational numbers. The values $\sqrt{8}$ and π are not rational numbers (they are called 'irrational numbers') because they cannot be expressed as a fraction. These numbers are decimals that continue on without ending or repeating.
- Prime number - A prime number is a number that is only evenly divisible by 1 and itself.
- Prime factor - A prime factor is a prime number that divides evenly into another number. For example, 3 is a prime factor of 21, because 3 is a prime number and 21 is evenly divisible by 3.
- Least common multiple - The least common multiple is the smallest number that is evenly divisible by all numbers in a given set.
- Greatest common factor - The greatest common factor is the greatest number that all numbers in a set are evenly divisible by.
- Quotient - The result of a division operation. For example, the quotient of 10 and 5 is 2.
- Product - The result of a multiplication operation. For example, the product of 6 and 3 is 18.
- Sum - The result of an addition operation. For example, the sum of 4 and 7 is 11.
- Difference - The result of a subtraction operation. The difference between two numbers can be thought of as the distance between them on a number line. For example, the difference of 12 and 8 is 4.
- Factor - A factor is a number divides evenly into a given number. For example, 4 is a factor of 8, because 8 is evenly divisible by 4.
- Coefficient - A coefficient is a number that multiplies a variable and that denotes how many instances of that variable are represented together. This number is written in front of, or to the left of, the variable. There is generally no multiplication sign between the coefficient and the variable. For example, in the term '3x', 3 is the coefficient.
- Term - A term is a number or variable or a product of number(s) and/or variable(s) that does not contain an operation symbol. For example, in the expression $y + 4x + 7$, y, 4x, and 7 are separate terms.

- Expression - An expression is a group of one or more numbers variables, and/or terms that are combined together with operations. There is no equal sign in an expression. For example, $7x - (2x + 3) \div 4$ is an expression.
- Variable - A variable is an unknown value represented by a letter in an expression or equation. A variable can represent one value or a set of values. For example, in the equation $2x + 4 = 10$, x is a variable and has one value. In the equation $y = 8x + 1$, x and y can have multiple values as long as they both make the equation true.
- Equation - An equation is a relationship equating two expressions. An equation can be distinguished from an expression by the equal sign. For example, $4x = 12$ is an equation because it has an equal sign.
- Inequality - An inequality is a comparison between two or more expressions that are not necessarily equal; one might be greater or less than another. Because of this, when solving an inequality for a variable, the solution is a range of values. For example, $5a + 2 \leq 22$ is an inequality because it has a "less than or equal to" symbol between the two expressions.

Mathematics Practice Test #1

Practice Questions

1. Antonio wants to buy a roll of border to finish an art project. At four different shops, he found four different borders he liked. He wants to use the widest of the borders. The list shows the width, in inches, of the borders he found.

$$1\frac{7}{10}, 1.72, 1\frac{3}{4}, 1.695$$

Which roll of border should Antonio buy if he wants to buy the widest border?

a. $1\frac{7}{10}$
b. 1.72
c. $1\frac{3}{4}$
d. 1.695

2. Daniella wrote a decimal and a fraction which were equivalent to each other. Which pair of numbers could be the pair Daniella wrote?

a. $0.625, \frac{7}{8}$
b. $0.375, \frac{3}{8}$
c. $0.75, \frac{7}{5}$
d. $0.45, \frac{4}{5}$

3. Glenda poured salt into three salt shakers from a box that contained 19 ounces of salt. She poured 5 ounces of salt into one shaker. She divided what was left evenly into the other two shakers. Which equation best represents this scenario?

a. 19-5-2(7)=0
b. 5+2+7=19
c. 19-2-7-7=0
d. 19-2(5)-7=0

4. Large boxes of canned beans hold 24 cans of beans and small boxes hold 12 cans. One afternoon, Gerald brought 4 large boxes of canned beans and 6 small boxes of canned beans to the food bank. How many cans of beans did Gerald bring to the food bank that afternoon?

a. 168
b. 192
c. 288
d. 360

5. **Enrique used a formula to find the total cost, in dollars, for repairs he and his helper, Jenny, made to a furnace. The expression below shows the formula he used, with 4 being the number of hours he worked on the furnace and 2 being the number of hours Jenny worked on the furnace.**

$$20 + 35(4 + 2) + 47$$

What is the total cost for repairing the furnace?

a. \$189
b. \$269
c. \$277
d. \$377

6. **One morning at Jim's café, 25 people ordered juice, 10 ordered milk, and 50 ordered coffee with breakfast. Which ratio best compares the number of people who ordered milk to the number of people who ordered juice?**

a. 5 to 7
b. 5 to 2
c. 2 to 7
d. 2 to 5

7. **At the middle school Vanessa attends, there are 240 Grade 6 students, 210 Grade 7 students, and 200 Grade 8 students. Which ratio best compares the number of students in Grade 8 to the number of students in Grade 6 at Vanessa's school?**

a. 5 : 6
b. 5 : 11
c. 6 : 5
d. 7 : 8

8. **A display at the bottom of the laptop computer Erica was using showed that the battery had a 70% charge. Which decimal is equivalent to 70%?**

a. 0.07
b. 70.0
c. 7.0
d. 0.7

9. **The drawing shows a chart used to record completed Math assignments. A checkmark is used to show which assignments are finished.**

Math Assignment

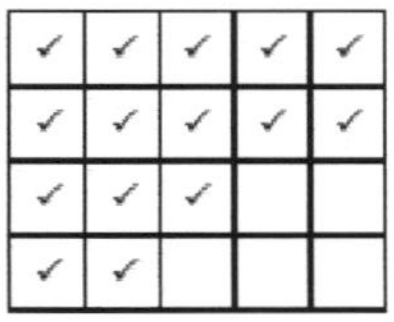

Which of the following shows the percentage of Math assignments in the chart which are finished?

a. 15%
b. 25%
c. 55%
d. 75%

10. Harold learned that 6 out of 10 students at his school live within two miles of the school. If 240 students attend Grade 6 at his school, about how many of these students should Harold expect to live within two miles of the school?

a. 24
b. 40
c. 144
d. 180

11. A unit of liquid measure in the English System of Measure is the gill. The table, shown here, gives conversions from gills to fluid ounces.

Conversion Table

Gills	Fluid Ounces
2	8
4	16
5	20
6	24
10	40

Which equation best describes the relationship between gills, *g*, and fluid ounces, *f*?

a. $f = 8g - 8$
b. $f = 2g + 4$
c. $f = 4g$
d. $4f = g$

12. The table below shows changes in the area of several trapezoids as the lengths of the bases, b_1 and b_2, remain the same and the height, *h*, changes.

Trapezoids

b_1 (in feet)	b_2 (in feet)	h (in feet)	A (in square feet)
5	7	2	12
5	7	4	24
5	7	6	36
5	7	8	48

Which formula best represents the relationship between *A*, the areas of these trapezoids, and *h*, their heights?

a. $A = 5h$
b. $A = 6h$
c. $A = 7h$
d. $A = 12h$

13. This table shows lengths, widths, and areas of four rectangles. In each rectangle, the length remains 40 meters, but the width changes.

Rectangles

Length	40 meters	40 meters	40 meters	40 meters
Width	20 meters	30 meters	40 meters	50 meters
Perimeter	120 meters	140 meters	160 meters	180 meters

Which formula best represents the relationship between *P*, the perimeters of these rectangles, and *w*, their widths?

a. $P = w + 80$
b. $P = 2w + 80$
c. $P = 2(2w + 40)$
d. $P = 10(w + 40)$

14. Thomas drew a polygon with vertices: *A*, *B*, *C*, and *D*. He measured the angles formed and recorded the information shown here.

$$m\angle A = 70°, m\angle B = 80°, m\angle C = 120°, m\angle D = 90°$$

Which of the angles that Thomas drew is an obtuse angle?

a. $\angle A$
b. $\angle B$
c. $\angle C$
d. $\angle D$

15. In Δ*RST*, shown here, $m\angle S$ is 20° less than $m\angle R$.

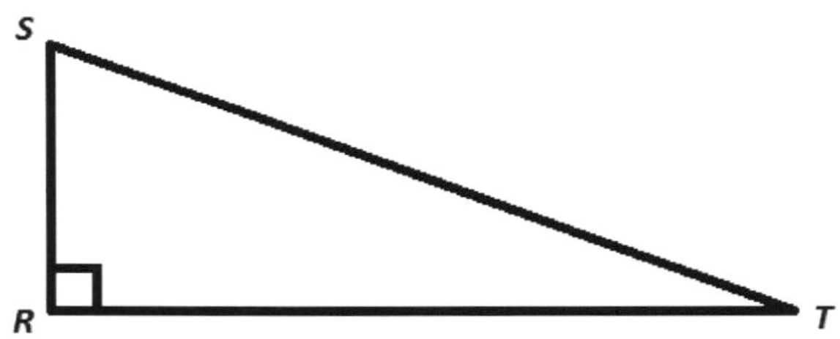

What is the measure of $\angle T$?

a. 110°
b. 70°
c. 50°
d. 20°

16. Ellen measured ∠*R* in the parallelogram shown here and found it to be 35°. She knows that ∠*R* and ∠*T* have equal measures. She also knows ∠*S* and ∠*V* are equal in measure.

What is the measure of ∠***V***?

a. 215°
b. 145°
c. 70°
d. 35°

17. Which expressions are equivalent to 4(2n-6)? Select all that apply.

1. 4n(2-6)
2. 8n-24
3. 8n+24
4. 2(2n-6)+2(2n-6)
5. 5(2n-6)-(2n-6)

18. A store buys sodas from the manufacture for $3.60 a case. There are 24 sodas in a case. They sell them for $.35 per soda. How much profit do the make on one soda?

____

19. Jessica wrote down the times required for five girls to run a race. The times are shown in this list.

25.1 seconds, 24.9 seconds, 25.2 seconds, 24.8 seconds, 25.0 seconds

What time is closest to the total for all five runners?

a. 1 minute and 5 seconds
b. 1 minute and 25 seconds
c. 2 minutes and 5 seconds
d. 2 minutes and 25 seconds

20. This drawing shows an equilateral triangle and a ruler.

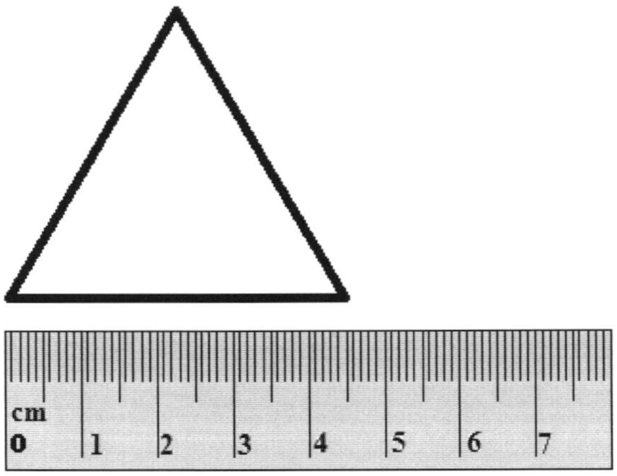

Which is closest to the perimeter of the triangle?

a. 4.5 centimeters
b. 9.0 centimeters
c. 13.5 centimeters
d. 20.3 centimeters

21. The drawing shows a protractor and a trapezoid.

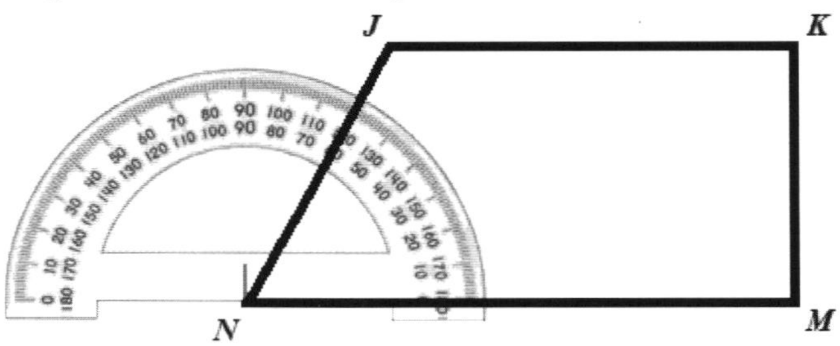

Which is closest to the measure of $\angle JNM$?

a. 61°
b. 79°
c. 119°
d. 121°

22. Given the equation $a^2 + (2b - c) \times d$, solve for a=2, b=5, c=8, and d=4.

____

23. Mega Book Store is selling books for 30% off. James wants to buy 3 books. The regular prices of the books are \$8, \$12, and \$15. What is the total price he should expect to pay during the sale?

a. \$35
b. \$25
c. \$24.50
d. \$23.50

24. Stephen researched the topic of solar-powered lights for his science project. He exposed 10 new solar lights to five hours of sunlight. He recorded the number of minutes each light continued to shine after dark in the list below.

63, 67, 73, 75, 80, 91, 63, 72, 79, 87

Which of these numbers is the mean of the number of minutes in Stephen's list?

a. 28
b. 63
c. 74
d. 75

25. Grade 6 students at Fairview Middle School were asked to name their favorite of six school subjects. The plot below shows a summary of their answers. Each X represents 5 students.

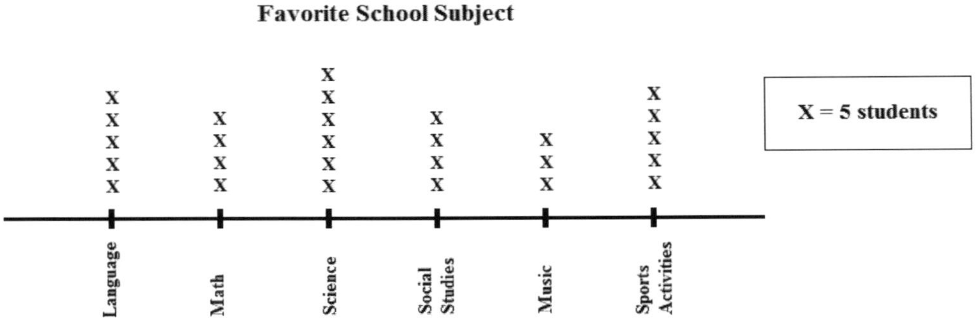

Which graph best represents the data in the plot?

a.

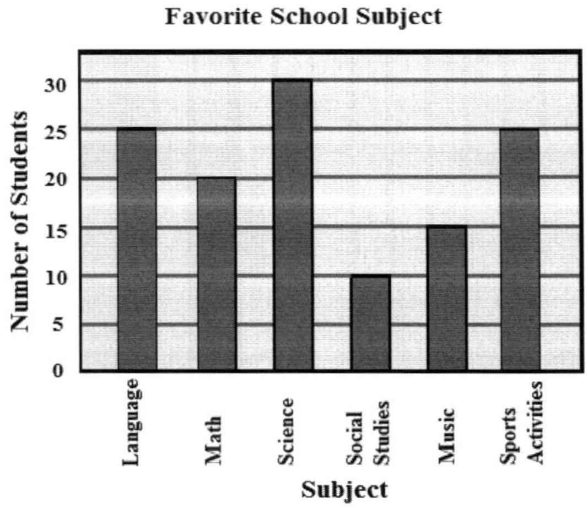

c.

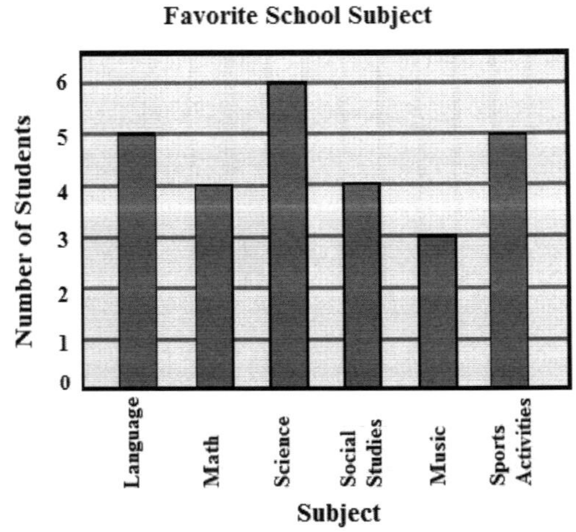

b.

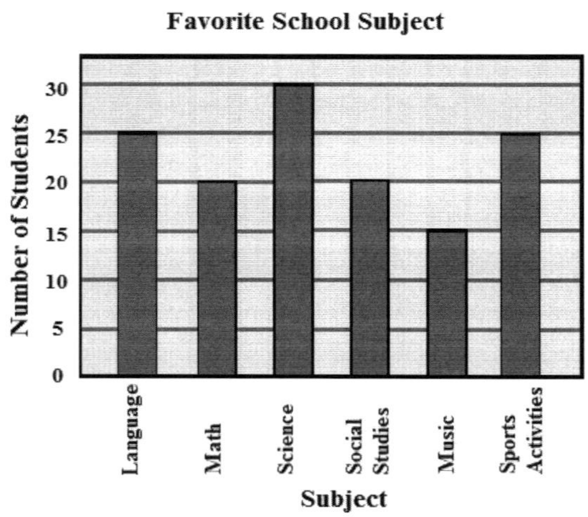

d.

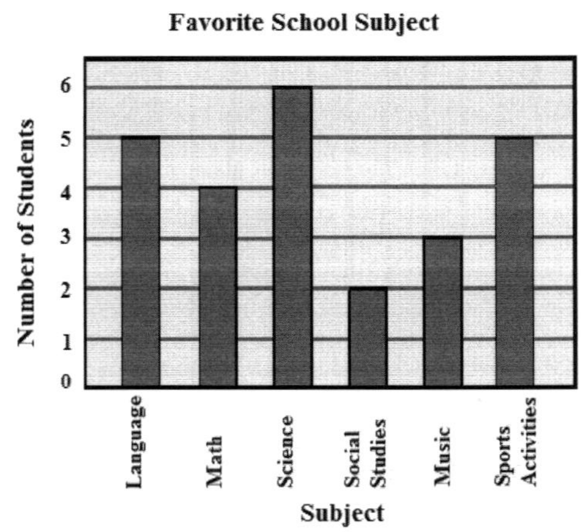

26. **Sammie had $120 he had earned doing chores for people in his neighborhood. When school started, he spent $50 for shirts, $30 for jeans, and $40 for school supplies. Which graph best represents how Sammy spent his $120?**

a.

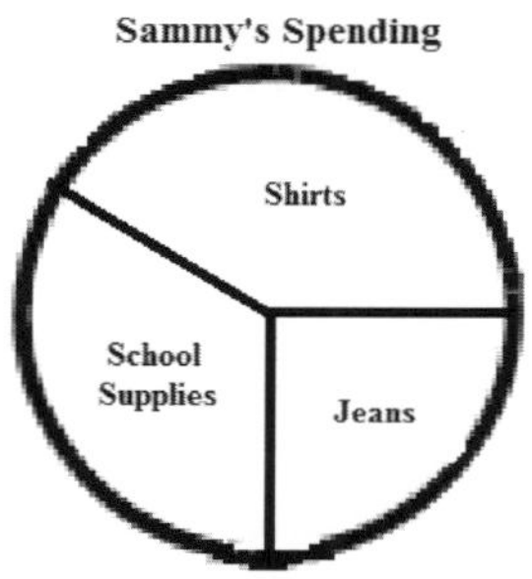

c.

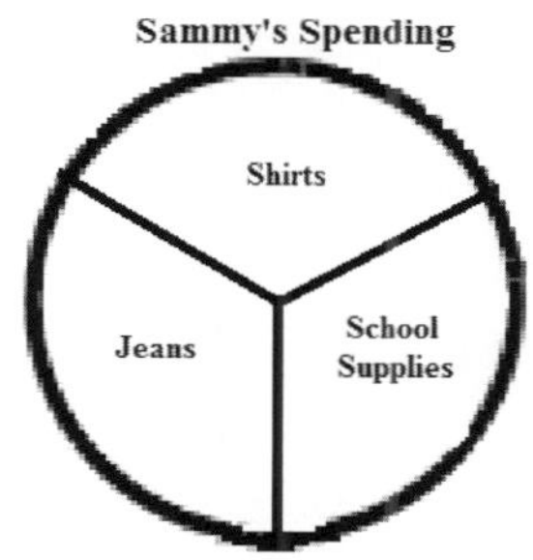

b.

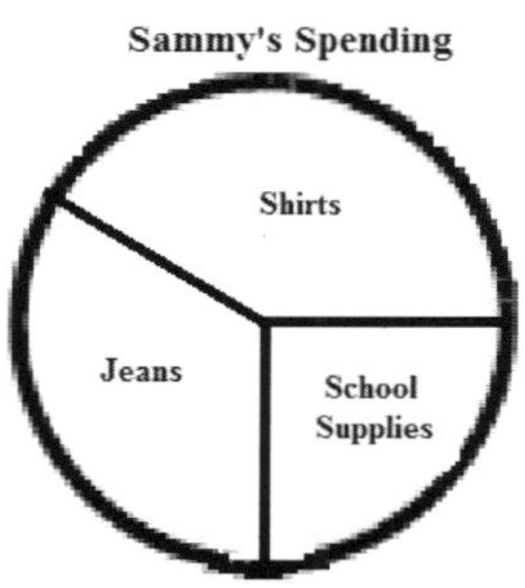

d.

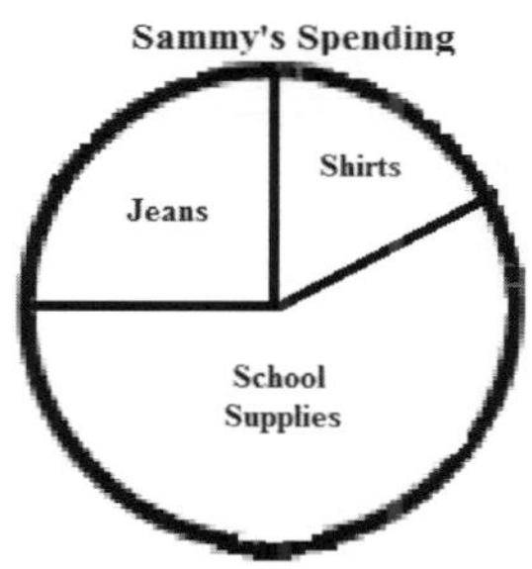

27. **James and his driving partner, Larissa, recently drove a truck from Dallas, TX to Los Angeles, CA. The total distance they drove was 1,380 miles. James is paid $0.35 per mile he drives and Larissa is paid $0.30 per mile she drives. What additional information is needed to find the amount James should be paid for the trip?**

a. The total number of hours each person drove
b. The total number of miles each person drove
c. The total amount of fuel the truck used
d. The total weight of the truck and cargo

28. **Petra installed 10 light fixtures at a new warehouse that was being built. Each of the fixtures required 3 light bulbs. The bulbs come in packages of 5 and cost $8 per package. What was the total cost for the bulbs required for all of the fixtures Petra installed at the warehouse?**

a. $16
b. $48
c. $120
d. $240

29. Anna and other members of her club sold caps to commemorate their city's 100th birthday. The caps sold for $14 and came in four colors. The club made $3,360 in total sales from selling the caps. The graph below shows the part of the total sales that each color represented.

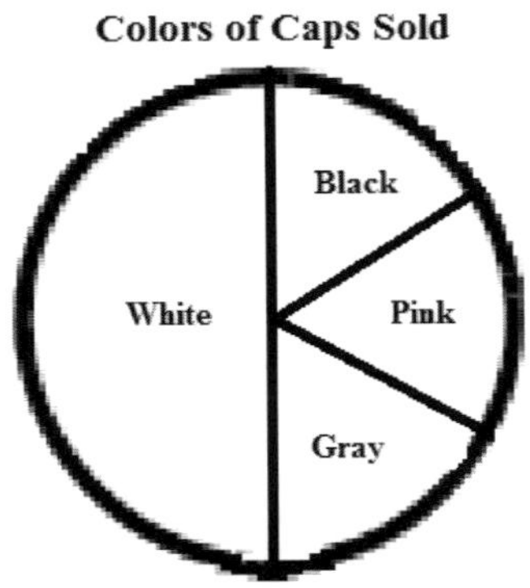

Which number is closest to the combined number of white and pink caps sold by Anna's club members?

a. 40
b. 80
c. 120
d. 160

30. Gabe has 6 pencils. The lengths of his pencils in inches are shown on the number line below. What is the mean length of the pencils?

a. 7 in.
b. $7\frac{1}{4}$ in.
c. $7\frac{1}{2}$ in.
d. $6\frac{3}{4}$ in.

31. Jason wants to put dry fertilizer on the grass in his front yard. The yard is 20 feet wide and 45 feet long. Each pound of the fertilizer he plans to use is enough for 150 square feet. Which procedure could Jason use to determine the correct amount of fertilizer to use on the entire yard?

a. Divide 150 by 20 and divide 150 by 45, and then add those quotients together
b. Add 20 and 45, double that total, and then divide that total by 150
c. Multiply 20 by 45, and then subtract 150 from that product
d. Multiply 20 by 45, and then divide that product by 150

32. An electronics store sells laptops for \$475. They are on sale for \$380. Which equation below represents this? Let *r* represent the regular price of laptops and *s* represent the sale price.

a. $r = .8s$
b. $s = .2r$
c. $s = .7r$
d. $s = .8r$

33. Kerianne collected the weights of her friends. What is the range of her friends' weight?

55 lbs, 63 lbs, 48 lbs, 72 lbs, 61 lbs, 68 lbs

____

34. What is the greatest common factor of 66 and 24?

____

35. Point *A* on the graph below is reflected across the x-axis and then translated 3 units left. At what coordinates does it end up?

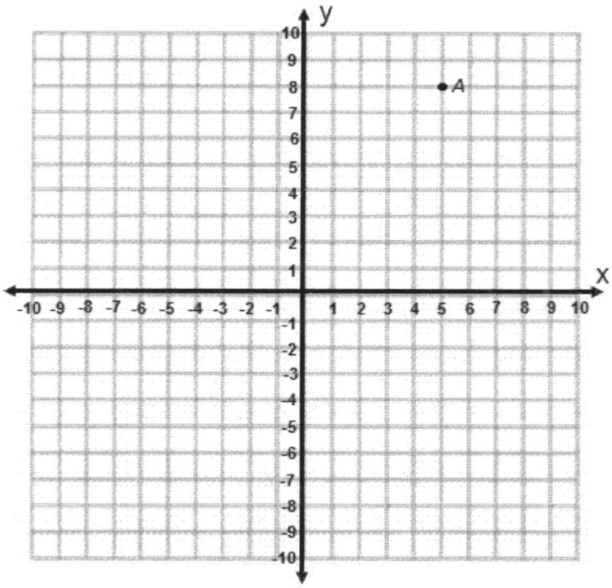

a. $(2,8)$
b. $(2,-8)$
c. $(-2,8)$
d. $(5,-8)$

36. Candace's shoelace broke. She measured the unbroken shoelace and finds that she needs a replacement lace that is at least 16 inches long. The store has the following lengths available.

$$15\frac{7}{10}, 16.25, \frac{47}{3}, 15.5$$

Which one of the following lace lengths would be long enough to replace the broken shoelace?

a. $15\frac{7}{10}$
b. 16.25
c. $\frac{47}{3}$
d. 15.5

37. Nadia is working summer jobs. She earns $5 for every dog she walks, $2 for bringing back a trashcan, $1 for checking the mail, and $5 for watering the flowers. Nadia walks 3 dogs, brings back 5 trashcans, checks the mail for 10 neighbors, and waters the flowers at 6 houses. Which expression can be used to find out how much money Nadia earned?

a. $2(5) +$6(10) + $1
b. $10(6) + $1 + $5
c. $5(3+6) + $2(5) + $1(10)
d. $15 + $10 + $16

38. Only 8% of the dogs were solid white. Which decimal is equivalent to 8%?

a. 0.08
b. 80.0
c. 8.0
d. 0.8

39. Use this grid to answer the question.

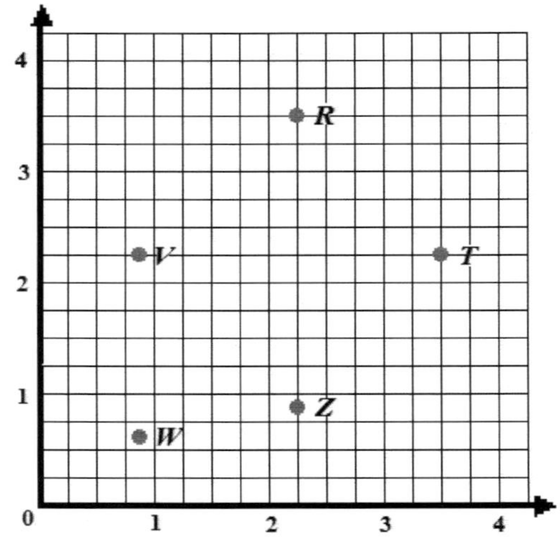

Which of the points on the grid best represents the point at $(2\frac{1}{4}, \frac{7}{8})$?

a. T
b. V
c. W
d. Z

40. Part A: A restaurant is trying to attract a younger crowd. They think that they have managed to attract more young people but wanted to graph their results to see. The ages of 40 guests are given below. Create a histogram to show the results.

23	26	21	42	35	29	53	31
19	24	27	30	22	37	21	25
22	26	30	34	27	20	50	41
32	23	18	20	39	22	33	35
25	30	27	19	24	42	47	21

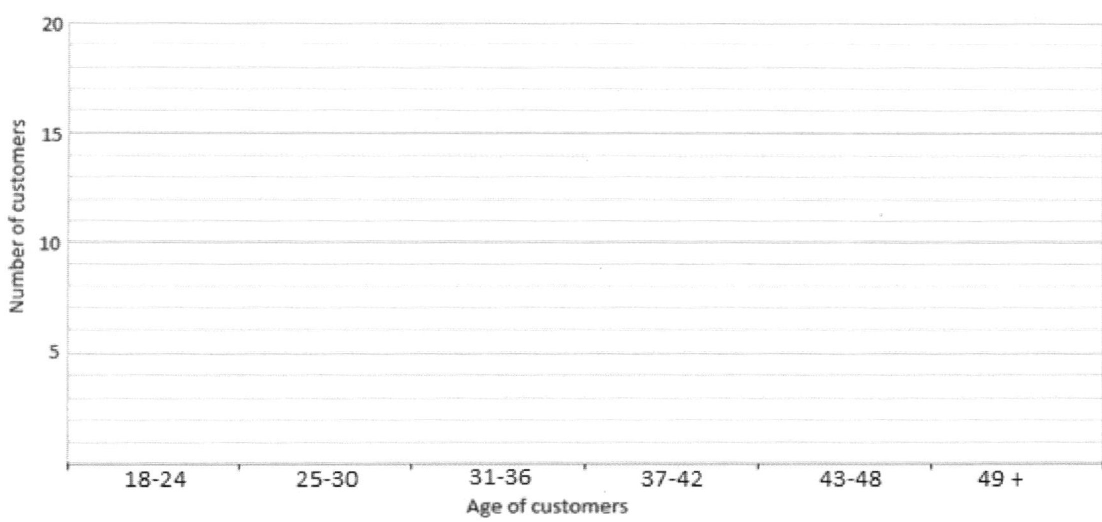

Part B: If they wanted the median age of the customers to be in the 24-30 range were they successful?

____

Answers and Explanations

1. C: To answer this question correctly, convert all numbers to decimal form to make them easy to compare. Since two of the numbers are already in decimal form, we only need to convert $1\frac{7}{10}$ and $1\frac{3}{4}$ to decimal form.

$$7 \div 10 = 0.7, \text{so } 1\frac{7}{10} = 1.7$$

$$\text{and } 3 \div 4 = 0.75, \text{so } 1\frac{3}{4} = 1.75$$

Therefore, by comparing place values from left to right of 1.7, 1.72, 1.75 and 1.695, we see that 1.695 is least, 1.7 is next greatest, 1.72 is next, and 1.75 is greatest. So, Antonio should buy the border that is $1\frac{3}{4}$ inches wide.

2. B: To answer this question, one method that can be used is to convert all the fractions to decimal form so it is easier to compare them to each other. This can be done by simply dividing, since the fraction sign means division.

$$7 \div 8 = 0.875$$

$$3 \div 8 = 0.375$$

$$7 \div 5 = 1.4$$

$$4 \div 5 = 0.8$$

So, the only pair of numbers in which the fraction is equivalent to the decimal is in answer B.

3. A: She starts with 19 ounces and then subtracts 5. Then she has 14 ounces and divides that by 2 which gives her 7ounces per shaker. Thus the equation: 19-5-2(7)=0

4. A: Multiply 24 by 4 to get 96 and multiply 12 by 6 to get 72. Then, add 96 and 72 to get the correct answer, 168.

5. C: To solve this formula, follow the order of operations. First, add what is in the parenthesis, 4 + 2, to get 6. Then, multiply the 6 by 35 to get 210. Last, we should add 20 + 210 + 47 to get 277.

6. D: Note that the ratio asked for is the number of people who ordered milk to the number who ordered juice. The number of people who ordered coffee does not matter here. This compares 10 to 25, and the order is important here. Since the ratio is with the number of people who ordered milk first, the 10 must come first. So, the ratio is 10 to 25, but the ratio can be written in simpler form by dividing both numbers in the ratio by 5, to get the ratio: 2 to 5.

7. A: One way to answer this question is to name the ratio: 200 to 240, then write the ratio in simplest terms by dividing both terms by the greatest common factor, 40, to get 5 to 6. It should be noted that the number of Grade 7 students is not important for this problem. Also, the order of the ratio matters. Since it asks for the ratio using the number of Grade 8 students first, the ratio is 200 to 240 and not the other way around.

8. D: To correctly write a percent as a decimal, the percent sign is dropped and the number is rewritten with the decimal point two places to the left. This is because a percent is always a value out of 100 and the second place after the decimal point is the hundredths place. So, 70% = 0.70 and the zero at the end after the decimal can be dropped.

9. D: There are 15 of the 20 assignments with check marks indicating a finished assignment. Since the fraction $\frac{1}{20}$ represents 5%, then 15 times 5% gives 75% of the assignments finished.

10. C: One way to find this answer is to set up a proportion: $\frac{6}{10} = \frac{G}{240}$, in which G represents the number of Grade 6 students living within two miles of the school. To solve the proportion, we should cross-multiply. So, 10 times G = 6 times 240. This gives the equation:

$10G$ = 1,440. To solve the equation we divide both sides of the equation by 10, which gives G = 144.

11. C: Looking at the chart, a pattern can be seen in the relationship between the number of gills and the number of fluid ounces. Each number of gills in the first column, when multiplied by 4, gives the number of fluid ounces in the second column. So, f equals 4 times g, or $f = 4g$.

12. B: The formula for the area of trapezoids is not necessarily needed here to do this problem. Since the relationship between the area, A, and the height, h, can be seen in the chart, looking at the third and fourth columns to see if there is a pattern will show a relationship between the variables. Each value in the area column is equal to 6 times the value in the height column. So, we get $A = 6h$.

13. B: To answer this question, start with the perimeter formula, $P = 2(l + w)$ and substitute values that are known to remain the same. So, $P = 2(l + w)$ becomes $P = 2(40 + w)$. Then we distribute, multiplying both numbers inside the parenthesis by 2 and get $P = 80 + 2w$. Writing the variable first in the expression gives us: $P = 2w + 80$.

14. C: An obtuse angle measures between 90 and 180 degrees and $\angle C$ is the only choice which measured in that range.

15. D: The box symbol shown at $\angle R$ means that $\angle R$ measures 90°. Since we are told $m\angle S$ is 20° less than $m\angle R$, subtract 90 –20 to get 70. This means that $m\angle S$ = 70°. The sum of $m\angle R$ and $m\angle S$ is found by adding: 90 +70 = 160. The sum of all angles in a triangle always adds up to 180°, so subtracting 180 – 160 results in a difference of 20. So, $m\angle T$ is 20°.

16. B: The angles opposite each other in a parallelogram are equal in measure. So, $\angle R$ has an equal measure to $\angle T$, or 35°. The sum of the measures of these two angles is 35 + 35 = 70. The sum of the measures of all four angles of a quadrilateral is 360°. We subtract 360 – 70 to get 290. So, 290° is the sum of the measures of the other two equal angles, $\angle S$ and $\angle V$. Then we divide 290 by 2 to get 145. We know that $\angle V$ has a measure of 145°.

17. II, V: First distribute in the 4 to get $8n - 24$. Then do the same for all of the answer choices and see which ones equal $8n - 24$.

18. $.20: First find what it costs the store per coke. So, divide $3.60 by 24 to get $.15 per soda. Then they sell them for $.35 per soda so they make $.20 per soda.

19. C: A close estimate for the total time for all five runners is 125 seconds, which is found by adding 25.1 + 24.9 + 25.2 + 24.8 + 25.0. Then, to convert seconds to minutes, divide by 60 seconds (since there are 60 seconds in a minute) to get 2 with remainder of 5, or 2 minutes and 5 seconds.

20. C: The ruler is used to determine the length of one side of the triangle, which is about 4.5 centimeters. Since this is an equilateral triangle, all three sides are of equal length. To find the perimeter, we add up all of the sides. However, since they are all the same length, we can just multiply 4.5 centimeters by 3 to get 13.5 centimeters.

21. A: Since segment NM lies along the right side of the protractor, we read the inside scale. The segment NM passes between 60° and 70°, much closer to the 60°, so the correct answer is 61°.

22. 12 : First plug all of the numbers into the equation. $2^2 + (2(5) - 8) \times 4$. Then follow the order of operations. $2^2 + 2 \times 4 = 4 + 2 \times 4 = 4 + 8 = 12$.

23. C: First add the costs of all 3 books together to get \$35. Then find out what 30% of \$35 is. This can be done by multiplying it times .3 to get \$10.50. Then subtract \$10.50 from \$35 and you have the sale price of \$24.50.

24. D: The mean is just the average. To calculate this, find the total of all 10 numbers by adding. Then, divide that total by 10 because that is the number of data points. The total is 750, so the mean of this group of numbers is 75

25. B: Notice that the vertical scale should be 0 to 30 by 5's since each of the X's in the plot represent 5 students. Also, each column should represent a number from the line plot. For example, since Language and Sports Activities both show 5 X's, and each X represents 5 students, 5 times 5 = 25. The subjects of Math and Social Studies both show 4 X's, so 4 times 5 = 20. All of the values are found in this way and the only chart that shows these values is B.

26. A: The appropriate fractions can be found by putting the amount of money spent on each category over the total amount of money spent. $\frac{50}{120}$ is a little less than half, since half of 120 is 60. $\frac{30}{120}$ simplifies to $\frac{1}{4}$ and $\frac{40}{120}$ simplifies to $\frac{1}{3}$. This means that Sammy spent almost $\frac{1}{2}$ his money on shirts, $\frac{1}{4}$ of his money on jeans, and $\frac{1}{3}$ of his money on school supplies. The graph in A best represents those fractions.

27. B: Since each person is paid by the number of miles driven, one must know not the total miles for the trip, but the miles each person drove. The fuel, weight, or hours do not matter for this problem.

28. B: To answer this question, find the total number of bulbs required by multiplying 10 by 3. The number of packages of bulbs required can be found by dividing this total number of bulbs, 30, by 5, to find that 6 packages are needed. Then, multiplying 6 by the cost per package, 8, we find that the total cost for all the bulbs needed was \$48.

29. D: To answer this question, the total number of caps sold must be found by dividing the total sales, 3,360, by the price of each cap, 14. 3,360 ÷ 14 = 240, so 240 caps were sold in total. So, looking at the graph, it appears that about half of the caps were white, around 120. The graph also shows that the other 3 colors were sold in about equal numbers, so dividing the other half, 120, by 3, gives around 40. Then, adding 120 white caps and 40 pink caps, gives an answer of 160. The club had close to 160 combined sales of white and pink caps.

30. B: First add all of the lengths together to get $43\frac{1}{2}$ inches. Then divide by 6 to get the mean. $43\frac{1}{2} \div 6 = 7\frac{1}{4}$

31. D: This procedure first finds the area to be fertilized, by multiplying the length and width of the rectangular yard. Then, it divides that area by the area each pound of fertilizer will cover.

32. D: \$380 is 80% of \$475, and answer choice D is the only one that represents this. s=.8r

33. 24: Begin by arranging the different weights from least to greatest:

48 lbs, 55 lbs, 61 lbs, 63 lbs 68 lbs, 72 lbs. Range is the difference between the highest and lowest values in a set of data; therefore, 72 – 48 = 24.

34. 6: To find the greatest common factor first factor both numbers completely. The factors of 66 include 1, 2, 3, 6, 11, 22, 33, and 66. The factors of 24 include 1, 2, 3, 4, 6, 8, 12, and 24. The greatest factor that they have in common is 6.

35. B: After the reflection and the translation the new point would be here:

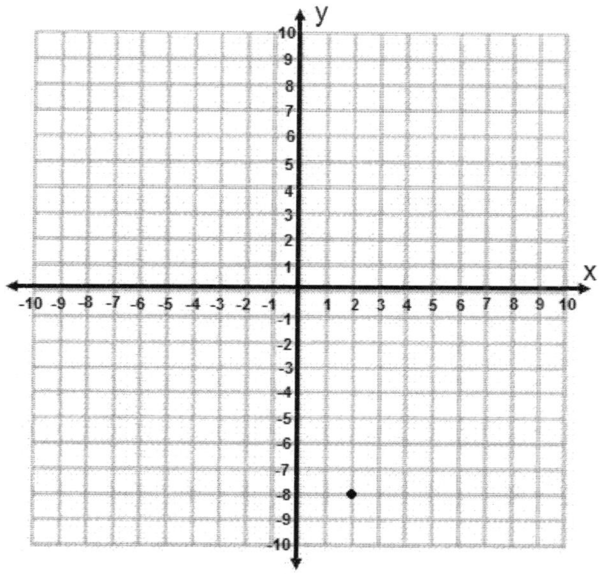

and that is the point (2, -8)

36. B: It is easier to think as the required 16 inches as 16.00 and convert all answer choices to a decimal to compare. Anything greater than 16.00 would be sufficient. $15\frac{7}{10}$ is equal to 15.7, $\frac{47}{3}$ is equivalent to 15.67 and 15.5 remains 15.5. These three choices are all slightly less than the required 16.00 inches; therefore making 16.25 inches the only adequate choice.

37. C: Since she earns \$5 for walking dogs and watering flowers, this term can be combined to simplify the equation. The other terms for bringing back trashcans and checking the mail are straight multiplication.

38. A: To correctly write a percent as a decimal, the percent sign is dropped and the number is rewritten with the decimal point two places to the left. If there is not two digits in the percent, a zero is used as a place holder. This is because a percent is always a value out of 100 and the second place after the decimal point is the hundredths place. So, 8% = 0.08.

39. D: Each of the units represents $\frac{1}{4}$. The point Z is 9 units right of the y-axis or $\frac{9}{4}$ units, which is equivalent to $2\frac{1}{4}$. The point R is also 9 units from the y-axis, or $\frac{9}{4}$, which is equivalent to $2\frac{1}{4}$. Be careful to notice that coordinate pairs always come in the order of the x-coordinate and then the y-

coordinate, and is defined by the pair of numbers. The y- coordinate for Z is $\frac{7}{8}$, while Point R has a y-coordinate of $3\frac{1}{2}$.

40. Part A: Count the number of customers in each age group and draw a bar on the histogram that represents that.

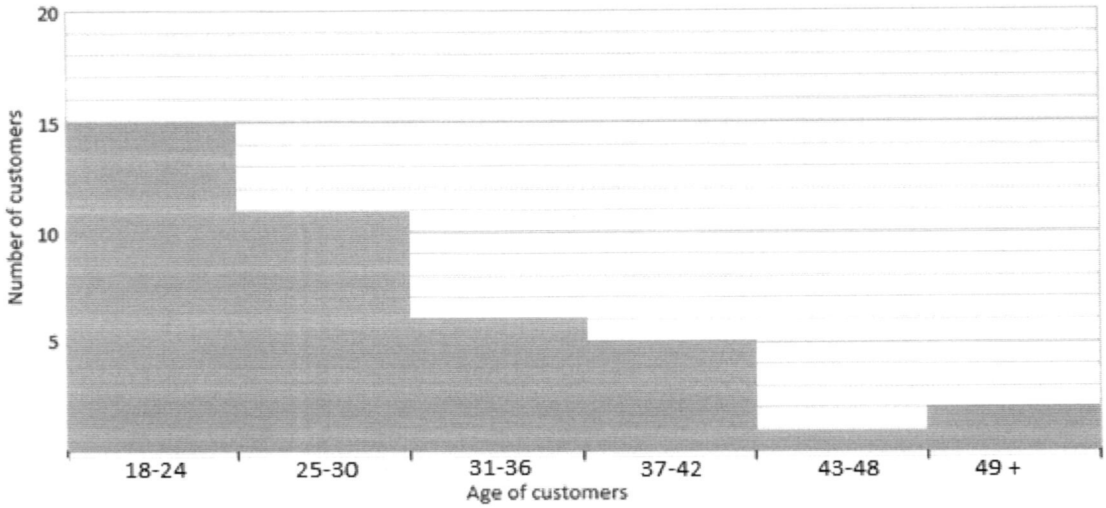

Part B: Yes: The median is the middle number of the group. Since there are 40 numbers there is no middle number so the median is the mean of the 20th and 21st number. Since this problem does not ask for a specific number there is no reason to write out the numbers and find the 20th and 21st. Instead you can see that the 25-30 age range encompasses numbers 16-26, so yes the median is in that range.

Mathematics Practice Test #2

Practice Questions

1. Four students measured the length of the pencil each was using. The list shows the lengths, in centimeters, of the four pencils.

17.03 cm, 17.4 cm, 17.31 cm, 17.09 cm

Which list shows the lengths of the pencils in order, from shortest to longest?

a. 17.4 cm, 17.31 cm, 17.09 cm, 17.03 cm
b. 17.03 cm, 17.09 cm, 17.4 cm, 17.31 cm
c. 17.4 cm, 17.03 cm, 17.09 cm, 17.31 cm
d. 17.03 cm, 17.09 cm, 17.31 cm, 17.4 cm

2. Castor collects only baseball and football cards. He has 40 baseball cards and 10 football cards. Which decimal best shows the part of his entire card collection represented by his baseball cards?

a. 0.8
b. 0.75
c. 0.4
d. 0.25

3. Which expression best shows the prime factorization of 630?

a. $2 \times 3 \times 105$
b. $2 \times 5 \times 7 \times 9$
c. $2 \times 3^2 \times 5 \times 7$
d. $2^2 \times 3^2 \times 5 \times 7$

4. Place the following numbers on the number line in the correct location:

$$-\frac{5}{3}, -\frac{2}{5}, 1.3, 1\frac{3}{5}$$

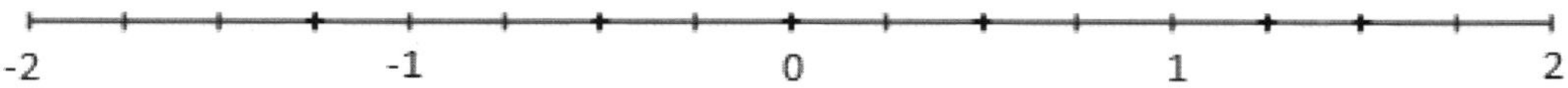

5. A club is making necklaces in school colors. They plan to use an equal number of blue beads and silver beads on each necklace. The blue beads come in bags of 60 and the silver beads come in bags of 80. What is the smallest number of bags of each color the club can purchase to have an equal number of each color bead with no beads left when the necklaces are finished?

a. 3 bags of blue and 4 bags of silver
b. 4 bags of blue and 3 bags of silver
c. 40 bags of blue and 30 bags of silver
d. 80 bags of blue and 60 bags of silver

6. Evan measured the amount of rain in the gauge over the weekend. On Saturday, he measured $1\frac{6}{10}$ inches and on Sunday, $\frac{8}{10}$ inches. What is the total amount of rain, in inches, Evan measured on those two days, written in the simplest form?

a. $1\frac{14}{20}$
b. $1\frac{4}{10}$
c. $1\frac{2}{5}$
d. $2\frac{2}{5}$

7. Rafael purchased 8 new tires for the two family cars. The price of each tire was $144, including taxes. He agreed to make 18 equal monthly payments, interest-free, to pay for the tires. What will be the amount Rafael should pay each month?

a. $16
b. $32
c. $64
d. $128

8. Part A: In the graph below what is the area of the smaller figure? Each square on the graph is one square unit.

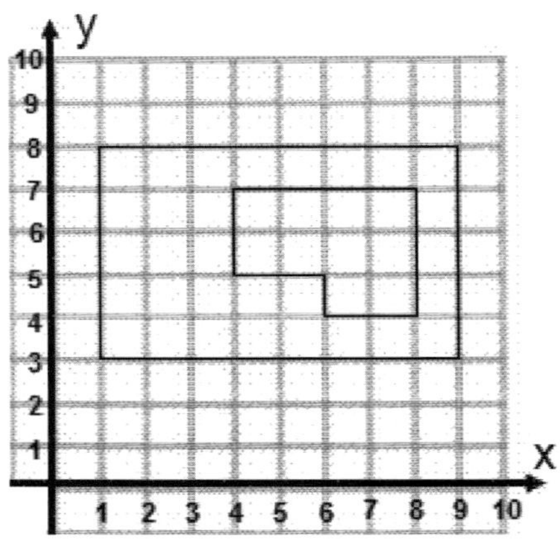

____

Part B: The area of the smaller figure is what fraction of the larger one?

____

9. William needs to find the value of the expression below. What is the value of this expression? $3^2 \times 2 - 4(3 - 1)$

a. 28
b. 18
c. 14
d. 10

10. Elena counted the number of birds that came to her bird bath one afternoon. While she watched, 20 sparrows, 16 finches, 4 wrens, and 10 jays came to the bird bath. Which ratio, in simplest form, compares the number of finches that Elena counted to the number of sparrows?

a. 4 : 5
b. 4 : 9
c. 16 : 20
d. 20 : 36

11. One cold afternoon at a small café, 20 people drank hot tea, 45 drank coffee, and 15 drank hot chocolate. Which ratio compares the number of people who drank coffee to the number who drank tea?

a. 4 to 13
b. 4 to 9
c. 9 to 4
d. 3 to 1

12. Part A: A lake near Armando's home is reported to be 80% full of water. Which fraction is equivalent to 80% and in simplest form?

a. $\frac{1}{80}$
b. $\frac{8}{10}$
c. $\frac{4}{5}$
d. $\frac{80}{1}$

Part B: If the lake is currently 12 feet deep, how deep would it be when it is completely full?

____

13. The rectangle in this drawing is divided into equal-sized parts, with some of them shaded a darker color.

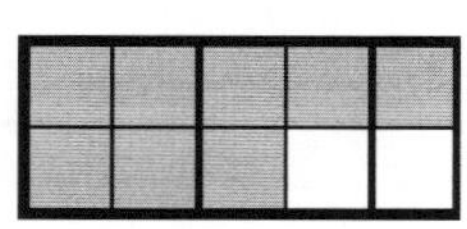

What percent best represents the part of the rectangle that is shaded a darker color?

a. 8%
b. 20%
c. 53%
d. 80%

14. Annette read that out of 20 televisions sold in her state last year, 3 were Brand V. If a furniture store near her home sold 360 televisions last year, about how many should Annette expect to be Brand V?

a. 18
b. 54
c. 1,080
d. 2,400

15. Thomas has mapped out his neighborhood on the graph below. He marked his house with the Point H, he marked his school with the point S, and he marked the park with the point P. Each square on the graph represents .25 miles. In the morning he walks to school, and after school he walks to the park. How far has he walked?

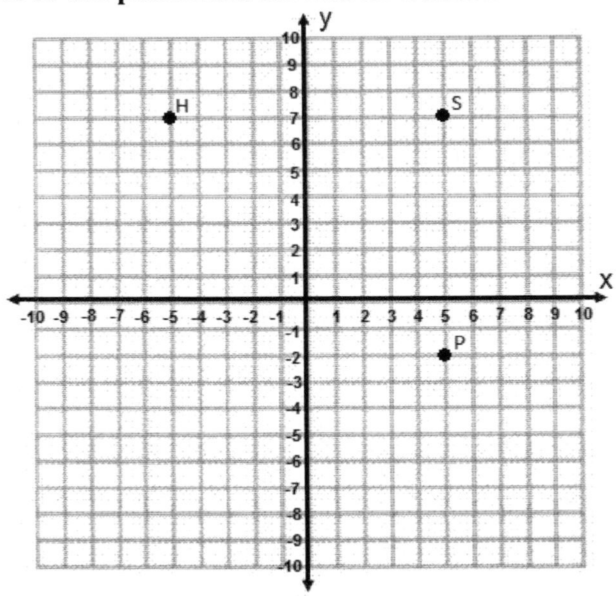

____

16. The table below gives the positions of several terms in a sequence and the values of those terms.

Sequence

Position of term, *n*	Value of Term
1	1
2	6
3	11
4	16
5	21
n	?

Which rule can be used to find the value of *n*?

a. 5n
b. 6n
c. 5n − 4
d. 6n − 5

17. Julia has a cell phone contract with a monthly charge of $45. She bought a phone with a one-time price of $50 with that contract. Which table best represents the total of all charges which should be paid at the end of each month of the contract?

a.

Number of Months	1	2	3	4	5	6
Total Charges	$45	$90	$135	$180	$225	$270

b.

Number of Months	1	2	3	4	5	6
Total Charges	$95	$140	$185	$230	$275	$320

c.

Number of Months	1	2	3	4	5	6
Total Charges	$95	$190	$285	$380	$475	$570

d.

Number of Months	1	2	3	4	5	6
Total Charges	$50	$95	$140	$185	$230	$275

18. This table shows bases, heights, and areas of four triangles. In each triangle, the base remains the same and the height changes.

Triangles

Base, *b*	30 yards	30 yards	30 yards	30 yards
Height, *h*	20 yards	40 yards	60 yards	80 yards
Area, *A*	300 square yards	600 square yards	900 square yards	1200 square yards

Which formula best represents the relationship between *A*, the areas of these triangles, and *h*, their heights?

a. $A = \frac{h}{30}$
b. $A = \frac{h}{15}$
c. $A = 30h$
d. $A = 15h$

19. An automobile mechanic charges $65 per hour when repairing an automobile. There is also a charge for the parts required. Which equation can the mechanic use to calculate the charge, *c*, to repair an automobile which requires *h* hours and *p* dollars worth of parts?

a. $c = 65(h + p)$
b. $c = 65h + p$
c. $c = 65p + h$
d. $c = h + p$

20. **Greg knows that in the triangle below, $m\angle X$ is 50° more than $m\angle V$.**

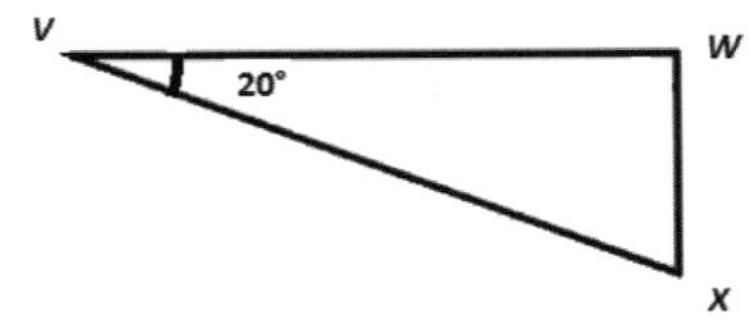

What is the measure of $\angle W$?

a. 20°
b. 50°
c. 70°
d. 90°

21. **Silvia knows that in this shape, $\angle M$ is equal in measure to $\angle K$, and that the measure of $\angle N$ is 4 times the measure of $\angle K$.**

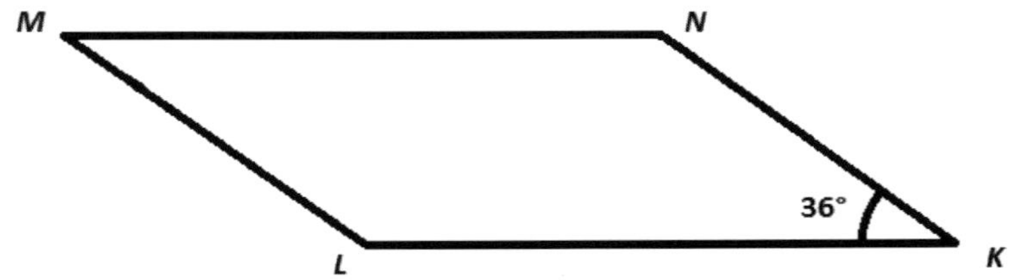

What is the measure of $\angle L$?

a. 36°
b. 72°
c. 144°
d. 288°

22. **There are five points labeled on this grid.**

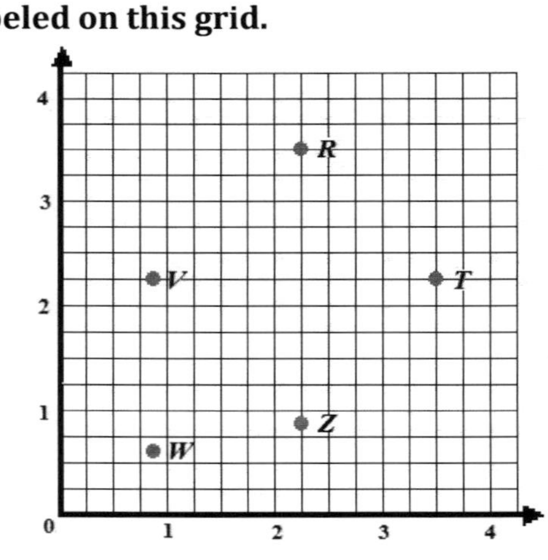

Which of the points on the grid best represents the point at $(3\frac{1}{2}, 2\frac{1}{4})$?

a. *R*
b. *T*
c. *V*
d. *W*

23. Curtis measured the temperature of water in a flask in science class. The temperature of the water was 35°C. He carefully heated the flask so that the temperature of the water increased about 2°C every 3 minutes. Approximately how much had the temperature of the water increased after 20 minutes?

a. 10°C
b. 13°C
c. 15°C
d. 35°C

24. Carlos helped in the library by putting new books on the shelves. Each shelf held between 21 and 24 books. Each bookcase had 5 shelves and Carlos filled 2 of the bookcases. Which number is nearest to the number of books Carlos put on the shelves?

a. 100
b. 195
c. 215
d. 240

25. Several angles and a protractor are shown in this drawing.

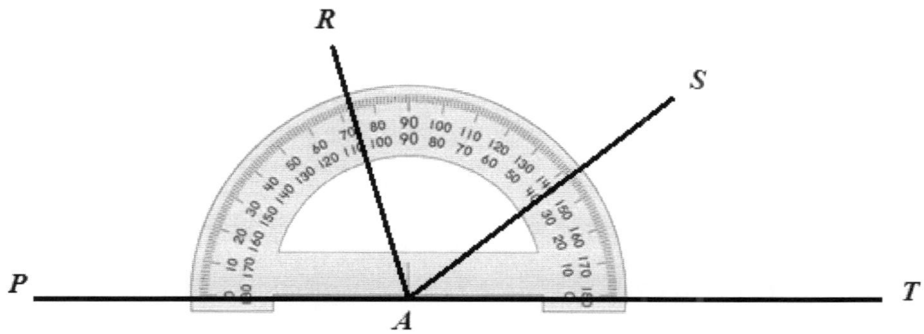

Which measure, in degrees, is closest to the measure of $\angle PAS$?

a. 37°
b. 43°
c. 143°
d. 157°

26. A lamp Sara decided to order online comes in four colors: brown, tan, white, and yellow. The shade for the lamp can be one of two styles: round or square. Which list shows all the possible combinations for a lamp of one color and one style for its shade that Sara can order?

a.

Brown, Round
Tan, Round
White, Square
Yellow Square

b.

Brown, Tan
Tan, White
White, Yellow
Yellow, Round
Round Square

c.

Brown, Tan
Brown, White
Brown, Yellow
Tan, White
Tan, Round
Tan Square

d.

Brown, Round
Tan, Round
White, Round
Yellow, Round
Brown Square
Tan, Square
White, Square
Yellow, Square

27. Alma collected coins. In the bag where she kept only dimes, she had dimes from four different years. She had 20 dimes minted in 1942, 30 minted in 1943, 40 minted in 1944, and 10 minted in 1945. If Alma reached into the bag without looking and took a dime, what is the probability that she took a dime minted in 1945?

a. $\frac{2}{5}$
b. $\frac{3}{10}$
c. $\frac{1}{5}$
d. $\frac{1}{10}$

28. Jacob recorded the high temperature in his backyard each day for six days. The list below shows those high temperatures.

61°, 54°, 58°, 63°, 71°, 71°

Which of these temperatures is the median of the ones in Jacob's list?

a. 17°
b. 62°
c. 63°
d. 71°

29. Mr. Smith paid $60 for a kit to build a dollhouse for his granddaughter. He also paid $10 for tools, $20 for paint, and $10 for other supplies to build the dollhouse. Which graph best represents the dollhouse expenses Mr. Smith had?

a.

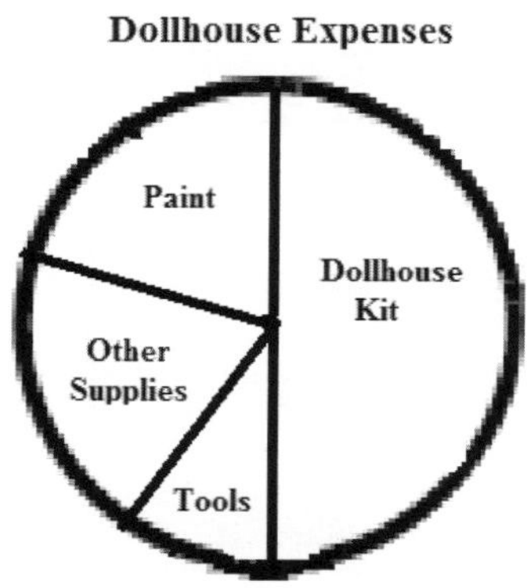

c.

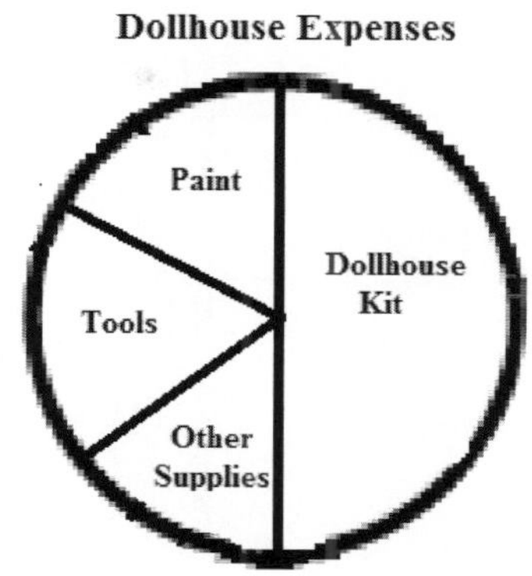

b.

d.

30. People who attended an orchestra concert at Johnson Middle School were asked to which of five age groups they belonged. The data is recorded in this graph.

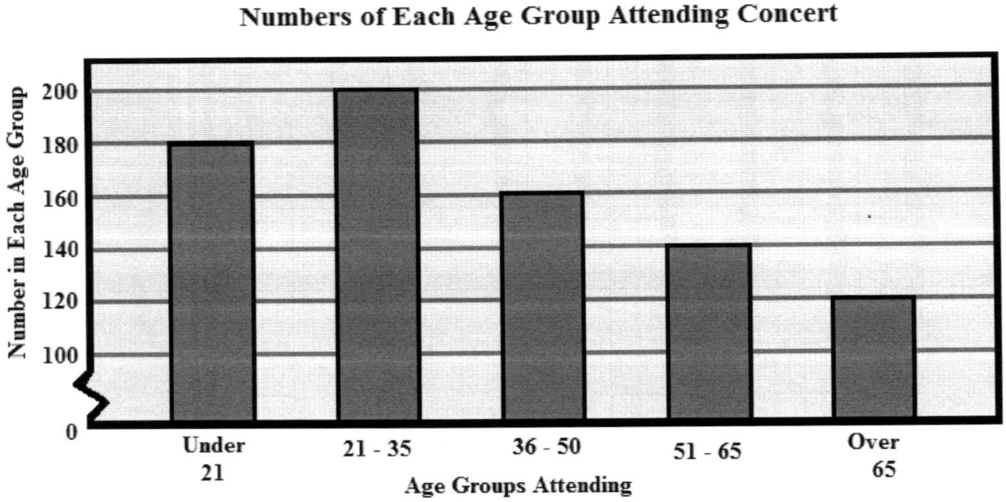

Which table correctly represents the data recorded in the graph?

a.

Number of Each Age Group Attending Concert

Age Group (in years)	Under 21	21 – 35	36 – 50	51 – 65	Over 65
Number in Group	180	200	160	140	120

b.

Number of Each Age Group Attending Concert

Age Group (in years)	Under 21	21 – 35	36 – 50	51 – 65	Over 65
Number in Group	180	220	180	160	140

c.

Number of Each Age Group Attending Concert

Age Group (in years)	Under 21	21 – 35	36 – 50	51 – 65	Over 65
Number in Group	180	200	140	120	100

d.

Number of Each Age Group Attending Concert

Age Group (in years)	Under 21	21 – 35	36 – 50	51 – 65	Over 65
Number in Group	180	200	160	120	120

31. Harlan plans to make stew for a large group. The recipe he uses requires 150 carrots. He knows that he can buy large bags of carrots for $3.75 each. What additional information does Harlan need to find the amount of money the carrots will cost for his stew?

a. The amounts of other vegetables he will need for the stew
b. The number of people he expects to eat the stew
c. The price each person attending the event paid
d. The number of carrots in a large bag of carrots

32. The cashier at Weekender Video Arcade recorded the number of tokens sold on Thursday, Friday, Saturday, and Sunday during one weekend. The graph shows the number of tokens sold on each of those four days.

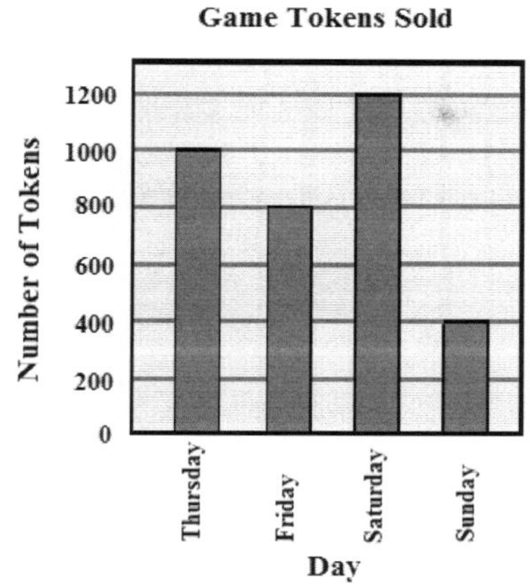

If the tokens sell for $1.25, what amount of money should the cashier have received for tokens sold on Friday and Saturday combined?

a. $1,500
b. $2,000
c. $2,500
d. $2,250

33. Part A: It took Hailey 18 minutes to jog from her house to the park. If the park is 2.5 miles away how long did it take her to go 1 mile?

____

Part B: If she keeps the same pace how long will it take her to go from the park to her friend's house that is 3.5 miles away?

____

34. Mr. Foster wants to put new carpet on the floor of his rectangular playroom. The playroom is 27 feet long and 18 feet wide. He has found an inexpensive carpet that is priced $14 per square yard. What would be a reasonable price for enough carpet to cover the floor of his playroom?

a. $486
b. $756
c. $1,260
d. $2,268

35. The rectangular floor of a garage has an area of 198 square feet. Andy knows that the floor is 7 feet longer than it is wide. What is length of the floor of the garage?

a. 11 feet
b. 14 feet
c. 18 feet
d. 92 feet

36. Timothy brought 12 of his toy cars to the baby sitters. These toy cars represent 30% of his toy car collection. What is the total number of cars in Timothy's collection?

____

37. Kenneth needs to repaint a wall in his bathroom. The wall is 8 feet high and 14 feet long. Part of the wall is covered with tile and he will not paint that part. The part of the wall covered by tile is 14 feet long and 42 inches high. Which expression could Kenneth use to find the area of the part of the wall he needs to repaint?

a. $14 \times 8 - (42 + 8)$
b. $14 \times 8 - (42 \times 14)$
c. $14 \times 8 - [(42 \div 12) \times 14]$
d. $2(14 + 8) - [(42 \div 12) + 14]$

38. Arlene had a garden for flowers. The rectangular garden was 10 feet wide and 16 feet long. In the garden, she planted daisies in a rectangular plot 5 feet wide and 10 feet long. She also planted pansies in a square plot 6 feet on each side. If Arlene planted no other flowers, how much area in her garden could still be planted?

a. 13 square feet, because $2(10 + 16) - [2(5 + 10) + 2(6 + 6)] = 13$
b. 38 square feet, because $2(10 + 16) - (5 \times 10) + (6 \times 6) = 38$
c. 74 square feet, because $10 \times 16 - [(5 \times 10) + (6 \times 6)] = 74$
d. 146 square feet, because $10 \times 16 - (5 \times 100) + (6 \times 6) = 146$

39. There are five points labeled on this grid.

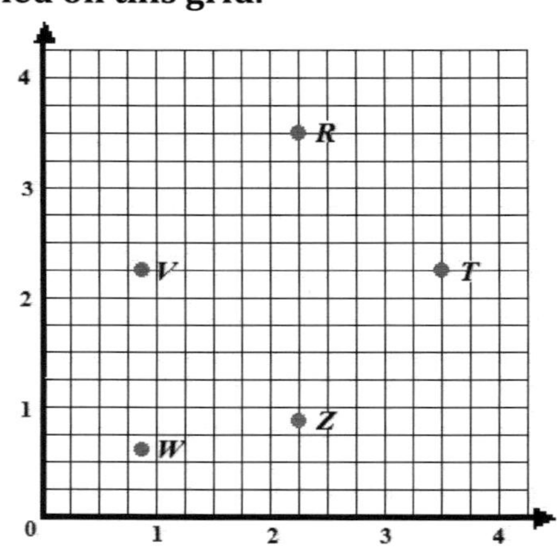

Which of the coordinates on the grid best represents the point R?

a. $(3\frac{1}{2}, 2\frac{1}{2})$
b. $(2\frac{1}{4}, 3\frac{1}{2})$
c. $(3\frac{1}{2}, 4\frac{1}{2})$
d. $(2\frac{1}{4}, 3\frac{1}{4})$

40. A fair was open for 4 days. The attendance to the fair during those 4 days is recorded below as well as the number of ride tickets sold.

Day	Number of entrants	Number of tickets sold
1	102	510
2	114	912
3	108	756
4	131	1048

Part A: How many tickets were sold per entrant on day 2?

____

Part B: What is the average number of tickets sold per entrant over the entire 4 day?

____

Answers and Explanations

1. D: To correctly order the numbers in this question, making the decimals all have the same number of digits by adding as many zeros as necessary to the numbers with fewer digits makes them easier to compare. Here, only 17.4 has fewer digits than the others, so add one zero to make it 17.40 (*this does not change the value*). Now, by comparing place values from left to right of 17.03, 17.4, 17.31, and 17.09, we see that 17.03 is the shortest, 17.09 is the next longest, 17.31 is the third longest, and 17.4 is the longest. Notice the question asked for shortest to longest, not longest to shortest.

2. A: In order to answer this question, we add the number of baseball and football cards to realize that there are 50 total cards in Castor's collection, 40 of which are baseball cards. To convert this to a decimal, we need to divide 40 by 50. This gives the correct answer, 0.8.

3. C: There is more than one way to solve this problem. One method is to use the fact that the number ends in 0. This means 10 is a factor. So, 10 × 63 = 630. 10 has prime factors of 2 and 5. 63 has factors of 7 and 9 and the 9 has two factors of 3. Putting the prime factors in order, least to greatest, and showing the two factors of 3 with an exponent of 2 gives us the answer: $2 \times 3^2 \times 5 \times 7$.

4. $-\frac{5}{3}$ is going to be slightly more than the $-1\frac{3}{4}$ mark on the number line. $-\frac{2}{5}$ is going to be a little more than $-\frac{1}{2}$ mark. 1.3 is going to be a little more than the $1\frac{1}{4}$ mark. $1\frac{3}{5}$ is going to be a little more than the $1\frac{3}{4}$ mark.

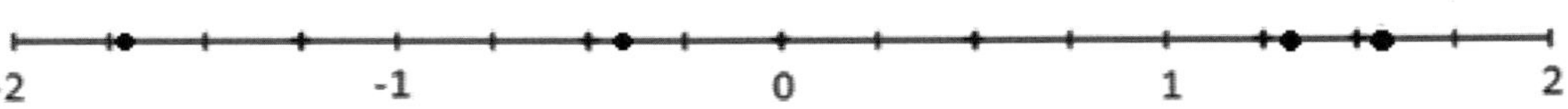

5. B: There is more than one way to solve this problem. One method is to find the least common multiple of 60 and 80. To do this, first find the prime factors of each number.

60 = 2 × 2 × 3 × 5

80 = 2 × 2 × 2 × 2 × 5

The factors common to 60 and 80 are 2, 2, and 5. The factors that are not common to both numbers are two factors of 2 from 80 and a factor of 3 from 60. To find the least common multiple, multiply all the factors without repetition. That is, multiply the common factors (2, 2, and 5) and the other factors (2, 2, and 3) together:

2 × 2 × 2 × 2 × 3 × 5 = 240

240 is the least common multiple. This is the total number of beads needed of each color. To find how many bags the club will need to purchase, divide this total by the number of beads that come in each bag for each color bead. 240 ÷ 60 = 4 (4 bags of blue). 240 ÷ 80 = 3 (3 bags of silver).

6. D: To answer this question, note that the fractions have common denominators. When adding fractions with common denominators, we need to add only the numerators, so, the sum of $\frac{6}{10}$ and $\frac{8}{10}$ is $\frac{14}{10}$. This should then be written as a mixed number, $1\frac{4}{10}$, which is found by dividing 14 by 10 which gives the whole number and the remainder becomes your new numerator over the same denominator of 10. The fraction $\frac{4}{10}$ can also be written as $\frac{2}{5}$ by dividing numerator and denominator by the common factor of 2. Therefore, $\frac{14}{10}$ is equivalent to $1\frac{2}{5}$. Be careful here to remember the 1 from the original $1\frac{6}{10}$ amount given in the problem, which must be added to the $1\frac{2}{5}$ to make a total of $2\frac{2}{5}$.

7. C: First, multiply the cost of each tire, \$144, by the number of tires, 8, to get \$1,152. Then, divide \$1,152 by the number of months, 18, to get the amount paid each month, \$64.

8. Part A: 10: The number of square units inside the figure is 10.

Part B: $\frac{1}{4}$: The larger figure is 8 by 5 so it is 40 square units. So, it is $\frac{10}{40} = \frac{1}{4}$.

9. D: To simplify this expression, use the order of operations.

$$3^2 \times 2 - 4(3 - 1)$$

$$= 3^2 \times 2 - 4(2)$$

$$= 9 \times 2 - 4(2)$$

$$= 18 - 8$$

$$=10$$

10. A: The ratio asked for is the number of finches compared to the number of sparrows. This compares 16 to 20, but the ratio can be written in simpler form by dividing both numbers in the ratio by 4, to get the ratio of 4 to 5. It is important to notice the order of the ratio. Since the number of finches is written before the number of sparrows, the ratio must be 16 to 20 and not 20 to 16. Also, note that the number of wrens or jays does not matter here.

11. C: The ratio compares the number of coffee drinkers to the number of tea drinkers, in that order, so the ratio is 45 to 20. Note that the ratio of 20 to 45 would be incorrect. The ratio of 45 to 20 can then be written in simpler terms by dividing both terms by 5 to get 9 to 4. Notice that the number of hot chocolate drinkers is not important in this problem.

12. Part A: C: The 80% means 80 out of 100, which can be written as $\frac{80}{100}$. This fraction can be written in lowest terms by dividing both the numerator and denominator by the greatest common factor of 20, to get the fraction, $\frac{4}{5}$.

Part B: 15 feet: If the lake is 12 feet deep at 80% full then you can just divide 12 by .8 to get 15 feet.

13. D: The number of shaded parts is 8 and the total number of parts is 10. This can be written as the ratio: $\frac{8}{10}$. Since percent is always a ratio with a denominator of 100, multiply both terms of the ratio by 10 to get the ratio: $\frac{80}{100}$, which can be written as 80%.

14. B: One method that can be used to answer this question is to write and solve the proportion: $\frac{3}{20} = \frac{V}{360}$, where V stands for the number of Brand V televisions that were sold at the furniture store. To solve the proportion, we can cross multiply: 20 times V and 3 times 360, which gives the equation: $20V = 1{,}080$. We solve this equation by dividing both sides of the equation by 20 to get $V = 54$.

15. 4.75: Point H is located at (-5, 7), and Point S is located at (5, 7). The distance between these is 10 units on the graph or 2.5 miles. Point P is located at (5, -2). The distance between it and Point S is 9 units on the graph or 2.25 miles. So, Thomas walked a total of 4.75 miles.

16. C: Notice that there is a difference of 5 between the values in Column 2. This gives the "5" in front of *n*. Then, notice that if you multiply the position of the term by 5, the value is less than that product, by 4. So, the rule is $5n$ -4.

17. B: There is a one-time charge of $50 for the price of the phone and a $45 monthly charge in the first month for a total of $95. Then, a charge of $45 only is added for every month after that. Since the chart shows the total charge each month, adding $45 to the total due from the first month gives a total of $140 for the first 2 months. Then, $45 is added for the next month, for a total of $185 for the first 3 months, $230 for 4 months, $275 for 5 months, and $320 in total charges for the first 6 months.

18. D: The formula for the area of a triangle can be used here, but it is not necessary. To find the relationship between the heights and areas, look at the last two rows. A pattern can be seen that each value for the area, *A*, is just 15 times the value of the height, *h*. So, the formula is: $A = 15h$.

19. B: The amount charged for hours worked will require us to multiply the number of hours by $65. The charge for parts is not changed by the number of hours worked. So, the equation needs to show 65 times *h*, the number of hours, plus *p*, the price of the parts. So, the correct equation is: $c = 65h + p$.

20. D: To find $m\angle W$, we must first find the measure of $\angle X$. We know $m\angle X$ is 50° more than $m\angle V$. Since $m\angle V$ = 20°, then $m\angle X$ = 20° + 50° = 70°. So, $m\angle V + m\angle X$ = 90°. It is important here to know that the sum of the three angles of any triangle is 180°. Since $m\angle V + m\angle X$ = 90°, then 90°+ $m\angle W$ = 180°. So, $m\angle W$ =90°.

21. C: Since we are told that $m\angle N$ is 4 times $m\angle K$, we can find the $m\angle N$ by multiplying 36° by 4 to get 144°. Knowing $\angle M$ measures 36° because it is equal to $m\angle K$ gives us the measures of three of the angles. The sum of the four angles of a quadrilateral always equals 360°. So, we add the measures of the three angles that we know and then subtract that total from 360°:

360 – (36 + 144 +36) = 360 – 216 = 144. The measure of $\angle L$ is 144°.

22. B: Each of the units represents $\frac{1}{4}$. The point *T* is 14 units right of the *y*-axis or $\frac{14}{4}$ units, which is equivalent to $3\frac{1}{2}$. The point *T* is also 9 units from the *x*-axis, or $\frac{9}{4}$, which is equivalent to $2\frac{1}{4}$. Be careful to notice that coordinate pairs always come in the order of the *x*-coordinate and then the *y*-coordinate, which is why Point *R* would be incorrect.

23. B: The water temperature increased by about 2 °C every 3 minutes, or $\frac{2}{3}$ of a degree Celsius every minute. Multiplying the increase in degrees per minute by the total number of minutes yields

$$\frac{2\ °\text{C}}{3\ \text{min}} \times 20\ \text{min} = \frac{40}{3}, \text{or } 13.33°$$

Since the problem asks for the increase in temperature and not the total temperature that results after the increases, 13 is the closest to our answer.

24. C: First, since there are 5 shelves on each of the 2 bookcases, we multiply 5 by 2 to get 10 shelves total. Then, we find the minimum and maximum number of books that could have filled the shelves. Since 21 times 10 is 210 and 24 times 10 is 240, The number of books he shelved must be between 210 and 240. Answer D is 240, which would mean that every shelf was filled with the maximum number of books, which is not as likely.

25. C: Since segment PA lies along the left side of the protractor, we should read the outside scale. The segment SA passes between 140° and 150°, much closer to 140°, so the correct answer is 143°.

26. D: This list is the only one which lists all the possible ways Sara can order the lamp. Each of the four color choices can be chosen, and they can all be combined with one of two styles. In total, there are eight possibilities.

27. D: By adding all of the dimes, we find that there are a total of 100 dimes in the bag. 10 of them were minted in 1945. The probability, then, of choosing a dime minted in 1945 is 10 out of 100, which is equivalent to the fraction $\frac{1}{10}$.

28. B: To find the median of a set of data, first arrange the numbers in numerical order. Since this is an even numbered list, the two most central numbers are 61 and 63. Midway between these numbers is 62.

29. D: By adding up all of Mr. Smith's expenses for the dollhouse, \$60 + \$10 + \$20 + \$10, you find that his expenses totaled \$100. Mr. Smith spent \$60 on the kit, which is more than $\frac{1}{2}$ his expenses ($\frac{1}{2}$ of \$100 would be \$50), $\frac{1}{10}$ of his expenses on tools ($\frac{1}{10}$ of \$100 = \$10), $\frac{1}{5}$ of his expenses on paint ($\frac{1}{5}$ of \$100 = \$20), and $\frac{1}{10}$ of his expenses on other supplies. This is the only graph that correctly shows these fractions.

30. A: This table is the only one with the correct numbers from the graph for each category.

31. D: Since Harlan knows the cost of each bag of carrots, and also how many total carrots he needs, he also needs to know the number of carrots in each bag to find the number of bags he needs to buy. Then, he can multiply the number of bags by the price to find the amount of money the carrots for his stew will cost.

32. C: Though the graph shows the numbers of tokens sold on Thursday through Sunday, we are only asked about those sold on Friday and Saturday. So, we add those numbers together to get 800 + 1,200 = 2,000. Then, since each of the 2,000 tokens sold for \$1.25 each, the 2,000 should be multiplied by \$1.25 to get \$2500.

33. Part A: 7.2 minutes: If it takes her 18 minutes to jog 2.5 miles then just divide 18 by 2.5 to get 7.2 minutes.

Part B: 25.2 minutes: If she keeps the same pace then it would take her 7.2 minutes times 3.5 miles. This equals 25.2 minutes.

34. B: It is necessary to find the area of the floor by multiplying the dimensions together. However, since the dimensions are given in feet and we only know the price of carpeting per square yard, converting the dimensions from feet to yards first is helpful. Since there are 3 feet in a yard, dividing each of the dimensions by 3 will give us the measurements in yards. So, 18/3 = 6 and 27/3 = 9. So, the floor is 6 yards by 9 yards, which is an area of 54 square yards. Last, we multiply 54 by \$14, since each square yard costs \$14 and there are 54, so the price of the carpet should be \$756.

35. C: Guess and check is one way to find the correct answer. We know the length times the width gives the area of the garage floor, 198 square feet. We might guess that the width is 9. We know that the length is 7 more than the width, so, then the length would be 16. 9 times 16 is 144. We would see that our first guess is too low, so we guess higher. We might guess 12 for the width. The length is 7 more, so the length would be 19. 12 times 19 is 228, but this is too high. When we try 11 for the width, we find the length to be 18. 11 times 18 is 198, so the width of the garage floor is 11 and the length is 18. Be careful to note that the question asks for the length and not the width.

36. 40: If 12 of his cars represents 30% of his collection the divide by 3 to find 10% and then multiply by 10 to get 100%. $12 \div 3 = 4 \times 10 = 40$.

37. C: We multiply the length and wide of the wall to find the area of the entire wall. So, 8 × 14. Then, we want to subtract the area of the tiled section that does not need to be painted from the area of the entire wall. However, the height of the tiled section is given in inches, while all the other dimensions in the problem are given in feet. So, we must convert this to feet. Since we are going from a smaller unit to a larger unit (inches to feet), we want to divide. We need to divide 42 by 12 since that is the conversion factor (12 inches in 1 foot). Then we multiply the height (in feet) by the length to find the area covered by the tile. So, this is 14 times the 42 divided by 12. Last, we subtract the two areas to find the area of the part of the wall Kenneth will repaint.

38. C: The area of the garden should be found by multiplying 10 times 16 to get 160. Then the area of the daisy plot can be found by multiplying 5 times 10 to get 50, and the area of the pansy plot can be found by multiplying 6 times 6 to get 36. We then add the 50 square feet and 36 square feet to get 86 square feet, which is the area the two plots (daisy and pansy) cover. To find the area of the garden that can still be planted, subtract that from the total area of 160 square feet to get 74 square feet.

39. B: Each of the units represents $\frac{1}{4}$. The point R is 9 units to the right of the *y*-axis or $\frac{9}{4}$, which is equivalent to $2\frac{1}{4}$. Point R is also 14 units above the *x*-axis or $\frac{14}{4}$, which is equivalent to $3\frac{1}{2}$. Be careful to notice that coordinate pairs always come in the order of the *x*-coordinate and then the *y*-coordinate.

40. D: Only answer D correctly shows each amount of birdfeed being subtracted from the original total amount of 10 cups that originally given to Xander.

How to Overcome Test Anxiety

Just the thought of taking a test is enough to make most people a little nervous. A test is an important event that can have a long-term impact on your future, so it's important to take it seriously and it's natural to feel anxious about performing well. But just because anxiety is normal, that doesn't mean that it's helpful in test taking, or that you should simply accept it as part of your life. Anxiety can have a variety of effects. These effects can be mild, like making you feel slightly nervous, or severe, like blocking your ability to focus or remember even a simple detail.

If you experience test anxiety—whether severe or mild—it's important to know how to beat it. To discover this, first you need to understand what causes test anxiety.

Causes of Test Anxiety

While we often think of anxiety as an uncontrollable emotional state, it can actually be caused by simple, practical things. One of the most common causes of test anxiety is that a person does not feel adequately prepared for their test. This feeling can be the result of many different issues such as poor study habits or lack of organization, but the most common culprit is time management. Starting to study too late, failing to organize your study time to cover all of the material, or being distracted while you study will mean that you're not well prepared for the test. This may lead to cramming the night before, which will cause you to be physically and mentally exhausted for the test. Poor time management also contributes to feelings of stress, fear, and hopelessness as you realize you are not well prepared but don't know what to do about it.

Other times, test anxiety is not related to your preparation for the test but comes from unresolved fear. This may be a past failure on a test, or poor performance on tests in general. It may come from comparing yourself to others who seem to be performing better or from the stress of living up to expectations. Anxiety may be driven by fears of the future—how failure on this test would affect your educational and career goals. These fears are often completely irrational, but they can still negatively impact your test performance.

Elements of Test Anxiety

As mentioned earlier, test anxiety is considered to be an emotional state, but it has physical and mental components as well. Sometimes you may not even realize that you are suffering from test anxiety until you notice the physical symptoms. These can include trembling hands, rapid heartbeat, sweating, nausea, and tense muscles. Extreme anxiety may lead to fainting or vomiting. Obviously, any of these symptoms can have a negative impact on testing. It is important to recognize them as soon as they begin to occur so that you can address the problem before it damages your performance.

The mental components of test anxiety include trouble focusing and inability to remember learned information. During a test, your mind is on high alert, which can help you recall information and stay focused for an extended period of time. However, anxiety interferes with your mind's natural processes, causing you to blank out, even on the questions you know well. The strain of testing during anxiety makes it difficult to stay focused, especially on a test that may take several hours. Extreme anxiety can take a huge mental toll, making it difficult not only to recall test information but even to understand the test questions or pull your thoughts together.

Effects of Test Anxiety

Test anxiety is like a disease—if left untreated, it will get progressively worse. Anxiety leads to poor performance, and this reinforces the feelings of fear and failure, which in turn lead to poor performances on subsequent tests. It can grow from a mild nervousness to a crippling condition. If allowed to progress, test anxiety can have a big impact on your schooling, and consequently on your future.

Test anxiety can spread to other parts of your life. Anxiety on tests can become anxiety in any stressful situation, and blanking on a test can turn into panicking in a job situation. But fortunately, you don't have to let anxiety rule your testing and determine your grades. There are a number of relatively simple steps you can take to move past anxiety and function normally on a test and in the rest of life.

Physical Steps for Beating Test Anxiety

While test anxiety is a serious problem, the good news is that it can be overcome. It doesn't have to control your ability to think and remember information. While it may take time, you can begin taking steps today to beat anxiety.

Just as your first hint that you may be struggling with anxiety comes from the physical symptoms, the first step to treating it is also physical. Rest is crucial for having a clear, strong mind. If you are tired, it is much easier to give in to anxiety. But if you establish good sleep habits, your body and mind will be ready to perform optimally, without the strain of exhaustion. Additionally, sleeping well helps you to retain information better, so you're more likely to recall the answers when you see the test questions.

Getting good sleep means more than going to bed on time. It's important to allow your brain time to relax. Take study breaks from time to time so it doesn't get overworked, and don't study right before bed. Take time to rest your mind before trying to rest your body, or you may find it difficult to fall asleep.

Along with sleep, other aspects of physical health are important in preparing for a test. Good nutrition is vital for good brain function. Sugary foods and drinks may give a burst of energy but this burst is followed by a crash, both physically and emotionally. Instead, fuel your body with protein and vitamin-rich foods.

Also, drink plenty of water. Dehydration can lead to headaches and exhaustion, especially if your brain is already under stress from the rigors of the test. Particularly if your test is a long one, drink water during the breaks. And if possible, take an energy-boosting snack to eat between sections.

Along with sleep and diet, a third important part of physical health is exercise. Maintaining a steady workout schedule is helpful, but even taking 5-minute study breaks to walk can help get your blood pumping faster and clear your head. Exercise also releases endorphins, which contribute to a positive feeling and can help combat test anxiety.

When you nurture your physical health, you are also contributing to your mental health. If your body is healthy, your mind is much more likely to be healthy as well. So take time to rest, nourish your body with healthy food and water, and get moving as much as possible. Taking these physical steps will make you stronger and more able to take the mental steps necessary to overcome test anxiety.

Mental Steps for Beating Test Anxiety

Working on the mental side of test anxiety can be more challenging, but as with the physical side, there are clear steps you can take to overcome it. As mentioned earlier, test anxiety often stems from lack of preparation, so the obvious solution is to prepare for the test. Effective studying may be the most important weapon you have for beating test anxiety, but you can and should employ several other mental tools to combat fear.

First, boost your confidence by reminding yourself of past success—tests or projects that you aced. If you're putting as much effort into preparing for this test as you did for those, there's no reason you should expect to fail here. Work hard to prepare; then trust your preparation.

Second, surround yourself with encouraging people. It can be helpful to find a study group, but be sure that the people you're around will encourage a positive attitude. If you spend time with others who are anxious or cynical, this will only contribute to your own anxiety. Look for others who are motivated to study hard from a desire to succeed, not from a fear of failure.

Third, reward yourself. A test is physically and mentally tiring, even without anxiety, and it can be helpful to have something to look forward to. Plan an activity following the test, regardless of the outcome, such as going to a movie or getting ice cream.

When you are taking the test, if you find yourself beginning to feel anxious, remind yourself that you know the material. Visualize successfully completing the test. Then take a few deep, relaxing breaths and return to it. Work through the questions carefully but with confidence, knowing that you are capable of succeeding.

Developing a healthy mental approach to test taking will also aid in other areas of life. Test anxiety affects more than just the actual test—it can be damaging to your mental health and even contribute to depression. It's important to beat test anxiety before it becomes a problem for more than testing.

Study Strategy

Being prepared for the test is necessary to combat anxiety, but what does being prepared look like? You may study for hours on end and still not feel prepared. What you need is a strategy for test prep. The next few pages outline our recommended steps to help you plan out and conquer the challenge of preparation.

Step 1: Scope Out the Test

Learn everything you can about the format (multiple choice, essay, etc.) and what will be on the test. Gather any study materials, course outlines, or sample exams that may be available. Not only will this help you to prepare, but knowing what to expect can help to alleviate test anxiety.

Step 2: Map Out the Material

Look through the textbook or study guide and make note of how many chapters or sections it has. Then divide these over the time you have. For example, if a book has 15 chapters and you have five days to study, you need to cover three chapters each day. Even better, if you have the time, leave an extra day at the end for overall review after you have gone through the material in depth.

If time is limited, you may need to prioritize the material. Look through it and make note of which sections you think you already have a good grasp on, and which need review. While you are studying, skim quickly through the familiar sections and take more time on the challenging parts.

Write out your plan so you don't get lost as you go. Having a written plan also helps you feel more in control of the study, so anxiety is less likely to arise from feeling overwhelmed at the amount to cover.

Step 3: Gather Your Tools

Decide what study method works best for you. Do you prefer to highlight in the book as you study and then go back over the highlighted portions? Or do you type out notes of the important information? Or is it helpful to make flashcards that you can carry with you? Assemble the pens, index cards, highlighters, post-it notes, and any other materials you may need so you won't be distracted by getting up to find things while you study.

If you're having a hard time retaining the information or organizing your notes, experiment with different methods. For example, try color-coding by subject with colored pens, highlighters, or post-it notes. If you learn better by hearing, try recording yourself reading your notes so you can listen while in the car, working out, or simply sitting at your desk. Ask a friend to quiz you from your flashcards, or try teaching someone the material to solidify it in your mind.

Step 4: Create Your Environment

It's important to avoid distractions while you study. This includes both the obvious distractions like visitors and the subtle distractions like an uncomfortable chair (or a too-comfortable couch that makes you want to fall asleep). Set up the best study environment possible: good lighting and a comfortable work area. If background music helps you focus, you may want to turn it on, but otherwise keep the room quiet. If you are using a computer to take notes, be sure you don't have any other windows open, especially applications like social media, games, or anything else that could distract you. Silence your phone and turn off notifications. Be sure to keep water close by so you stay hydrated while you study (but avoid unhealthy drinks and snacks).

Also, take into account the best time of day to study. Are you freshest first thing in the morning? Try to set aside some time then to work through the material. Is your mind clearer in the afternoon or evening? Schedule your study session then. Another method is to study at the same time of day that you will take the test, so that your brain gets used to working on the material at that time and will be ready to focus at test time.

Step 5: Study!

Once you have done all the study preparation, it's time to settle into the actual studying. Sit down, take a few moments to settle your mind so you can focus, and begin to follow your study plan. Don't give in to distractions or let yourself procrastinate. This is your time to prepare so you'll be ready to fearlessly approach the test. Make the most of the time and stay focused.

Of course, you don't want to burn out. If you study too long you may find that you're not retaining the information very well. Take regular study breaks. For example, taking five minutes out of every hour to walk briskly, breathing deeply and swinging your arms, can help your mind stay fresh.

As you get to the end of each chapter or section, it's a good idea to do a quick review. Remind yourself of what you learned and work on any difficult parts. When you feel that you've mastered the material, move on to the next part. At the end of your study session, briefly skim through your notes again.

But while review is helpful, cramming last minute is NOT. If at all possible, work ahead so that you won't need to fit all your study into the last day. Cramming overloads your brain with more information than it can process and retain, and your tired mind may struggle to recall even previously learned information when it is overwhelmed with last-minute study. Also, the urgent nature of cramming and the stress placed on your brain contribute to anxiety. You'll be more likely to go to the test feeling unprepared and having trouble thinking clearly.

So don't cram, and don't stay up late before the test, even just to review your notes at a leisurely pace. Your brain needs rest more than it needs to go over the information again. In fact, plan to finish your studies by noon or early afternoon the day before the test. Give your brain the rest of the day to relax or focus on other things, and get a good night's sleep. Then you will be fresh for the test and better able to recall what you've studied.

Step 6: Take a Practice Test

Many courses offer sample tests, either online or in the study materials. This is an excellent resource to check whether you have mastered the material, as well as to prepare for the test format and environment.

Check the test format ahead of time: the number of questions, the type (multiple choice, free response, etc.), and the time limit. Then create a plan for working through them. For example, if you have 30 minutes to take a 60-question test, your limit is 30 seconds per question. Spend less time on the questions you know well so that you can take more time on the difficult ones.

If you have time to take several practice tests, take the first one open book, with no time limit. Work through the questions at your own pace and make sure you fully understand them. Gradually work up to taking a test under test conditions: sit at a desk with all study materials put away and set a timer. Pace yourself to make sure you finish the test with time to spare and go back to check your answers if you have time.

After each test, check your answers. On the questions you missed, be sure you understand why you missed them. Did you misread the question (tests can use tricky wording)? Did you forget the information? Or was it something you hadn't learned? Go back and study any shaky areas that the practice tests reveal.

Taking these tests not only helps with your grade, but also aids in combating test anxiety. If you're already used to the test conditions, you're less likely to worry about it, and working through tests until you're scoring well gives you a confidence boost. Go through the practice tests until you feel comfortable, and then you can go into the test knowing that you're ready for it.

Test Tips

On test day, you should be confident, knowing that you've prepared well and are ready to answer the questions. But aside from preparation, there are several test day strategies you can employ to maximize your performance.

First, as stated before, get a good night's sleep the night before the test (and for several nights before that, if possible). Go into the test with a fresh, alert mind rather than staying up late to study.

Try not to change too much about your normal routine on the day of the test. It's important to eat a nutritious breakfast, but if you normally don't eat breakfast at all, consider eating just a protein bar. If you're a coffee drinker, go ahead and have your normal coffee. Just make sure you time it so that the caffeine doesn't wear off right in the middle of your test. Avoid sugary beverages, and drink enough water to stay hydrated but not so much that you need a restroom break 10 minutes into the test. If your test isn't first thing in the morning, consider going for a walk or doing a light workout before the test to get your blood flowing.

Allow yourself enough time to get ready, and leave for the test with plenty of time to spare so you won't have the anxiety of scrambling to arrive in time. Another reason to be early is to select a good seat. It's helpful to sit away from doors and windows, which can be distracting. Find a good seat, get out your supplies, and settle your mind before the test begins.

When the test begins, start by going over the instructions carefully, even if you already know what to expect. Make sure you avoid any careless mistakes by following the directions.

Then begin working through the questions, pacing yourself as you've practiced. If you're not sure on an answer, don't spend too much time on it, and don't let it shake your confidence. Either skip it and come back later, or eliminate as many wrong answers as possible and guess among the remaining ones. Don't dwell on these questions as you continue—put them out of your mind and focus on what lies ahead.

Be sure to read all of the answer choices, even if you're sure the first one is the right answer. Sometimes you'll find a better one if you keep reading. But don't second-guess yourself if you do immediately know the answer. Your gut instinct is usually right. Don't let test anxiety rob you of the information you know.

If you have time at the end of the test (and if the test format allows), go back and review your answers. Be cautious about changing any, since your first instinct tends to be correct, but make sure you didn't misread any of the questions or accidentally mark the wrong answer choice. Look over any you skipped and make an educated guess.

At the end, leave the test feeling confident. You've done your best, so don't waste time worrying about your performance or wishing you could change anything. Instead, celebrate the successful completion of this test. And finally, use this test to learn how to deal with anxiety even better next time.

Review Video: Test Anxiety
Visit mometrix.com/academy and enter code: 100340

Important Qualification

Not all anxiety is created equal. If your test anxiety is causing major issues in your life beyond the classroom or testing center, or if you are experiencing troubling physical symptoms related to your anxiety, it may be a sign of a serious physiological or psychological condition. If this sounds like your situation, we strongly encourage you to seek professional help.

How to Overcome Your Fear of Math

Not again. You're sitting in math class, look down at your test, and immediately start to panic. Your stomach is in knots, your heart is racing, and you break out in a cold sweat. You're staring at the paper, but everything looks like it's written in a foreign language. Even though you studied, you're blanking out on how to begin solving these problems.

Does this sound familiar? If so, then you're not alone! You may be like millions of other people who experience math anxiety. Anxiety about performing well in math is a common experience for students of all ages. In this article, we'll discuss what math anxiety is, common misconceptions about learning math, and tips and strategies for overcoming math anxiety.

What Is Math Anxiety?

Psychologist Mark H. Ashcraft explains math anxiety as a feeling of tension, apprehension, or fear that interferes with math performance. Having math anxiety negatively impacts people's beliefs about themselves and what they can achieve. It hinders achievement within the math classroom and affects the successful application of mathematics in the real world.

Symptoms and Signs of Math Anxiety

To overcome math anxiety, you must recognize its symptoms. Becoming aware of the signs of math anxiety is the first step in addressing and resolving these fears.

Negative Self-Talk

If you have math anxiety, you've most likely said at least one of these statements to yourself:

- "I hate math."
- "I'm not good at math."
- "I'm not a math person."

The way we speak to ourselves and think about ourselves matters. Our thoughts become our words, our words become our actions, and our actions become our habits. Thinking negatively about math creates a self-fulfilling prophecy. In other words, if you take an idea as a fact, then it will come true because your behaviors will align to match it.

Avoidance

Some people who are fearful or anxious about math will tend to avoid it altogether. Avoidance can manifest in the following ways:

- Lack of engagement with math content
- Not completing homework and other assignments
- Not asking for help when needed
- Skipping class
- Avoiding math-related courses and activities

Avoidance is one of the most harmful impacts of math anxiety. If you steer clear of math at all costs, then you can't set yourself up for the success you deserve.

Lack of Motivation

Students with math anxiety may experience a lack of motivation. They may struggle to find the incentive to get engaged with what they view as a frightening subject. These students are often overwhelmed, making it difficult for them to complete or even start math assignments.

Procrastination

Another symptom of math anxiety is procrastination. Students may voluntarily delay or postpone their classwork and assignments, even if they know there will be a negative consequence for doing so. Additionally, they may choose to wait until the last minute to start projects and homework, even when they know they need more time to put forth their best effort.

Physiological Reactions

Many people with a fear of math experience physiological side effects. These may include an increase in heart rate, sweatiness, shakiness, nausea, and irregular breathing. These symptoms make it difficult to focus on the math content, causing the student even more stress and fear.

Strong Emotional Responses

Math anxiety also affects people on an emotional level. Responding to math content with strong emotions such as panic, anger, or despair can be a sign of math anxiety.

Low Test Scores and Performance

Low achievement can be both a symptom and a cause of math anxiety. When someone does not take the steps needed to perform well on tests and assessments, they are less likely to pass. The more they perform poorly, the more they accept this poor performance as a fact that can't be changed.

Feeling Alone

People who experience math anxiety feel like they are the only ones struggling, even if the math they are working on is challenging to many people. Feeling isolated in what they perceive as failure can trigger tension or nervousness.

Feeling of Permanency

Math anxiety can feel very permanent. You may assume that you are naturally bad at math and always will be. Viewing math as a natural ability rather than a skill that can be learned causes people to believe that nothing will help them improve. They take their current math abilities as fact and assume that they can't be changed. As a result, they give up, stop trying to improve, and avoid engaging with math altogether.

Lack of Confidence

People with low self-confidence in math tend to feel awkward and incompetent when asked to solve a math problem. They don't feel comfortable taking chances or risks when problem-solving because they second-guess themselves and assume they are incorrect. They don't trust in their ability to learn the content and solve problems correctly.

Panic

A general sense of unexplained panic is also a sign of math anxiety. You may feel a sudden sense of fear that triggers physical reactions, even when there is no apparent reason for such a response.

Causes Of Math Anxiety

Math anxiety can start at a young age and may have one or more underlying causes. Common causes of math anxiety include the following:

The Attitude of Parents or Guardians

Parents often put pressure on their children to perform well in school. Although their intentions are usually good, this pressure can lead to anxiety, especially if the student is struggling with a subject or class.

Perhaps your parents or others in your life hold negative predispositions about math based on their own experiences. For instance, if your mother once claimed she was not good at math, then you might have incorrectly interpreted this as a predisposed trait that was passed down to you.

Teacher Influence

Students often pick up on their teachers' attitudes about the content being taught. If a teacher is happy and excited about math, students are more likely to mirror these emotions. However, if a teacher lacks enthusiasm or genuine interest, then students are more inclined to disengage.

Teachers have a responsibility to cultivate a welcoming classroom culture that is accepting of mistakes. When teachers blame students for not understanding a concept, they create a hostile classroom environment where mistakes are not tolerated. This tension increases student stress and anxiety, creating conditions that are not conducive to inquiry and learning. Instead, when teachers normalize mistakes as a natural part of the problem-solving process, they give their students the freedom to explore and grapple with the math content. In such an environment, students feel comfortable taking chances because they are not afraid of being wrong.

Students need teachers that can help when they're having problems understanding difficult concepts. In doing so, educators may need to change how they teach the content. Since different people have unique learning styles, it's the job of the teacher to adapt to the needs of each student. Additionally, teachers should encourage students to explore alternate problem-solving strategies, even if it's not the preferred method of the educator.

Fear of Being Wrong

Embarrassing situations can be traumatic, especially for young children and adolescents. These experiences can stay with people through their adult lives. Those with math anxiety may experience a fear of being wrong, especially in front of a group of peers. This fear can be paralyzing, interfering with the student's concentration and ability to focus on the problem at hand.

Timed Assessments

Timed assessments can help improve math fluency, but they often create unnecessary pressure for students to complete an unrealistic number of problems within a specified timeframe. Many studies have shown that timed assessments often result in increased levels of anxiety, reducing a student's overall competence and ability to problem-solve.

Debunking Math Myths

There are lots of myths about math that are related to the causes and development of math-related anxiety. Although these myths have been proven to be false, many people take them as fact. Let's go over a few of the most common myths about learning math.

Myth: Men Are Better at Math Than Women

Math has a reputation for being a male-dominant subject, but this doesn't mean that men are inherently better at math than women. Many famous mathematical discoveries have been made by women. Katherine Johnson, Dame Mary Lucy Cartwright, and Marjorie Lee Brown are just a few of the many famous women mathematicians. Expecting to be good or bad at math because of your gender sets you up for stress and confusion. Math is a skill that can be learned, just like cooking or riding a bike.

Myth: There Is Only One Good Way to Solve Math Problems

There are many ways to get the correct answer when it comes to math. No two people have the same brain, so everyone takes a slightly different approach to problem-solving. Moreover, there isn't one way of problem-solving that's superior to another. Your way of working through a problem might differ from someone else's, and that is okay. Math can be a highly individualized process, so the best method for you should be the one that makes you feel the most comfortable and makes the most sense to you.

Myth: Math Requires a Good Memory

For many years, mathematics was taught through memorization. However, learning in such a way hinders the development of critical thinking and conceptual understanding. These skill sets are much more valuable than basic memorization. For instance, you might be great at memorizing mathematical formulas, but if you don't understand what they mean, then you can't apply them to different scenarios in the real world. When a student is working from memory, they are limited in the strategies available to them to problem-solve. In other words, they assume there is only one correct way to do the math, which is the method they memorized. Having a variety of problem-solving options can help students figure out which method works best for them. Additionally, it provides students with a better understanding of how and why certain mathematical strategies work. While memorization can be helpful in some instances, it is not an absolute requirement for mathematicians.

Myth: Math Is Not Creative

Math requires imagination and intuition. Contrary to popular belief, it is a highly creative field. Mathematical creativity can help in developing new ways to think about and solve problems. Many people incorrectly assume that all things are either creative or analytical. However, this black-and-white view is limiting because the field of mathematics involves both creativity and logic.

Myth: Math Isn't Supposed To Be Fun

Whoever told you that math isn't supposed to be fun is a liar. There are tons of math-based activities and games that foster friendly competition and engagement. Math is often best learned through play, and lots of mobile apps and computer games exemplify this.

Additionally, math can be an exceptionally collaborative and social experience. Studying or working through problems with a friend often makes the process a lot more fun. The excitement and satisfaction of solving a difficult problem with others is quite rewarding. Math can be fun if you look for ways to make it more collaborative and enjoyable.

Myth: Not Everyone Is Capable of Learning Math

There's no such thing as a "math person." Although many people think that you're either good at math or you're not, this is simply not true. Everyone is capable of learning and applying mathematics. However, not everyone learns the same way. Since each person has a different learning style, the trick is to find the strategies and learning tools that work best for you. Some people learn best through hands-on experiences, and others find success through the use of visual aids. Others are auditory learners and learn best by hearing and listening. When people are overwhelmed or feel that math is too hard, it's often because they haven't found the learning strategy that works best for them.

Myth: Good Mathematicians Work Quickly and Never Make Mistakes

There is no prize for finishing first in math. It's not a race, and speed isn't a measure of your ability. Good mathematicians take their time to ensure their work is accurate. As you gain more experience and practice, you will naturally become faster and more confident.

Additionally, everyone makes mistakes, including good mathematicians. Mistakes are a normal part of the problem-solving process, and they're not a bad thing. The important thing is that we take the time to learn from our mistakes, understand where our misconceptions are, and move forward.

Myth: You Don't Need Math in the Real World

Our day-to-day lives are so infused with mathematical concepts that we often don't even realize when we're using math in the real world. In fact, most people tend to underestimate how much we do math in our everyday lives. It's involved in an enormous variety of daily activities such as shopping, baking, finances, and gardening, as well as in many careers, including architecture, nursing, design, and sales.

Tips and Strategies for Overcoming Math Anxiety

If your anxiety is getting in the way of your level of mathematical engagement, then there are lots of steps you can take. Check out the strategies below to start building confidence in math today.

Focus on Understanding, Not Memorization

Don't drive yourself crazy trying to memorize every single formula or mathematical process. Instead, shift your attention to understanding concepts. Those who prioritize memorization over conceptual understanding tend to have lower achievement levels in math. Students who memorize may be able to complete some math, but they don't understand the process well enough to apply it to different situations. Memorization comes with time and practice, but it won't help alleviate math anxiety. On the other hand, conceptual understanding will give you the building blocks of knowledge you need to build up your confidence.

Replace Negative Self-Talk with Positive Self-Talk

Start to notice how you think about yourself. Whenever you catch yourself thinking something negative, try replacing that thought with a positive affirmation. Instead of continuing the negative thought, pause to reframe the situation. For ideas on how to get started, take a look at the table below:

Instead of thinking...	Try thinking...
"I can't do this math." "I'm not a math person."	"I'm up for the challenge, and I'm training my brain in math."
"This problem is too hard."	"This problem is hard, so this might take some time and effort. I know I can do this."
"I give up."	"What strategies can help me solve this problem?"
"I made a mistake, so I'm not good at this."	"Everyone makes mistakes. Mistakes help me to grow and understand."
"I'll never be smart enough."	"I can figure this out, and I am smart enough."

Practice Mindfulness

Practicing mindfulness and focusing on your breathing can help alleviate some of the physical symptoms of math anxiety. By taking deep breaths, you can remind your nervous system that you are not in immediate danger. Doing so will reduce your heart rate and help with any irregular breathing or shakiness. Taking the edge off of the physiological effects of anxiety will clear your mind, allowing your brain to focus its energy on problem-solving.

Do Some Math Every Day

Think about learning math as if you were learning a foreign language. If you don't use it, you lose it. If you don't practice your math skills regularly, you'll have a harder time achieving comprehension and fluency. Set some amount of time aside each day, even if it's just for a few minutes, to practice. It might take some discipline to build a habit around this, but doing so will help increase your mathematical self-assurance.

Use All of Your Resources

Everyone has a different learning style, and there are plenty of resources out there to support all learners. When you get stuck on a math problem, think about the tools you have access to, and use them when applicable. Such resources may include flashcards, graphic organizers, study guides, interactive notebooks, and peer study groups. All of these are great tools to accommodate your individual learning style. Finding the tools and resources that work for your learning style will give you the confidence you need to succeed.

Realize That You Aren't Alone

Remind yourself that lots of other people struggle with math anxiety, including teachers, nurses, and even successful mathematicians. You aren't the only one who panics when faced with a new or challenging problem. It's probably much more common than you think. Realizing that you aren't alone in your experience can help put some distance between yourself and the emotions you feel about math. It also helps to normalize the anxiety and shift your perspective.

Ask Questions

If there's a concept you don't understand and you've tried everything you can, then it's okay to ask for help! You can always ask your teacher or professor for help. If you're not learning math in a traditional classroom, you may want to join a study group, work with a tutor, or talk to your friends. More often than not, you aren't the only one of your peers who needs clarity on a mathematical concept. Seeking understanding is a great way to increase self-confidence in math.

Remember That There's More Than One Way To Solve A Problem

Since everyone learns differently, it's best to focus on understanding a math problem with an approach that makes sense to you. If the way it's being taught is confusing to you, don't give up. Instead, work to understand the problem using a different technique. There's almost always more than one problem-solving method when it comes to math. Don't get stressed if one of them doesn't make sense to you. Instead, shift your focus to what does make sense. Chances are high that you know more than you think you do.

Visualization

Visualization is the process of creating images in your mind's eye. Picture yourself as a successful, confident mathematician. Think about how you would feel and how you would behave. What would your work area look like? How would you organize your belongings? The more you focus on something, the more likely you are to achieve it. Visualizing teaches your brain that you can achieve whatever it is that you want. Thinking about success in mathematics will lead to acting like a successful mathematician. This, in turn, leads to actual success.

Focus on the Easiest Problems First

To increase your confidence when working on a math test or assignment, try solving the easiest problems first. Doing so will remind you that you are successful in math and that you do have what it takes. This process will increase your belief in yourself, giving you the confidence you need to tackle more complex problems.

Find a Support Group

A study buddy, tutor, or peer group can go a long way in decreasing math-related anxiety. Such support systems offer lots of benefits, including a safe place to ask questions, additional practice with mathematical concepts, and an understanding of other problem-solving explanations that may work better for you. Equipping yourself with a support group is one of the fastest ways to eliminate math anxiety.

Reward Yourself for Working Hard

Recognize the amount of effort you're putting in to overcome your math anxiety. It's not an easy task, so you deserve acknowledgement. Surround yourself with people who will provide you with the positive reinforcement you deserve.

Remember, You Can Do This!

Conquering a fear of math can be challenging, but there are lots of strategies that can help you out. Your own beliefs about your mathematical capabilities can limit your potential. Working toward a growth mindset can have a tremendous impact on decreasing math-related anxiety and building confidence. By knowing the symptoms of math anxiety and recognizing common misconceptions about learning math, you can develop a plan to address your fear of math. Utilizing the strategies discussed can help you overcome this anxiety and build the confidence you need to succeed.

Thank You

We at Mometrix would like to extend our heartfelt thanks to you, our friend and patron, for allowing us to play a part in your journey. It is a privilege to serve people from all walks of life who are unified in their commitment to building the best future they can for themselves.

The preparation you devote to these important testing milestones may be the most valuable educational opportunity you have for making a real difference in your life. We encourage you to put your heart into it—that feeling of succeeding, overcoming, and yes, conquering will be well worth the hours you've invested.

We want to hear your story, your struggles and your successes, and if you see any opportunities for us to improve our materials so we can help others even more effectively in the future, please share that with us as well. **The team at Mometrix would be absolutely thrilled to hear from you!** So please, send us an email (support@mometrix.com) and let's stay in touch.

If you'd like some additional help, check out these other resources we offer for your exam:

http://MometrixFlashcards.com/NCReady

Online Resources

Due to our efforts to try to keep this book to a manageable length, we've created a link that will give you access to all of your online resources:

mometrix.com/resources719/ssncg6math

It's Your Moment, Let's Celebrate It!

Share your story @mometrixtestpreparation